# New Language Learning and Teaching Environments

**Series Editor**
Hayo Reinders, Department of Education;
Department of Languages, Anaheim University;
King Mongkut's University of Technology Thonburi,
Anaheim; Bangkok, New Zealand

*New Language Learning and Teaching Environments* is an exciting book series edited by Hayo Reinders. It explores emerging trends, innovations, and interdisciplinary approaches in language education. Since its launch in 2012, the series has published over 30 volumes, offering a multidisciplinary forum for researchers, educators, and practitioners interested in the evolving landscape of language learning and teaching. Books in the series aim to:

- Explore new developments in technology, pedagogy, policy, and curriculum design.
- Examine implementation and impact, showcasing how new ideas take shape in diverse educational settings.
- Take an interdisciplinary approach, connecting insights from linguistics, education, psychology, and technology.
- Blend research and practice, ensuring that contributions offer real-world relevance beyond purely theoretical discussions.

*New Language Learning and Teaching Environments* is the first series to provide an outlet for researchers to publish work of this nature, and the first stop for teachers interested in this area.

View the latest call for proposals.

Hayo Reinders · Joo-Kyung Park ·
Ju Seong Lee
Editors

# Innovation in Language Learning and Teaching

The Case of Korea

*Editors*
Hayo Reinders
King Mongkut's University of Technology
Thonburi, Thailand

Ju Seong Lee
Department of English Language Education
Education University of Hong Kong
Tai Po, New Territories, Hong Kong

Joo-Kyung Park
Department of English Language and Literature
Honam University
Gwangju, Korea (Republic of)

ISSN 2946-2932　　　　ISSN 2946-2940　(electronic)
New Language Learning and Teaching Environments
ISBN 978-3-031-83560-5　　ISBN 978-3-031-83561-2　(eBook)
https://doi.org/10.1007/978-3-031-83561-2

© The Editor(s) (if applicable) and The Author(s), under exclusive license to Springer Nature Switzerland AG 2025

This work is subject to copyright. All rights are solely and exclusively licensed by the Publisher, whether the whole or part of the material is concerned, specifically the rights of translation, reprinting, reuse of illustrations, recitation, broadcasting, reproduction on microfilms or in any other physical way, and transmission or information storage and retrieval, electronic adaptation, computer software, or by similar or dissimilar methodology now known or hereafter developed.
The use of general descriptive names, registered names, trademarks, service marks, etc. in this publication does not imply, even in the absence of a specific statement, that such names are exempt from the relevant protective laws and regulations and therefore free for general use.
The publisher, the authors and the editors are safe to assume that the advice and information in this book are believed to be true and accurate at the date of publication. Neither the publisher nor the authors or the editors give a warranty, expressed or implied, with respect to the material contained herein or for any errors or omissions that may have been made. The publisher remains neutral with regard to jurisdictional claims in published maps and institutional affiliations.

Cover credit: Luis Jou Garcia\\GettyImages

This Palgrave Macmillan imprint is published by the registered company Springer Nature Switzerland AG
The registered company address is: Gewerbestrasse 11, 6330 Cham, Switzerland

If disposing of this product, please recycle the paper.

# Contents

1 A Brief History of English Language Education in Korea 1
  *Joo-Kyung Park, Hayo Reinders, and Ju Seong Lee*

2 Innovation in Elementary English Education
  in Korea from the Perspective of Literacy Education 19
  *Hae-Ri Kim*

3 Transforming Language Education Through AI:
  Artificial Intelligence Digital Textbook (AIDT) 49
  *Sangmin-Michelle Lee and Junseong Bang*

4 Integrating Informal Digital Learning of English
  (IDLE) into Korean Middle School Contexts 73
  *Joohyun Bae*

5 Artificial Intelligence in Enhancing Korean High
  School Students' English Skills 97
  *Rakhun Kim*

| | | |
|---|---|---|
| 6 | An Innovative In-Service English Teacher Education Program: Toward a Closer Coupling of Knowledge and Practice<br>*Eun-kyoung Jang, Ahn S.-H. Gyemyong, and Mun Woo Lee* | 129 |
| 7 | English for Peacebuilding Purposes Writing Courses<br>*Jocelyn Wright* | 159 |
| 8 | Exploring Localized Adaptations of Critical Literacy Practices in Korean EFL Contexts<br>*Young-Mee Suh and Seonmin Huh* | 185 |
| 9 | Content and Language Integrated Programs at a Korean Science and Engineering University<br>*Eun Gyong Kim* | 213 |
| 10 | A Case Study of an AI-Assisted CLIL Approach: A College English Course for Global Citizenship and Global Competence in an EFL Setting<br>*Eun-Jou Oh* | 229 |
| 11 | ChatGPT and Google Bard in Critical-PBLL: Korean University Student Perspectives<br>*Mi Kyong Kim* | 259 |
| 12 | An Analysis of Flipped Learning Research Trends in Korean EFL Classrooms: Using Big Data Techniques<br>*Hye-Kyung Kim and Sumi Han* | 281 |
| 13 | ESP Research in Korea: Current Status and Implications for Korean ELT<br>*Jihyeon Jeon and Eun-Young Kwon* | 303 |
| 14 | Innovation in ELT in Korea: Looking to the Future<br>*Ju Seong Lee, Hayo Reinders, and Joo-Kyung Park* | 331 |
| Index | | 343 |

# Contributors

**Joohyun Bae**  Korea University, Seoul, South Korea

**Junseong Bang**  Ymatics Corp., Seoul, South Korea

**Ahn S.-H. Gyemyong**  Department of English Education, College of Education, Hanyang University, Seoul, South Korea

**Sumi Han**  Hallym University, Chuncheon, South Korea

**Seonmin Huh**  Division of English, General Education Center, Chungbuk National University, Cheongju, South Korea

**Eun-kyoung Jang**  Doonchon High School, Seoul, South Korea

**Jihyeon Jeon**  Ewha Womans University, Seoul, Korea

**Hae-Ri Kim**  Seoul National University of Education, Seoul, South Korea

**Hye-Kyung Kim**  Tech University of Korea, Siheung, South Korea

**Eun Gyong Kim**  School of Digital Humanities and Computational Social Sciences, Korea Advanced Institute of Science and Technology, Daejeon, South Korea

**Mi Kyong Kim**  Chodang University, Jeollannam-do, Republic of Korea

**Rakhun Kim**  Hongik University, Seoul, South Korea

**Eun-Young Kwon**  AI Industry Research Center, Kwangwoon University, Seoul, Korea

**Ju Seong Lee**  Department of English Language Education, B4-1/F-47, Education University of Hong Kong, Tai Po, Hong Kong

**Mun Woo Lee**  Department of English Language and Literature, Yonsei University, Seoul, South Korea

**Sangmin-Michelle Lee**  Kyung Hee University, Yongin, South Korea

**Eun-Jou Oh**  Korean Bible University, Seoul, South Korea

**Joo-Kyung Park**  Department of English Language and Literature, Honam University, Gwangju, Republic of Korea

**Hayo Reinders**  King Mongkut's University of Technology, Thonburi, Thailand

**Young-Mee Suh**  Department of English Education, Hanyang University, Seoul, South Korea

**Jocelyn Wright**  Mokpo National University, Mokpo, South Korea

# List of Figures

| | | |
|---|---|---|
| Fig. 2.1 | The "Ice Cream" illustration from *On Market Street* | 39 |
| Fig. 2.2 | The Child's drawing of the "Idea" | 40 |
| Fig. 2.3 | "Lazy Jane" by Shel Silverstein | 41 |
| Fig. 2.4 | The Child's poem | 42 |
| Fig. 3.1 | Middle school English AIDT, Teacher's view (Lee et al., 2025) | 52 |
| Fig. 3.2 | The architecture of AIDT (KERIS, 2024, p. 21, translated into English) | 53 |
| Fig. 3.3 | Bloom's Taxonomy (1956) and the High Touch and High Tech model (Adapted from KERIS [2024, p. 16]) | 60 |
| Fig. 3.4 | Transition from Equality to Equity in the AI-driven Learning Systems (Bang & Lee, 2024) | 66 |
| Fig. 4.1 | Mean scores of IDLE activities (*Note* IDLE1 = watching YouTube, IDLE2 = watching movies/drama, IDLE3 = watching memes, IDLE4 = watching instructional videos, IDLE5 = talking on social media, IDLE6 = writing comments) | 83 |
| Fig. 4.2 | Mediation model $^{***}p < 0.001$ | 85 |
| Fig. 5.1 | The basic framework of AI Digital Textbook (AIDT) | 99 |

# List of Figures

| | | |
|---|---|---|
| Fig. 5.2 | Hardware infrastructure supporting digital transformation in Korean educational settings | 101 |
| Fig. 5.3 | GPT to EXCEL and User Log | 108 |
| Fig. 5.4 | Corrective recast from AI Chatbot and learner's successful repair | 115 |
| Fig. 6.1 | Characteristics of the program outcomes | 143 |
| Fig. 7.1 | Virtual exhibit | 166 |
| Fig. 12.1 | Data structure | 289 |
| Fig. 12.2 | Publication trend over time | 290 |
| Fig. 12.3 | Top 10 journals by publication count | 291 |
| Fig. 12.4 | Top 10 authors by publication count | 292 |
| Fig. 12.5 | Top 10 affiliations by publication count | 293 |
| Fig. 12.6 | Top 10 author keywords by count | 294 |
| Fig. 13.1 | Sample results of a 2-gram frequency analysis using AntConc | 312 |
| Fig. 13.2 | Sample results of a 4-gram frequency analysis using AntConc | 313 |

# List of Tables

| | | |
|---|---|---|
| Table 4.1 | Descriptive statistics | 82 |
| Table 4.2 | Analysis of the mediation model | 85 |
| Table 4.3 | Action plans for IDLE integration | 88 |
| Table 4.4 | Lesson plans for three-stage continuum model of integrating IDLE | 90 |
| Table 5.1 | Procedure of the instruction | 106 |
| Table 5.2 | Instructional material shared across the two groups: list of discourse markers for Finding Main Idea (FMI) tasks | 107 |
| Table 6.1 | Activities of different sessions in the foundational course | 138 |
| Table 6.2 | Theme groups of each program | 139 |
| Table 6.3 | Books & articles for study & research in different theme groups | 140 |
| Table 6.4 | Activities of different sessions in the advanced course | 141 |
| Table 7.1 | Awards nominations | 168 |
| Table 9.1 | Students' evaluations of EFL courses (5.00) | 216 |
| Table 9.2 | Differences (%) in pre- and post-test scores (by year) among undergraduate EFL courses | 216 |
| Table 9.3 | Students' evaluations of content classes (/5.00) | 218 |

List of Tables

| | | |
|---|---|---|
| Table 9.4 | Students' evaluations of pre- and post-language classes (/5.00) | 218 |
| Table 9.5 | The most difficult part of the content lecture (multiple choices possible) | 219 |
| Table 9.6 | Survey results of ESL SW courses (out of 6.00) | 222 |
| Table 9.7 | ESP Scientific Writing courses | 223 |
| Table 9.8 | Students' preference over online vs. in-person instruction in Scientific Writing | 223 |
| Table 10.1 | Desired results with performance domains | 237 |
| Table 10.2 | Learning materials and modules of the College English I & II | 240 |
| Table 10.3 | Schedule of College English I and II | 242 |
| Table 10.4 | The results of students' perceptions surveys after CEI and CEII | 244 |
| Table 10.5 | Key themes from College English I, PR writing content analysis | 247 |
| Table 13.1 | Differences between EGP and ESP | 308 |
| Table 13.2 | Frequent vocabulary compilation: An AntConc analysis of article titles from *English for Specific Purposes* | 314 |
| Table 13.3 | Research categories in *English for Specific Purposes* | 315 |
| Table 13.4 | Publication status of ESP Papers in *English Teaching* by Period | 317 |
| Table 13.5 | Discourse types of ESP Research in *English Teaching* | 318 |
| Table 13.6 | Discourse areas and forms of EAP research in *English Teaching* (by discourse type) | 318 |
| Table 13.7 | Discourse settings and specific discourse forms of EOP research in *English Teaching* (by discourse type) | 319 |
| Table 13.8 | ESP studies from *English Teaching*: research content and methodology | 320 |

# 1
# A Brief History of English Language Education in Korea

Joo-Kyung Park, Hayo Reinders, and Ju Seong Lee

## Introduction

Throughout the history of English language education in Korea, there have been many changes and developments. Most of these have been driven by the Korean Government, or more precisely the Ministry of Education (MOE) of Korea. Particularly important have been the changes in the National Curriculums (NCs), which have served as the

---

J.-K. Park (✉)
Department of English Language and Literature, Honam University, Gwangju, Republic of Korea
e-mail: english58@hanmail.net

H. Reinders
King Mongkut's University of Technology, Thonburi, Thailand

J. S. Lee
Department of English Language Education, B4-1/F-47, Education University of Hong Kong, Tai Po, Hong Kong
e-mail: jslee@eduhk.hk

© The Author(s), under exclusive license to Springer Nature Switzerland AG 2025
H. Reinders et al. (eds.), *Innovation in Language Learning and Teaching*, New Language Learning and Teaching Environments,
https://doi.org/10.1007/978-3-031-83561-2_1

cornerstone for English language learning and teaching at all education levels in Korea. Based on global trends and national political, economic, and social needs, NCs define the status and role of English, set goals and objectives for English education, and provide guidelines for instructional and evaluation methods. According to Choi (2007), there have been six periods of major NC reforms, overlapping with political developments:

1. The end of the Joseon Dynasty (1883–1910): The beginning and expansion of English education.
2. The Japanese colonial time (1910–1945): The declination, revival, and oppression of English education.
3. After liberation from Japan till 1955, including the U.S. military government (1945–1955): The reestablishment of English education.
4. From the first Republic to the military rule (Supreme Council for National Reconstruction) (1955–1963): The development of English education (the First NC established in 1955).
5. From the Third to the Fifth Republic (1963–1992): The stabilization and stagnation of English education (the Second [1963], the Third [1973, 1974], the Fourth [1981], and the Fifth [1987, 1988] NC).
6. From the Citizens' government till the Participatory Government (1992–2008): The reform of English education (the Sixth [1992], the Seventh [1997], and the 2007 Revised NC) (Park & Kim, 2014, pp. 49–50).

Three more revised NCs were issued in 2009, 2015, and 2022 based on the Seventh NC,[1] continuing the educational reform process. Currently, the 2022 Revised NC is in use.

Since globalization in the 1990s, English has been considered one of the key subjects in enhancing the nation's international competitiveness. The 2007 Revised NC deserves special attention as it was the first to adopt the concept of English as a lingua franca (ELF),[2] viewing English ability as key in coping with the rapid changes in the globalized world.

---

[1] The NCs revised after the Seventh NC saw only partial changes and so were named after the year they were issued: The 2007/2009/2015/2022 Revised NC.
[2] English as a lingua franca (ELF) was used as an English translation of the Korean term 'gukjeeoroseoui yeongeo' in the 2007 and following NCs, which is used interchangeably with

In the 2022 Revised NC, this view is maintained and enhancement of learners' English communication competency is stated as the ultimate goal. That is, English is considered the most-widely used means of communication to acquire information, appreciate cultural diversity, creatively express one's thoughts, and interact collaboratively with participants in the English-speaking community (Ministry of Education, 2022, p. 3, cited in Park & Sung, 2024).

## Major Changes and Developments in English Education in Korea

Park and Kim (2014) summarize the changes from 1992 onwards and identify these as pertaining to the following seven areas:

First, a shift was made in ELT goals and instructional methods: (1) During the first NC period (1955–1962), American English was adopted as the standard and many American topics were included in secondary English textbooks (Moon, 2005); (2) During the fourth NC period (1981–1986), more emphasis was placed on developing oral over written language and a listening test was included in the college entrance exam in 1994; (3) During the seventh NC period (1997–2006), the main goal of ELT was to promote national development and globalization, focusing on building a positive attitude toward being a world citizen and acquiring everyday English communicative skills; (4) This period also saw an emphasis on learner-centered education, adopting open education and a differentiated curriculum.[3] More cultural content was included in language learning materials; (5) The 2007 NC adopted the concept

---

English as an international language (EIL), English as a global language (EGL), and/or World Englishes (WE) in Korea (Park & Sung, 2024).

[3] Open education is an educational philosophy that seeks to achieve holistic child development by providing effective education on basic skills, character, and creativity. In Korea, British and American open education was introduced into kindergarten education in the 1970s. From the mid-1990s, as the Ministry of Education began to encourage open education in earnest, it rapidly expanded (Encyclopedia of Korean culture, 2024). Differentiated curriculum is one way of realizing open education by providing students of different abilities with curriculum that cater to their own needs. In elementary and secondary English classes, students are divided into three leveled groups, low, intermediate, and advanced, who are given tasks with a differential degree of difficulty by differentiated curriculum.

of English as an International Language (EIL) and defined English as the language of 'intercultural speakers' not as that of 'native speakers' (Ministry of Education, Science, and Technology, 2008). However, it should be noted that there was a big discrepancy between the NC rhetoric and classroom reality and so the curriculum goals were mostly not successfully achieved.

Second, formal elementary English education was introduced in 1997. This had both positive and negative effects on ELT in Korea. On the positive side, notable improvement has been made in material development and teacher education. Not only elementary English textbooks used in schools but also diverse materials for teaching young learners were developed by local university professors and school teachers. A lot of mandatory as well as optional teacher education programs were offered for elementary school English teachers in order to develop their English proficiency and English teaching skills. At the same time, it has had a detrimental impact on learners, teachers, and parents. Some young learners have lost interest in learning English for different reasons: Some feel overburdened or tired of private English lessons forced by their parents; Some others, on the contrary, experience boredom or helplessness as they cannot follow the lessons. English classes in elementary schools have both children who can read high-level English books without difficulty and those who cannot write the alphabet properly even in the sixth grade (Song & Lee, 2013). Teachers were given a significant additional workload and some parents who were dissatisfied with the way English was taught in schools suffered the financial consequences of hiring private tutors or sending their children to 'hagwon' or language institute or even overseas.

Third, school classrooms nationwide were modernized with the help of information and communication technology. Advanced technology and high-speed Internet are actively incorporated into school education, supporting blended and multimedia-assisted language learning. This classroom modernization has continued until the present day, with Generative AI increasingly becoming part of the school education system. This has, however, created a 'digital divide' between teachers and students who have easy access to and strong skills in using technology and those who do not. This, along with the 'English divide'[4] has become a serious social issue.

Fourth, a large number of native English-speaking teachers (NESTs) came into the nation as assistant teachers, mainly through the two Korean Government programs that recruit them, the English Program in Korea (EPIK) and Teach and Learn in Korea (TaLK). It was expected that as a result Korean students would be exposed to authentic English input and become motivated to learn English. The expat teachers have brought not only new energy and changes to Korean English classrooms, but also new issues and problems, which will be discussed in the next section of this chapter.

Fifth, a number of English Villages[5] and other English immersion facilities were established in order to expose Korean learners to a semi-natural English-speaking environment, to promote English language and cultural understanding, to provide underprivileged learners with an equal educational opportunity and to lessen overseas study expenses (Park, 2009). Some skepticism and questions, however, were raised about the authenticity of the cultural representation of the facilities and their cost-effectiveness. It was also questioned whether such simulated facilities create real needs of English usage or not (Kim, 2006; Krashen, 2006; Park, 2006a).

Sixth, teaching English in English (TEE) in elementary and secondary schools and English-medium instruction (EMI) in universities were intensified. TEE, a policy of an obligatory use of classroom English in elementary and secondary schools, was adopted in 2001 (Park, 2019). The rationale behind the policy was that teacher's use of English would provide more input and foster communicative interaction with the students, which would lead to the communicative competence required in a global society (Lee, 2007). However, it was found that though the teachers perceived it as effective for a majority of instructional tasks, it

---

[4] English divide is a social division created within a society due to the lack of access to English by some of the members of the population (Martinez-Garcia, 2020).
[5] English Villages are "simulated English speaking theme parks designed for domestic language immersion experiences within Korea, which promotes a unique participation-reinforced English immersion edutainment space for general masses within Korea. Its objectives and visions feature three dominant ideological constructs: (i) global Koreans (ii) economical education alternatives (iii) experiential learning" (Lee, 2011, p. 1).

was not implemented fully, mainly due to a lack of teachers' English proficiency and confidence in their TEE ability (S-A Kim, 2002; S-Y Kim, 2002). Adopted and expanded by the Korean government's thrust and universities' efforts for internationalization, EMI in universities has experienced similar issues and problems to those of TEE: (1) undemocratic, unilateral, and mandatory policy implementation; (2) insufficient English abilities and confidence of both students and professors (Park, 2019).

Seventh, the National English Ability Test (NEAT) was introduced. It was implemented as a full-scale test as of 2012, and was intended to replace the English test of the College Scholastic Aptitude Test (CSAT) from 2015. However, the whole plan was discarded due to insufficient funding in 2014 by the then-new government. By adopting the direct assessment of speaking and writing skills as a test domain, with 'intelligibility' as the key evaluation factor, rather than 'native speaker' performance, NEAT could have had a powerful and positive washback effect and made a positive impact on ELT in Korea.

As discussed above, many new policies regarding ELT in Korea were developed and implemented particularly when each new government started. Some significant progress and development have been made but more often than not these were accompanied by many issues and challenges. Some of these have been persistent for decades.

## Major Issues and Challenges

ELT in Korea has gone through many changes and challenges driven by societal needs and changes both within and beyond Korea. These have resulted in frequent revisions of the NCs for the purpose of educational reforms, which have led to some improvements and progress as discussed above but also teacher fatigue and dissatisfaction and distrust with public English education. In order to move from rhetoric to true change, no less than a paradigm shift is required. The following key issues should be addressed:

First, Korean government policy for ELT is influenced by native speakerism. Though the NCs since 2007 continue to adopt the concept of

ELF/EIL, textbooks dominantly present a single-standard variety, American English in particular (Park, 2017; Park & Kim, 2014; Park & Sung, 2024; Shim, 2022). The 2015 English textbook writing guidelines issued by Korea Institute for Curriculum and Instruction (KICE) stipulate that English in textbooks should be 'natural' and 'authentic' standard varieties currently used in English-speaking countries (MOE and KICE, 2015), which may seem to encourage plurilingual presentations of English, but this appears limited to Englishes from within Kachruvian inner circle countries (Kachru, 1985). Also, expat teachers are recruited by EPIK and TaLK only from 'inner circle' countries, including the USA, UK, Canada, Australia, New Zealand, Ireland, and South Africa.[6] Eligibility of EPIK teachers[7] emphasizes their citizenship of an English-speaking nation more than their professional ELT credentials or teaching experience. Reflecting the concerns raised among various stakeholders, the EPIK recruitment policy was updated in 2015, and now a teaching credential is required. However, there have been concerns that the Korean government seems to privilege inner-circle varieties of English only and that the EPIK hires inexperienced NESTs and these inexperienced teachers make it harder for the program to achieve its goals in a timely and cost-effective manner (Shin et al., 2021). This shows a lack of understanding of ELT as a professional field among government officials, with some still believing that any native speaker of English can teach English (Park & Sung, 2024).

Second, Korean learners' and teachers' perceptions and attitudes towards English varieties and their speakers (including their own) appear to still be negatively influenced by native-speakerism. Shin (2020) pointed out that in contrast to official rhetoric ostensibly supporting varieties of English, even teachers who speak fluent English set native-speaker English, especially American English, as the norm and feel

---

[6] India was added in 2010 and one Indian teacher was hired with a lower salary than that for those from seven countries mentioned above. No more Indian teachers have been hired (Park & Sung, 2024).
[7] EPIK teachers must be citizens of one of the following countries: Australia, Canada, Ireland, New Zealand, United Kingdom, United States, or South Africa.; Hold a minimum of a Bachelor's degree from an accredited university; 3. Have a TEFL/TESOL/CELTA certificate (100+ hours), teaching license, or majored in Teaching, TESOL, Second Languages Studies, or any field of Education (EPIK, 2024).

burdened about teaching in English as they experience a lack of English proficiency. Korean English teachers with low professional self-esteem (Kim, 2011) underestimate their own English competence and lack confidence in themselves as legitimate English users, which in turn negatively influences and shapes their students' perceptions and understanding of English varieties and their speakers.

Third, elementary and secondary English textbooks can perpetuate cultural misrepresentations. The textbooks published during the earlier versions of NC were mostly centered on British and American English language and culture (Han & Bae, 2005). Reflecting the policy adopted in 2015 to integrate diverse cultures into English education (Ministry of Education, 2015), the recent English textbooks introduce various cultures. However, Park et al. (2022) found that the main interlocutors in the dialogues are white English native speakers, with more male than female. More efforts need to be made to integrate cultural components in a more balanced way in terms of race and gender.

Fourth, there is a lack of pre- and in-service training for NESTs in general, and in particular, training for both Korean teachers of English (KTEs) and NESTs for effective collaboration. Both KTEs and NESTs lack intercultural understanding, communication, and hands-on skills to effectively conduct 'team-teaching.' NESTs are marginalized by being assigned to teach classes unrelated to the curriculum or extracurricular classes with no test, which results in student misbehavior, disrespect, and demotivation, whereas KTEs are intimidated and lose face by being paired up with NESTs whose English language and cultural competence, based on NES norms, are superior. There is no proper training, however, for both groups of teachers to become empowered. Korean administrators at the regional offices of education and schools need education as they lack professional management skills due to deficiencies in communicative ability in English, intercultural understanding, and understanding of ELT as a professional discipline (Ahn & Lew, 2017; Park & Kim, 2014).

Kwon (2007) identified a number of persistent problems in ELT in Korea: (1) 'Incompetent teachers' whose English proficiency is not at the desired level; (2) Students who have low English proficiency and lose interest in learning English as they advance in school years; (3) Initiation of ELT-policy-making by outsiders, such as politicians. Park (2006b) suggested that ELT professionals and their organizations need to be more proactive in their outreach in order to empower English teachers, students, and the profession itself inside and outside of the classroom. Their professional expertise and experiences need to be seen and heard over those of 'false prophets', using a wide range of communication channels; (4) Private English education is prevalent, affecting public education and Korean families' finances; and (5) High expectations from parents and society put pressure on teachers and ELT professionals. After 17 years since Kwon's publication, however, the problems remain largely unresolved.

Shin (2020) pointed out that despite the policies and measures introduced by the South Korean government to emphasize the importance of English for its national competitiveness, English teaching in schools has not significantly improved. In-service English teachers continue to raise the question whether Communicative Language Teaching pedagogy developed in ESL environments is appropriate for Korea, where English is taught as a foreign language. Many teachers also experience reform fatigue due to frequent changes in policies for political purposes. Park and Sung (2024) claimed that what is lacking the most in ELT in Korea is a change in Korean stakeholders' perceptions of ELF and attitudes toward English varieties and speakers. The 2022 Revised NEC states the roles and the functions of English from an ELF or World Englishes (WE) perspective, but no concrete curricular and instructional directions are provided about how to include ELF or WE in content, teaching and learning activities, and evaluation guidelines. It seems that English education in Korea continues to be rooted in an English as a foreign language (EFL) perspective and native-speakerism. Accordingly, more work remains to be done.

## Introduction to the Chapters

As we have shown, the aspirations of the many top-down educational reforms that have been instigated over the years have not been realized. However, a significant amount of grassroots innovation is taking place across all educational sectors in Korea.

This edited volume explores what type of innovations in English language learning and teaching in Korea have been made, how and why. The book includes one chapter about innovation in elementary ELT, one about the AI Digital Textbook, or AIDT, which will be used in primary and secondary schools across the country starting in 2025, two about secondary ELT innovation and one about teacher education for secondary school teachers. the seven chapters about ELT innovation in higher education focus on topics ranging from English for Peace-building Purposes writing courses, Localized Adaptations of Critical Literacy Practices, Integrating Content and Language in Higher Education (ICLHE), an AI-Assisted Content Language Integrating Learning (CLIL) Approach, ChatGPT and Google Bard in Critical-Project-Based Language Learning (PBLL), Flipped Learning Research Trends, and Current Status and Implications of English for Specific Purposes (ESP) respectively.

In the next chapter, Hae-Ri Kim introduces the key innovations in elementary English literacy education in Korea, focusing on the results of collaborative research conducted by the author and practicing teachers. She provides a comprehensive perspective on innovations in elementary English literacy education being successfully applied in different situations and with learners of various proficiency levels and ages. In Chapter 3, Sangmin-Michelle Lee and Junseong Bang introduce AIDT, one of the most recent innovations in Korean education that aims to improve the quality of public education through personalized learning experiences. They explore three critical aspects of this transformation: the architecture and features of AIDT, the evolving roles of students and teachers in AI-enhanced personalized learning environments, and the considerations necessary for developing an AI-driven learning ecosystem. According to them, by providing learning content tailored to students' abilities and learning styles, AIDT will help individual students follow their optimal learning path and has the potential not only to improve the overall quality of public education but also to narrow achievement gaps between students and promote educational equity in Korea. They also claim that only by achieving synergy between ongoing technological advancement and meaningful engagement of teachers and students, we can fully realize the transformative potential of AI-based education and ensure that it serves its intended purpose of enhancing the learning experience while preserving educational integrity.

Joohyun Bae in Chapter 4 presents her research on Informal Digital Learning of English (IDLE) and Korean secondary learners' willingness to communicate. IDLE is often associated with Willingness to Communicate in a second language (L2 WTC). The study aims to examine whether English as an International Language (EIL) perceptions mediate the relationship between IDLE and L2 WTC of learners. Survey data was collected from 206 secondary school students in Korea. The results showed that EIL perception partially mediated the relationship between IDLE and L2 WTC, suggesting that learners who participate in IDLE activities have more positive EIL perceptions, which leads to a higher level of WTC. In Chapter 5, Rakhun Kim investigates the innovative application of Artificial Intelligence (AI) technology to enhance English language skills of Korean high school students, focusing on both productive and receptive skills. He presents two case studies that demonstrate the effectiveness of AI-driven language learning programs in improving reading comprehension for the Korean College Scholastic Aptitude Test (K-CSAT) and in enhancing English sentence production. The findings from these studies indicate that interactive engagement with generative AI significantly enhances Korean English learners' ability to identify main ideas through top-down processing, particularly when complemented by the guidance from human teachers for developing receptive skills. Subsequently, the discussion extends to productive skills, where AI's corrective feedback mechanisms further facilitate the development of complex sentence structures. The chapter suggests a holistic approach to implementing AI in English language education, calling for a collaborative effort between linguistics, second language acquisition (SLA) theory, and computer science.

In Chapter 6, the only one about teacher education, Eun-kyoung Jang, Ahn S.-H. Gyemyong, and Mun Woo Lee present an innovation that has been achieved through a one-year in-service English *language teacher education* (LTE) program in Seoul, Korea, nicknamed "Snowball". Initiated by a master teacher, the Snowball program features participants' learning by doing, instant feedback, and a long-term engagement. The program's *success* factors include *customized special interest groups, long-term action research, abundant sources of inspiration,* and *a culture of sharing*. They also share what didn't work with previous English LTE programs and then with Snowball, and finally some *lessons* learned on English LTE.

Jocelyn Wright in Chapter 7, the first one regarding innovations in ELT in higher education, describes two English for Peacebuilding Purposes (EPP) courses for A2–B2 level students she piloted in the Department of English Language and Literature at her university in 2022. In both courses, students explored their understandings and ideas about peace as a necessary process and desirable outcome as they produced different genres and registers through cyclical process writing. The first course, dedicated to the intrapersonal sphere, focused on expressive and reflective writing, and the second, dedicated to the interpersonal sphere, focused on interactive and responsive writing. She also discusses sources of inspiration for opening the courses, some points she took into consideration when designing, planning, implementing, and assessing them, and some adjustments she made (or expects to make) in 2023 based on observations, self-reflections, and student feedback to ensure that the process and course outcomes align. Young-Mee Suh and Seonmin Huh in Chapter 8 introduce the need for localized adaptations of critical literacy practices in EFL educational contexts and argue that localized adaptations should balance educator, curriculum and learner factors toward development of critical literacies. They suggest the implementation of critical literacies that balances language development with expansion of critical thinking, integrating both rational and affective connections within the content of the curriculum, thus balancing individual cognitive growth with social growth as a citizen of international communities. Chapter 9 by Eun Gyong Kim presents Integrating Content and Language in Higher Education (ICLHE), which, unlike in other contexts such as European institutions, has rarely been adopted by Korean universities. She examines a Korean science and engineering university's endeavors to provide integrated content and language education. At the university, the ICL approach is offered for newly-admitted undergraduate students in five subjects (biology, chemistry, math, physics, and programming) and for graduate classes as discipline-specific scientific writing courses. She shares the results of a content analysis of course materials, such as syllabi, lesson materials, and test materials and questionnaire surveys and interviews with students and professors were shown. These showed high levels of student and instructor satisfaction. The chapter shares the strengths and weaknesses of the classes and suggestions for their improvement.

Eunjou Oh in Chapter 10 depicts an interdisciplinary English language course that systematically integrates the tenets of global citizenship, global competence, and English language acquisition within CLIL. Constructed through the methodological framework of Backward Design (McTighe & Wiggins, 1999), the instructional model is strategically oriented toward the attainment of specific educational objectives. These objectives encompass the cultivation of global citizenship, the acquisition of global competence, proficiency in technology tools, and refinement of English communicative competence. She describes the instructional materials and instructional methodology, including an array of scaffolding such as machine translation tools, the use of L1, and collaborative learning methodologies. The learner perception surveys, pre-post assessments, and an English self-efficacy examination underscore the successful realization of stipulated educational objectives and manifest significant enhancements in competencies pertaining to reading, listening, speaking, and writing. The chapter highlights the interdisciplinary English course's role in not only fulfilling the essential function of language learning but also exploring its latent potential as a foundational subject for value-oriented learning in 21st-century liberal education at universities.

Chapter 11 by Mi Kyong Kim proposes an alternative learning approach: Project-Based Language Learning (PBLL), which is learner-centered Project-Based Learning (PBL) applied to language education, as coined by Beckett and Miller (2006). Incorporating PBL into general

English courses, PBLL shifts the focus to a student-driven inquiry-based teaching method, wherein learners construct knowledge about the English language and the subject of inquiry through their own explorations. Recent studies have begun to incorporate Artificial Intelligence (AI) technology-based learning tools to aid in the completion of Critical-PBLL tasks (M. Kim, 2023). She presents a Critical-PBLL framework for a general English course in her university, tailoring language interventions to learners' needs and proficiency levels. The chapter shares learner-driven inquiry processes that foster reflective and critical thinking, analyzes learners' English learning experiences, and examines the impact of these activities. Chapter 12 by Hye-Kyung Kim and Sumi Han looks into the innovative use and results of flipped learning in the unique cultural and educational setting of Korean EFL classrooms. A main focus is the bibliometric and keyword analysis of flipped learning trends in these classrooms, using the strength of big data technology. This fresh approach highlights the effective use of flipped learning and the big changes it can bring about. As Korean EFL classrooms deal with their special challenges and chances, adding tech-based methods such as flipped learning is a key move to improve educational quality. Jihyeon Jeon and Eun-young Kwon in Chapter 13 examine the current status of ESP in Korea and identify what is needed for improving ESP education in Korea, based on the results of their analysis of ESP research articles. The approach of ESP education, which focuses on developing curricula, crafting materials, and implementing programs that are specifically designed according to the learners' needs, appears to be a viable answer to the issue of 'personalization' in Korean ELT. A discussion on ESP education, therefore, must be included in discussing innovative teaching in Korea. However, the experience of ESP education is not shared or discussed visibly in Korea.

Finally, in the closing Chapter 14, we conclude with a number of lessons that can be drawn from the volume's innovations. We make a number of recommendations for the further development of the field of ELT in Korea.

# References

Ahn, S. & Lew, S. (2017). Native English-speaking teachers (NESTs) in Korea: Voices from two NESTs and one Korean English teacher. *Korean Journal of Teacher Education, 33*(2), 89–119.
Beckett, G., & Miller, P. (Eds.). (2006). *Project-based second and foreign language education: Past, present, and future.* Information Age Publishing.
Choi, Y. (2007). The history and policy of English language education in Korea. In Y. H. Choi & B. Spolsky (Eds.) *English education in Asia: History and policies* (pp. 33–66). Asia TEFL.
Encyclopedia of Korean Culture. (2024). *yeollingyoyuk* [open education]. Retrieved August 15, 2024, from the World Wide Web: https://encykorea.aks.ac.kr/Article/E0037042
EPIK. (2024). *Eligibility.* Retrieved August 15, 2024, from the World Wide Web: http://m.epik.go.kr/description/eligibility.php
Han, Y., & Bae, Y. (2005). An analysis of cultural content of high school and college English textbooks. *English Teaching, 60*(4), 47–70.
Kachru, B. (1985). Standards, codification and sociolinguistic realism: The English language in the outer circle. In R. Quirk & H. G. Widdowson (Eds.), *English in the world: Teaching and learning the language and literature* (pp. 11–30). Cambridge University Press.
Kim, H. (2011). Native speakerism affecting nonnative English teachers' identity formation: A critical perspective. *English Teaching, 66*(4), 53–71.
Kim, M. (2006). "English villages" in South Korea: What do they really promote? *NNEST Newsletter, 8*(2), 15–20.
Kim, M. (2023). PBL using AI technology-based learning tools in a college English class. *Korean Journal of General Education, 17*(2), 169–183.
Kim, S.-A. (2002). A critical reflection on the 'teaching English through English' classes in the Korean context. *English Teaching, 57*(4), 315–346.
Kim, S.-Y. (2002). Teachers' perceptions about teaching English through English. *English Teaching, 57*(1), 131–148.
Krashen, S. (2006). *English villages: Not a good investment.* Retrieved September 15, 2006, from the World Wide Web: http://sdkrashen.com/pipermail/krashen_sdkrashen.com/2006-April/000480.html
Kwon, O. (2007). Persistent problems and emerging issues in English education in Korea. *Foreign Language Education Research, 10*, 1–16.

Lee, J. (2007). Issues of EFL educational practice in Korea: A conceptual proposal for an alternative. *English Language & Literature Teaching, 13*(3), 41–56.

Lee, J. S. (2011). Globalization and language education: English Village in South Korea. *Language Research, 47*(1), 123–149.

Martinez-Garcia, M. T. (2020). Beyond the English Divide in South Korea. In C.-A. Huertas-Abril & M. E. Gómez-Parra (Eds.), *International approaches to bridging the language Gap* (pp. 214–233). https://doi.org/10.4018/978-1-7998-1219-7.ch013

McTighe, J., & Wiggins, G. (1999). *The understanding by design handbook*. Association for Supervision and Curriculum Development.

Ministry of Education. (2015). *National Curriculum of English (No. 2015–74 Supplementary 14)*. Ministry of Education.

Ministry of Education. (2022). *The 2022 Revised English National Curriculum*. Ministry of Education.

Ministry of Education and Korea Institute for Instruction and Evaluation. (2015). *Gaejeong gyoyukgwajongae ttareun gyokwayong doseo pyeonchan yueijeomgwa geomjeonggijun* (Points of note and standards for compiling textbooks of subject matters based on the revised curriculum). Ministry of Education and Korea Institute for Instruction and Evaluation.

Ministry of Education, Science, and Technology. (2008). *Chodeung hakkyo gyoyukgwajeong haeseol: Waegukeo – Yeongeo* [Elementary school curriculum explanatory booklet: Foreign language-English]. Ministry of Education, Science, and Technology.

Moon, E. (2005). A historical research on English textbooks in the formation stage of the contemporary educational system in Korea. *Foreign Languages Education, 2*(3), 245–269.

Park, H., Jeon, J., & Lee, S. (2022). An analysis of multicultural aspects found in English textbooks: Focusing on first-year middle school textbooks. *Korean Journal of English Language and Linguistics, 22*, 957–977.

Park, J. (2006a). Korea-Japan English camp: A case study of an English immersion program in Korea. *English Language & Literature Teaching, 14*(4), 141–160.

Park, J. (2006b). Professionalization of TEFL in Korea: The roads behind and ahead. *The Journal of Asia TEFL, 3*(4), 113–134.

Park, J. (2009). The development of English immersion education in Korea. *English 21, 2*(2), 1–20.

Park, J. (2019). English-medium instruction in the Korean higher education context: From an English as a lingua franca perspective. In K. Murata (Ed.),

*English-medium instruction from an English as a Lingua Franca perspective* (pp. 64–77). Routledge.

Park, J., & Kim, M. (2014). Teaching and learning of EIL in Korean culture and context. In M. Roby & R. M. Giri (Eds.), *The pedagogy of English as an international language: Perspectives from scholars, teachers, and students* (pp. 47–64). Springer.

Park, J., & Sung, K. (2024). ELT in South Korea from the perspectives of ELF and WE. In K. Murata (Ed.), *ELF and applied linguistics: Reconsidering applied linguistics research from ELF perspectives* (pp. 82–99). Routledge.

Park, T. (2017). A study on secondary school teachers' opinions about including British pronunciation in English listening assessment. *Secondary English Education, 10*(3), 3–21.

Shim, Y.-S. (2022). An analysis of the English section of Korea's college scholastic ability test from the ELF perspective. *Secondary English Education, 15*(2), 59–82.

Shin, H., Lee, J., Brawn, J., & Do, J. (2021). EPIK teachers' beliefs about language learning and teaching processes. *English Teaching, 76*(2), 81–105.

Shin, S. (2020). English language teacher education in South Korea: Changes and challenges. In A. B. M. Tsui (Ed.), *English language teaching and teacher education in East Asia: Global challenges and local responses* (pp. 159–174). Cambridge University Press.

Song, H., & Lee, H. (2013). *Yeongpoja sokchulhaneun chodeunghakkyo* [Elementary Schools with a high incidence of children who give up learning English]. Retrieved August 15, 2014, from the World Wide Web: https://www.khan.co.kr/national/education/article/201307222215045

# 2

# Innovation in Elementary English Education in Korea from the Perspective of Literacy Education

Hae-Ri Kim

## Introduction

In Korea, public education is carried out in accordance with the national curriculum, so changes in the curriculum have a great influence on school classes. When the first national-level curriculum was announced by the Ministry of Culture and Education in 1954, English was not included in the elementary school curriculum (Ministry of Culture and Education, 1954). As English grew in importance as a communication tool for people around the world, introducing English education in elementary schools became an important consideration. Therefore, elementary English education was introduced in 1982, with English classes being taught as special activities in elementary schools. At that time, elementary English was not part of the regular curriculum, and many problems arose, such as a lack of English teachers, no textbooks,

H.-R. Kim (✉)
Seoul National University of Education, Seoul, South Korea
e-mail: hrkim@snue.ac.kr

© The Author(s), under exclusive license to Springer Nature Switzerland AG 2025
H. Reinders et al. (eds.), *Innovation in Language Learning and Teaching*, New Language Learning and Teaching Environments,
https://doi.org/10.1007/978-3-031-83561-2_2

and inconsistent programs. Finally, elementary English was included in the sixth elementary school curriculum, announced in 1995. From 1997 onward, English was officially taught as a regular subject in grades three through six. In fact, the inclusion of English as a regular subject in elementary school was a major innovation in English education in Korea (Ministry of Education, 1995).

Another innovation in elementary English education involved changes in literacy education. When English was introduced in elementary school, basic teaching methods were used, such as those relied on in middle school classes, and the focus was mainly on oracy skills, for instance, developing listening and speaking ability through games. However, this situation began to change as the number of weekly English classes increased in elementary schools (Ministry of Education, Science and Technology, 2008). Although literacy education was emphasized and the amount of reading and writing began to increase, English textbooks[1] did not include activities for elementary school children unfamiliar with English letters to help them learn reading and writing systematically, and teachers did not know how to teach elementary school children appropriately, considering their cognitive and language levels. Therefore, along with supplementing textbooks and improving teacher education, collaborative research between teachers and scholars was actively conducted to come up with suitable materials and teaching methods for fostering English literacy. The author of this chapter was one of the scholars who attempted to find a way to supplement textbook-oriented classes through literature-based instruction, especially by utilizing literary works such as picture books and poems written for children.

This chapter examines the key innovations in elementary English literacy education in Korea, focusing on the results of collaborative research conducted by the author and practicing teachers. A comprehensive perspective will be provided to share innovations in elementary English literacy education being successfully applied in different situations and with learners of various proficiency levels and ages. Prior to

---

[1] In Korea, public education is carried out in accordance with the national curriculum, so English classes in schools must use textbooks recognized by the Ministry of Education. Since the curriculum sets limits on the number of vocabulary items and textbook pages, it is challenging to systematically present a diverse array of activities in textbooks.

exploring the research related to elementary English literacy education, I will briefly review the national elementary English curriculum, which has been revised five times since English was introduced in elementary school. This is because studies on literacy education were conducted to reflect the needs of learners and teachers while also reflecting the desired achievement levels and goals of the curriculum applied in each period.

## Understanding the Elementary English Curriculum

The curriculum, which determines the educational direction of elementary, middle, and high schools in Korea, has been revised over time in response to the changing world situation and shifts in the national, social, and educational environment. It ultimately aims to provide students with skills that will be needed in the society of the future. Since public education is based on the national curriculum, revisions of the curriculum have greatly influenced school classes and have affected education-related research. This section looks at the main elements of the sixth curriculum, when English was introduced in elementary school; the seventh curriculum, a revised curriculum that was issued three years later; and the 2008, 2011, 2015, and 2022 revised curricula. While the 2022 revised curriculum was announced in 2022, its English-teaching requirements will go into effect in 2025. As of now, textbooks currently being written will be used starting in 2025, and the Ministry of Education, local education offices, and schools are making necessary preparations.

Due to the government's globalization policy and high societal interest in English education, the Ministry of Education included English as a regular elementary school subject in the sixth curriculum (Ministry of Education, 1995). At that time, the overall emphasis for elementary English instruction was on basic English communicative skills, especially oral language skills, which caused an imbalance between spoken and written language skills. The level of achievement remained relatively unchanged when the seventh curriculum was issued in 1997 and applied until 2001 (Ministry of Education, 1997). In other words, the level of achievement set by the seventh curriculum for third-grade students only covered oral language-oriented activities, without any focus on written language. The letters of the alphabet and easy words were taught to read and write from the fourth grade onward.

In the 2008 revised English curriculum, there was a significant increase in English class hours in line with the government's policy to strengthen public education (Ministry of Education, Science and Technology, 2008). For example, the number of classes for third and fourth graders increased from one[2] to two periods per week, and those for fifth and sixth graders increased from two to three periods per week. This increase in class periods was reflected in the level of achievement, particularly influencing the early introduction and level of reading and writing. For example, "A rough understanding of the relationship between sound and letter" was added to the list of reading achievement goals in the 2008 revised curriculum, marking the start of phonics education. This was carried through in the 2011 and 2015 revised curriculums and emphasized more in the 2022 curriculum than in previous revisions.

Starting with the 2011 revised Elementary English Curriculum (Ministry of Education, Science and Technology, 2011), it was stated that English teaching and learning material should include content that helps foster creativity, logical and critical thinking, and problem-solving skills. These high-level abilities were also mentioned in the 2015 curriculum (Ministry of Education, 2015).

Finally, the 2022 revision (Ministry of Education, 2022), announced after the COVID-19 era, highlighted the skills that English learners will need in the society of the future. The ultimate goal of English education, "English communication competency," includes self-directed learning of English, understanding and exploring knowledge and information in various areas, and creatively expressing one's thoughts in English. Of particular note among the competencies is that of developing an empathetic understanding of humans and aesthetic sensitivity through literary works expressed in English.

In summary, the elementary English curriculum has been revised six times since English was introduced as a subject in elementary school, and each revised curriculum required that the trends of the times be reflected

---

[2] In Korean elementary schools, one period lasts for 40 minutes.

in English education. For instance, the achievement goals presented in the 2022 curriculum included "listening to or reading poetry, songs, and stories with empathy." This change suggests that learning materials will need to be presented in context in English education, that various materials of interest to learners should be used, and that elementary English education needs to go beyond basic communication skills centered on language patterns.

## Phonics as a Turning Point in Elementary English Literacy Education

The introduction of phonics techniques in the curriculum was a big change in literacy education. Because of a lack of class hours, children had previously had to learn the names of the letters of the alphabet in fourth grade and then begin reading words and sentences without understanding the relationship between spelling and sounds. When phonics began to be included in the elementary English textbooks, the focus was only on the initial consonant sound of a word. In the 2022 revised English curriculum, phonics receives more emphasis than in previous curricula thanks to the inclusion of rhymes as well as the sound of each letter at the level of phrases and sentences (Ministry of Education, 2022). In fact, once children are able to decode the initial consonant of a word, they can easily go on to read several words if they understand rhyming patterns. For example, the /at/ sound in "mat" is also found in "cat," "rat," "sat," and fat."

Among the earliest studies on teaching phonics in Korea, learners were taught how to read and write rhyming words but were not provided with opportunities to access rhyming patterns within a meaningful context, missing the opportunity to understand the meaning of decoded words. The positive effects of early literacy instruction were underscored in two studies that used picture books containing rhyming words in third- and fifth-grade classes.

In a study by H. Kim and S. Lee (2012), researchers used picture books to find ways for early English learners to simultaneously decode and understand words by learning rhyming patterns in context. The third-grade students who participated in the study read five picture books containing rhyming words, including *Hop on Pop* by Dr. Seuss (1963). Prior to the classes, children had difficulty identifying the various vowel sounds, but after learning how to decipher words by separating them according to onset and rhyme, they were able to understand and apply the principle of rhyming to reading and writing words. In addition, their ability to understand word meanings improved greatly because rhyming words were decoded in the context of stories. Overall, phonics classes dealing with rhyming patterns in context were meaningful in three different ways. First, the context provided by picture books positively affected the decoding and comprehension ability of children. Second, the context of the stories helped children make connections between written and spoken language. Third, children were able to use contextual clues to understand word meanings.

English is offered in Korean schools beginning in third grade. However, students who do not also study English through private education generally begin experiencing a learning gap in fifth grade, when the difficulty of reading demands increase. The fifth-grade English reading achievement criterion outlined in the current curriculum (Ministry of Education, 2015) is the ability to read and understand sentences. However, actual classrooms have mixed levels of students, with some unable to understand the relationships between sounds and letters or even decode the spellings of English words. In the classes containing students with mixed English ability levels, picture books with rhyming patterns improved all learners' English skills, regardless of level (J. Park & H. Kim, 2022). For example, lower-level fifth graders understood word decoding-oriented reading basics, while middle- and upper-level children were able to expand their literacy experience through an in-depth understanding of the principle of decoding. Therefore, in EFL situations, not only third graders who are beginners at English reading but also underachieving fifth graders can learn the principles of rhyming in context and improve their reading skills through picture books.

When English began being taught in elementary school, problems surrounding the introduction of written language and teaching methods began to occur. Therefore, phonics began to be introduced for teaching early reading, and the inefficiency of the techniques for teaching one-to-one correspondences between sounds and letters separately led to the study of teaching phonics in context. The introduction of phonics in English education was a turning point in elementary English education in Korea, and learning phonics in context proved to be more efficacious. Moreover, picture books can provide context for phonics-based early reading and help children both learn to decode words and learn their meanings. A study (Y. Yoon, 2023) that analyzed elementary English textbooks[3] found that the proportion of phonics rules differed slightly between textbooks, but the proportion gradually increased in 2011 and 2015 compared to the 2008 curriculum. When phonics was covered in textbooks, the focus was mainly on the initial consonant sound of words, without much context being provided. In teaching phonics, using a rhyme, which is a chunk made up of one or more vowels and consonants, is helpful for gaining reading fluency because English vowels can have several different sounds. Nevertheless, none of the English textbooks published so far have dealt with rhymes except for one published after the 2015 revised curriculum. It is expected that textbooks being developed based on the 2022 revised curriculum will contain higher-level phonics techniques, including rhymes in context.

## Integrating the Four Language Skills, with Reading as an Input Source

In English as a foreign language situation, the four language skills are generally taught and learned separately, in accordance with learner needs. For example, English education institutions in Korea offer separate classes on English reading, writing, listening, and conversation. In addition, the English achievement standards in the curricula distinguish between the four skills: listening, speaking, reading, and writing. In elementary English curricula, the emphasis was on fostering communicative ability through speaking emphasized, with the recommendation

---

[3] Since English textbooks are a certified textbook system in Korea, several textbooks for each subject are published after the curriculum is revised.

that writing components be linked to oracy. This meant that the level of reading achievement was lower than that of listening and speaking, with the importance of reading, which provides the necessary language input source for foreign language learners, being overlooked. Due to the development of media and technology, the distinctions between listening, speaking, reading, and writing have become unclear, and thus the 2022 revised English curriculum outlined the level of achievement through two areas: understanding and expression (Ministry of Education, 2022). "Understanding" includes listening, reading, and viewing, while "expression" includes speaking, writing, and presenting. Thus, the integration of language skills has become a priority.

In a foreign language environment where exposure to the target language is limited, reading is an important language input that can support the development of other language skills, such as listening, speaking, and writing (Cooper & Kiger, 2009; Richards & Renandya, 2002). Notably, reading is closely related to writing, and reading and writing have a positive effect on each other and play a complementary role in early language learning (Bernhardt, 1991; H. Kim & Y. Kang, 2009; H. Kim & S. Kim, 2010). In order to integrate the four language skills using reading as an input source, effective reading strategies are needed. Despite the importance of reading in foreign language education, the reality is that little research has been conducted on strategies for helping learners read well. Elementary English learners who lack reading strategies cannot arrive at the meaning of a text and end up translating words and phrases (Brown, 2000). Accordingly, in a study on teaching reading strategies (H. Kim & Y. Kim, 2010), children were taught strategies such as predicting, checking, visualizing, linking, asking, summarizing, and criticizing, and ended up being able to dynamically understand texts using such strategies.

In collaboration with elementary school teachers, the author conducted several studies that showed the impact of literacy experiences for students in different grades and possessing various English ability levels (H. Kim & Y. Jung, 2012; H. Kim & S. Kim, 2010; J. Kim & H. Kim, 2016; H. Kim & H. Lim, 2013; M. Lee & H. Kim, 2016; S. Yoon et al., 2018). For example, third graders with low English levels had positive experiences of reading and writing when they wrote double-entry journals in which they cited their favorite part of a picture book they had read and wrote down the reasons for it in two columns (H. Kim & S. Kim, 2010). Hence, children did not feel that writing was a burden and had a positive attitude toward reading and writing. If children are reading at an intermediate level, classes can focus more on systematic writing, using reading materials as input resources. M. Lee and H. Kim (2016) organized a writing workshop in which picture books were used as target language input and found that the fifth graders learned how to utilize them in their writing. In the writing workshop, the picture books served as a basis for the children to initiate and develop their writing. In the process of practicing, drafting, revising, and editing, efficient writing was possible because of systematic self-checking along with peer and teacher feedback.

In foreign language learning situations, learners' production skills are generally lower than their receptive skills. In elementary English classes with more of an emphasis on oral language skills, teachers use listening skills to improve children's speaking skills. This is because, on the one hand, the level of reading achievement in the curriculum is lower than that of speaking achievement, and, on the other hand, teachers are not familiar with materials or strategies that integrate speaking based on reading. However, speaking activities based on reading have an additional effect of naturally integrating reading and speaking as well as writing. For example, when children read English poems and engage in dramatization activities, the poems served as the target language input, helping them begin communicating orally by incorporating expressions from poems in their drama projects (J. Kim & H. Kim, 2016). Another example is using poems for two voices with a dialogue pattern, in which two people read one line at a time to build meaning. In a study focusing on poetry for two voices (S. Yoon et al., 2018), fifth graders improved their reading fluency by reading poems with their partners, and this type of reading led to collaborative writing in which partner sets could exchange and share ideas. Students became more confident at speaking as they improved their reading fluency by reading aloud.

In a study on implementing discussions on literature in elementary English classrooms, diverse genres of literature, such as narrative stories, dramas, and poems, were utilized, and listening, speaking, and writing could be integrated with reading (H. Kim & Y. Jung, 2012). The fifth graders in the study went through three transitional stages in which they gradually developed all four language skills of the target language. In the first stage, children came to understand the text through literary discussion activities, but English speaking was done at the word level, so it was necessary to raise their level of speaking. Therefore, in the second stage, sentences and patterns to be used in English discussions were introduced in mini-lessons, and children were given roles such as discussion leader, connector, and word wizard. In the final stage, minor roles were eliminated so that all children could have an opportunity to speak by leading the discussion in turn. While preparing for the discussion, they could improve their writing skills through writing discussion questions and expected answers in English.

In summary, language learners do not learn all four skills separately; rather, they often listen, read, write, and speak simultaneously, and the integration of all four skills supports language development as well as growth in literacy (Harste et al., 1984). The integration of the four language skills is more efficient when reading is a source of input, allowing for the improvement of all four skills in conjunction.

## A Shift in the Direction of Reading Instruction: The Transition to 'Reading to Learn'

In order for students to be competitive in the society of the future, they must be able to find, produce, and share information in English. This point began to be reflected in the 2015 revised English curriculum and proposed to develop knowledge information processing competencies in the 2022 revised English curriculum (Ministry of Education, 2022). In other words, in the previous curricula, the desired skills for the future were understanding knowledge and information in various fields and finding necessary information, but now it is required to have the competency to process knowledge and information by integrating the contents of other subjects in English classes. This is not only required in Korean situations but can also be seen as the current direction of literacy education, as schools prepare students for the decades ahead. It has been suggested that the direction of reading education should be shifted from "learning to read" to "reading to learn" because language learners will not be prepared for the demands of life beyond classrooms without a strong foundation in reading informational texts (National Reading Panel, 2000). 'Reading to learn' in which school subjects are integrated in English classes, is getting the attention of teachers, and many studies have been conducted in which diverse school subjects are integrated through children's literature or informational texts (H. Kim & E. Kim, 2012; H. Kim & J. Lee, 2009; H. Kim & H. Park, 2021; H. Kim & M. Yoo, 2013; J. Lee & H. Kim, 2020).

First, it is necessary to understand the genre and type of literary texts used in language classes that integrate the content of several subjects. Many teachers tend to think that informational texts are difficult for elementary school children with low language proficiency because they are written in a descriptive or expository style. However, the target information is also included in narrative picture books and poems for children, allowing language learners to easily obtain information while reading these literary texts. In fact, children who participated in a study conducted by H. Kim and J. Lee (2009) read picture books written in two different styles for each theme or subject. For example, to learn about 'growing plants,' they first read a picture book written in a narrative style and then read a picture book written in a descriptive style. Children were easily able to extract the relatively small amount of information presented in narrative style picture books, and this information helped them read more difficult informational texts, written in a descriptive style. The results showed that integrating English with other content allowed children to experience a new way of learning English reading and writing.

In a content integration study using poetry and stories dealing with the same subject in pairs, students exhibited different reading behaviors, text preferences, and reading achievements depending on the literary genre (H. Kim & E. Kim, 2012). When children read poems, they could easily memorize them by reading them several times and attending to rhythm and rhymes; when reading stories, they understood vocabulary and content matter better by focusing on illustrations and story structure elements such as the introduction, development, climax, and conclusion. Notably, lower-level learners preferred poems because they are short and easy to read, and upper-level learners preferred picture books because they could extract more information from them while enjoying interesting stories.

Meanwhile, in classes that integrated art, music, culture, and other subjects, students were not only able to read and acquire related information but also develop their aesthetic sensibility (H. Kim & E. Kim, 2010; H. Kim & M. Yoo, 2013; J. Lee & H. Kim, 2020). For example, students in a study by H. Kim and M. Yoo (2013) were able to extend their aesthetic sensibilities by reading books about great artists and imitating their techniques to develop their own artworks. They also expanded their knowledge of art and broadened their perspective on the arts. By learning English through famous artworks, students were able to have a rich language experience and gain knowledge that could serve as a sophisticated topic of conversation in international society, beyond the level of simple daily conversation.

In summary, reading in English to obtain information provides a meaningful communication context, boosting motivation to learn. English literary texts of various difficulty levels and styles can serve as ideal language materials for foreign language learners with various English ability levels, helping them achieve two goals: improving their language skills and acquiring information.

## Cultivating Creative Thinking Competencies in Literacy Education

Creativity has been raised as one of the major issues in elementary English education, and research on how to encourage creativity in English classes began after cultivating creative thinking was mentioned in the 2011 revised English curriculum (Ministry of Education, Science and Technology, 2011). Since then, creativity has been continuously emphasized in elementary English education, and in the 2022 revised English curriculum, six competencies, including creative thinking, were listed as core competencies (Ministry of Education, 2022). Although several studies (H. Jung, 2013; H. Kang, 2012; G. No, 2013) presented skeptical opinions on the possibility of fostering creativity in elementary English classes, many studies have been conducted on ways to teach creatively and teach creativity, including instruction using creative education techniques (J. Cho & H. Kim, 2016; I. Lee & H. Kim, 2015; B. Lim, & H. Kim, 2023; H. Shin & H. Kim, 2018). Some of the instructional techniques that have been explored are discussions, debates, inquiry-based learning, projects, creative problem solving, cooperative learning, and improving creative language skills through literary works.

Creativity can be divided into the categories of linguistic, literary, and everyday creativity, and McCallum (2012) notes that literary creativity is influenced by verbal creativity and the creativity of the reader. In other words, literary creativity is based on reader response theory (Rosenblatt, 1994), which suggests that a text can have different meanings for different readers. In addition, using literary works in language classes is useful for fostering creativity in that learners are provided with various perspectives, encounter various genres, and develop the ability to respond appropriately in consideration of language use and other positions in the context (Jones, 2016).

In foreign language classes, creativity can be fostered even if students of the target language have a low proficiency level. In other words, if appropriate learning materials and teaching methods are used, fourth-grade children with low levels of English can engage in creative activities in English. In a study by H. Shin and H. Kim (2018), alphabet picture books with various difficulty levels were used. Some featured words, while others featured phrases, sentences, or stories. At the end of the study, students were able to express creative ideas in an original, flexible manner in English in post-reading activities. Through the course of the study, children were fascinated by the unique illustrations of picture books and created their own works by imitating them. For example, *On Market Street* by Arnold and Anita Lobel (1981) presents a word for each letter of the alphabet; accompanying this is a unique illustration of a human figure formed from the object represented by the word. After reading this book, children selected a letter and then a word beginning with the letter, going on to create human figures using appropriate pictures. Most students chose nouns that are easy to express with pictures, but one child selected the abstract concept "idea" as an "I" word and then expressed it creatively through a human figure made from exclamation marks and lightbulbs. The "Ice cream" illustration (Fig. 2.1) from *On Market Street* is shown in the Appendix, next to the child's drawing (Fig. 2.2).

Sixth graders with high cognitive levels can engage in creative writing activities above their vocabulary level. In a study by H. Kim and Y. Kang (2009), children began to read English poetry and use it as a model. Then, they were able to gradually move to the stage of writing creatively, coming up with their own unique thoughts and forms. In other words, poems for children can be a source of interest for children, inspiring them to continue learning and making reading enjoyable. Further, the characteristics of poetry, including simplicity, rhythm, rhymes, and images, combine to make a strong impact on language learners. For example, children creating concrete poetry were able to strengthen and expand their poetic meaning by creating visually stimulating images. After reading Shel Silverstein's "Lazy Jane (1974)," which is written vertically, with only one word per line, one child created a visual effect by writing a poem inside a drawing of a long tree and drawing herself next to it. See Figs. 2.3 and 2.4 in the Appendix (Silverstein's "Lazy Jane" and the child's poem, respectively) for an illustration of the creative stimuli that poetry can give to children. Children also expressed their experiences or ideas in figurative languages such as similes and metaphors after reading poems.

I. Lee and H. Kim (2015) conducted an action research study and explored the idea that, among the genres of picture books, fantasy is more effective than realistic works for inspiring children to write creatively. By teaching strategies such as building up vocabulary, guiding cooperative learning, and teaching thinking skills and the steps of process writing, the researchers helped children develop their writing. Various literary experiences mentioned above fostered students' written communication and creative writing skills as well. Students were able to express their ideas creatively by referring to several literary aspects of fantasy stories. A recent study by B. Lim and H. Kim (2024) explored children's responses to picture books in three genres, such as traditional folklore, parody, and fantasy. The results of the study presented that while children's responses in all three genres were creative, different patterns were shown depending on the genre in cultivating creative thinking competency.

On the other hand, using postmodern picture books that have story structures differing from those of traditional picture books can change learners' thinking methods (Goldstone, 2004). Traditional texts develop in chronological order, allowing readers to easily follow the plot, but postmodern structures require readers to read more dynamically because multiple stories are presented nonlinearly in a single picture book or have a self-referential structure. J. Cho and H. Kim (2016) attempted to teach creative English writing to fifth graders using postmodern picture books. To foster participants' creativity, the researchers integrated activities for developing thinking skills, such as brainstorming, synectics, group discussions, and role-plays. They found that children in the study could build up their creative writing skills by interpreting the nonlinear structure of postmodern picture books and develop their writing skills by solving problems creatively through activities for developing thinking skills. In a study focusing on metafiction techniques of postmodern picture books (K. Park & H. Kim, 2023), children were able to actively engage in creative activities to rewrite story endings with different thoughts from the authors.

In summary, studies using literary works show that literary creativity and linguistic creativity can be naturally linked, and exposure to different genres of literary works can result in different patterns of creativity. It is also important to create a suitable environment for developing learners' creative potential (Fleith et al., 2022). In other words, creative writing can be further activated if appropriate activities are combined when using picture books as language input materials in foreign language learning situations. In addition, writing processes that allow learners to experience creative thinking processes and reconstruct meanings in order to express their thoughts creatively reflect their problem-solving processes and results, so further research on ways to provide creative teaching methods is needed.

# Enhancing Critical Thinking Skills to Overcome Prejudice

Critical thinking skills have been mentioned in all the revised curricula since they were first suggested in the 2011 revised English curriculum. This seems to come from the perception that it is a great loss to allow students in English classes conducted during the information age to deal with information while lacking logical and critical thinking processes. It is necessary to use literary works that touch upon and help remove learners' stereotypes since textbooks have limitations when it comes to cultivating critical thinking skills in elementary English classes.

Traditional folktales are familiar to children as oral literature and employ easy language and repetitive patterns, so they are learning materials with a low level of linguistic difficulty, even for elementary school children learning a foreign language. A study by H. Kim and E. Park (2011) focused on the linguistic advantages of folktales, which can help children improve their language skills while reading from a critical perspective and developing high-level thinking skills. Before the study, children expressed prejudices about characters' appearances and fell back on typical stereotypes. In other words, the princess is pretty, the prince is handsome, the prince saves the princess, and the stepmother, wolf, and dinosaur represent evil. However, by reading the stories and discussing them from the characters' point of view, they were able to overcome their prejudices and expand their way of thinking. They stopped evaluating characters solely through appearance, came to think that the princess could save the prince, and began judging the situation from the wolf's point of view.

When a folktale and a related parody were used in tandem, learners were repeatedly exposed to the same vocabulary and similar sentence structures but in different contexts (Y. Kim & H. Kim, 2016). For example, the folktale "Three Little Pigs" and a parody, *The True Story of the 3 Little Pigs* by Jon Scieszka and Lane Smith (1989), were paired together. Children first read the folktale, which had lower linguistic demands, then read the parody, which contained more difficult language and satirical elements. Through this reading activity, children made improvements in reading and writing, based on their English level, and were able to develop their critical thinking skills by overcoming simple stereotypes of good and evil implied in folktales. They were also able to independently develop criteria for moral judgment through parody and satire.

The genre of multicultural picture books can also help improve children's critical thinking. After reading traditional folktales and parodies, children mainly were able to change their view of characters and think critically in a way that deviated from stereotypes. However, when they read multicultural picture books, they showed interest in world cultures and people and became critical of cultural prejudice (H. Kim & E. Kim, 2010; K. Park & H. Kim, 2019). For example, students in a study by H. Kim and E. Kim (2010) responded to multicultural literature positively, becoming more interested in world culture, developing a logical and critical view of the world, and overcoming cultural prejudices.

In sum, English learners can overcome biases and prejudices by reading traditional folktales, parodies, and multicultural literature. These studies are based on the work of Freire and Ramos (2000), in which readers need to constantly challenge the power relationship between readers and writers by reading the text critically and becoming active participants rather than passively accepting the writer's ideas. It may seem difficult to get elementary school children to think critically in foreign language learning situations. However, if appropriate texts and strategies are used, children will have the opportunity to develop critical thinking skills while improving their English communication skills.

## Improving Problem-Solving Abilities in Elementary English Classes

Problem-solving in English classes has been an element of task-based language learning, a learning method that aims to provide meaningful, practical communication opportunities through carrying out various tasks (Y. Bae & K. Park, 2009). However, as suggested in the 2022 revised curriculum, learners will actively work to solve community problems through English based on their understanding of cultural identity and diversity as members of local, national, and global communities. To achieve this goal, it is necessary to develop and implement programs for exploring real-life problems and enhance learners' ability to solve them while integrating various subjects in English classes.

In a study that developed and applied a complex problem-solving program, it was reported that problem-solving skills could be improved in elementary English classes (H. Kim et al., 2021). The sixth graders participating in this study were able to improve their English production skills by answering step-by-step questions to solve problems after reading picture books. In addition, they were able to achieve personal growth by reflecting on their lives while exploring and solving problems.

In English classes that integrated social studies subjects using informational picture books, learners were exposed to various language input sources, and through this, they began to recognize the responsibilities and rights of democratic citizens (H. Kim & H. Park, 2021). In addition, they tried to solve the problems presented in the books while communicating with one another. Also, they showed a willingness to find solutions and practice global citizenship by drawing links between the picture books and the real world.

Of the 127 elementary school teachers in an online community of elementary school teachers who participated in a survey, only 23 (18%) had experience teaching problem-solving skills in English classes, but 97 (76.4%) responded that teaching such skills in English classes is necessary, and 95 (74.8%) believed it would be possible (H. Kim & Y. Kim, 2024). In summary, English classes dealing with problem-solving are not currently being conducted, but teachers recognize that this is one of the core competencies of the future.

## Incorporating Edtech into Literacy Activities

The development of English teaching methods has been accompanied by the evolution of technology, for example, the audio-lingual method was possible because language content could be recorded on cassette tapes and played back. The use of technology has also had a great influence on elementary English classes. In the era of the sixth national curriculum, some educational content appeared through the medium of VHS tapes, but as PCs became more popular, CD-ROMs became more convenient. In the 2022 revision, various media and ICT (information and communications technology) tools were proposed to be used in class and as learning aids to reflect the shift toward an educational environment containing digital and AI (artificial intelligence) resources.

In elementary English classes, diverse types of teaching and learning techniques, such as online platforms, digital tools, and mobile applications, could be integrated. In a study by E. Jang and H. Kim (2020), the possibility of adapting mobile application-based writing using picture books was explored. Sixth graders in this study enjoyed writing using the functions of mobile applications and learned how to utilize mobile app dictionaries and translators, developing strategies for using the translation software to write sentences. Through this process, learners were able to improve their writing skills.

Meanwhile, face-to-face classes may not be possible in the event of a future pandemic like COVID-19, so research on English teaching methods for such a situation is also needed. In fact, literature-based reading instruction could be carried out either online or offline by developing a smarlogue ("smart" and "analogue") type English reading program (H. Kim, 2020; K. Park, 2022). Through a smarlogue reading program, it is possible to read literature that relates to a textbook unit or integrates the content of the subject.

In short, what technology is currently doing through written language is extending our ideas of literacy education. For hundreds of years, we have relied on two major means of communication: face-to-face speech and words written or printed on paper. However, alternative forms of written communication, such as web-based texts, email, CD-ROMs, audio books, online databases, the Internet, and text messaging have become widespread. Technology has also made an on-off blended library system possible in an extensive reading program (K. Song et al., 2013).

## Conclusion

In this chapter, the author considered innovation in elementary English education, especially focusing on factors related to literacy, and for this purpose, she presented the results obtained through cooperative research with teachers. As mentioned at the beginning of this chapter, teaching English as a regular subject in elementary schools is one of the innovations that occurred in the history of English education in Korea, and we have seen further innovation and continual developments in the field since then. This is due to the fact that elementary English, which began as a special activity in public schools in the 1980s, was difficult to teach systematically throughout the country. Starting in 1997, when English became a regular subject in elementary schools, the stress was placed on basic everyday English, language education based on communication, and English education centered on oracy.

However, the importance of literacy education emerged in elementary English education, reflecting the trends of the times, and creativity, the improvement of thinking skills, and the use of edtech were introduced into elementary English education as important educational content and tools. In addition, stories began to be used in English classes as storytelling content; they were mainly used as a means of teaching linguistic elements such as English vocabulary and sentence patterns. Now, going beyond storytelling and the focus only on teaching English skills, various genres of children's literature such as poetry, drama, and picture books have begun to be used. In other words, English classes applying appropriate teaching methods are being conducted in accordance with the genre of literature or the theme of the story. These changes and developments in elementary English education are the result of efforts by teachers and scholars to overcome limitations in actual classrooms and prejudice against English education as a foreign language. The author hopes that these innovations in elementary English education can be used to lay the foundation for providing high-quality English education to the children of the future.

# Appendix

See Figs. 2.1, 2.2, 2.3 and 2.4.

**Fig. 2.1** The "Ice Cream" illustration from *On Market Street*

Fig. 2.2 The Child's drawing of the "Idea"

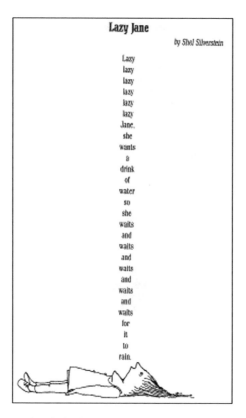

**Fig. 2.3** "Lazy Jane" by Shel Silverstein

Fig. 2.4 The Child's poem

# References

Bae, Y., & Park, K. (2009). A developmental study on the application of collaborative problem solving in English instruction. *Journal of Educational Technology, 25*(1), 137–170.

Bernhardt, D. B. (1991). *Reading development in a second language: Theoretical, empirical, and classroom perspectives*. Ablex Publishing Corp.

Brown, H. D. (2000). *Principles of language learning and teaching* (4th ed.). Prentice-Hall.

Cho, J. H., & Kim, H.-R. (2016). Teaching of creative writing in primary EFL context using postmodern picture books. *The 21$^{st}$ Century Association of English Language and Literature, 29*(2), 283–307.

Cooper, J. D., & Kiger, N. D. (2009). *Literacy: Helping children construct meaning* (7th ed.). Houghton Mifflin.

Fleith, D. D. S., Renzulli, J. S., & Westberg, K. L. (2022). Effects of a creativity training program on divergent thinking abilities and self-concept in monolingual and bilingual classrooms. *Creativity Research Journal, 14*(3), 373–386.

Freire, P., & Ramos, M. B. (2000). *Pedagogy of the oppressed*. Continuum.

Goldstone, B. (2004). The postmodern picture book: A new subgenre. *Language Arts, 81*(3), 196–204.

Harste, J., Woodward, V., & Burke, C. (1984). *Language stories and literacy lessons*. Heinemann.

Jang, E.-J., & Kim, H.-R. (2020). A Study of teaching writing in English instruction based on mobile applications using picture books. *Multimedia-Assisted Language Learning, 23*(4), 207–232.

Jones, R. H. (2016). Creativity and language. In R. H. Jones & J. C. Richards (Eds.), *Creativity in language teaching: Perspectives from research and practice* (pp. 16–31). Routledge.

Jung, H. Y. (2013). Teachers' perception of the application of creativity education to English lessons at elementary schools. *Educational Science Research, 44*(4), 147–168.

Kang, H. D. (2012). The effects of creativity & character education on elementary English education. *Primary English Education, 18*(1), 173–196.

Kim, H.-R. (2020). Developing a smarlogue type primary English reading program to prepare for the post-corona era. *Primary English Education, 26*(4), 181–204.

Kim, H.-R., & Jung, Y. H. (2012). Implementing literature discussion for primary English learners using children's literature based on the framework of action research. *Primary English Education, 18*(1), 247–281.

Kim, H.-R., & Kang, Y.-O. (2009). A study of the reading-writing connection in primary schools through the use of English poetry for children. *Primary English Education, 15*(1), 147–183.

Kim, H.-R., & Kim, E. (2010). A study of integrating culture into elementary English through response journal writing based on children's multicultural literature. *Primary English Education, 16*(2), 81–110.

Kim, H.-R., & Kim, E. Y. (2012). A study of reading-writing through content-based integrated teaching using poetry-story connection in a primary EFL classroom. *Primary English Education, 18*(2), 111–145.

Kim, H.-R., & Kim, S. J. (2010). A study of English writing through response journals using literary text in primary schools. *Studies in English Education, 15*(1), 196–220.

Kim, H.-R., & Kim, Y. (2024). A study of teachers' perceptions and suggestions for enhancing problem-solving skills in primary English. *Journal of the Korea English Education Society, 23*(1), 55–82.

Kim, H.-R., & Kim, Y.-M. (2010). Teaching of reading strategies in primary English through the use of children's literature. *Primary English Education, 16*(3), 85–121.

Kim, H.-R., & Lee, J. Y. (2009). A study of integrating content and language through the use of content-based literary texts in EFL primary English education. *Primary English Education, 15*(3), 135–161.

Kim, H.-R., & Lee, S.-Y. (2012). A study of teaching beginning reading based on rhymes using storybooks. *Primary English Education, 18*(3), 65–96.

Kim, H.-R., & Lim, H. (2013). Action research on developing production skills through questioning strategies for primary EFL learners based on children's literature. *Journal of the Korea English Education Society, 12*(1), 29–55.

Kim, H.-R., & Park, E. H. (2011). A study of primary English literacy education through critical reading of folktales. *The Journal of Teaching English Literature, 15*(2), 199–222.

Kim, H.-R., & Park, H. (2021). Exploring primary English and global citizenship education using informational picture books based on social studies and language integration. *The Journal of Linguistic Science, 99*, 189–222.

Kim, H.-R., Park, K.-J., & Kim, Y. (2021). Development of a complex-problem solving program base on subject integration to improve English communication skills of primary learners. *The Journal of Korea Elementary Education, 32*(Supplement), 31–50.

Kim, H.-R., & Yoo, M.-J. (2013). A study of English-art integrated lessons using informational texts in a primary EFL setting. *Primary English Education, 19*(2), 25–47.

Kim, J. M., & Kim, H.-R. (2016). Aspects of communication in EFL primary instruction based on English poetry for children and dramatizing activities. *Primary English Education, 22*(2), 35–56.

Kim, Y., & Kim, H.-R. (2016). A study of teaching primary English and developing critical thinking skills through connecting folktales and parodies. *Studies in English Education, 21*(4), 175–205.

Lee, I.-S., & Kim, H.-R. (2015). Action research on developing creative English writing skills among Korean primary school students: Focusing on using fantasy picture books. *English Language Teaching, 27*(1), 135–155.

Lee, J., & Kim, H.-R. (2020). The impact of integrating music into primary English instruction using informational texts. *Primary English Education, 26*(2), 25–47.

Lee, M. H., & Kim, H.-R. (2016). The effects of writing workshop in primary English using children's literature featuring social problems. *Foreign Languages Education, 23*(4), 139–170.

Lim, B. R., & Kim, H.-R. (2023). Exploration of creativity research trends and instructional guidance in primary English education. *Primary English Education, 29*(3), 5–31.

Lim, B. R., & Kim, H.-R. (2024). The patterns of creative thinking competency in elementary learners analyzed in English classes utilizing genre-specific picture books. *Primary English Education, 30*(1), 5–25.

McCallum, A. (2012). *Creativity and learning in secondary English: Teaching for a creative classroom.* Routledge.

Ministry of Culture and Education. (1954). *National curriculum of Korea.* Ministry of Culture and Education.

Ministry of Education. (1995). *Elementary school curriculum—General, English—Announcement by Ministry of Education No. 1995-7.* Ministry of Education.

Ministry of Education. (2015). *English curriculum: Announcement by Ministry of Education No. 2015-74 [Annex 14].* Ministry of Education.

Ministry of Education. (2022). *English curriculum: Announcement by Ministry of Education No. 2022-33 [Annex 14].* Ministry of Education.

Ministry of Education. (1997). *Foreign language curriculum (1): Announcement by Ministry of Education No.1997-15.* Ministry of Education.

Ministry of Education, Science and Technology. (2008). *Foreign language curriculum (1): Announcement by Ministry of Education, Science and Technology No. 2008 – 160 [Annex 14].* Ministry of Education, Science and Technology.

Ministry of Education, Science and Technology. (2011). *English curriculum: Announcement by Ministry of Education, Science and Technology No. 2011–361 [Annex 14].* Ministry of Education, Science and Technology.

National Reading Panel. (2000). *Report of the National Reading Panel: Teaching children to read, and evidence-based assessment of the scientific research literature on reading and its implications for reading instruction: Reports of the subgroups.* National Institute for Child Health and Human Development.

No, G. (2013). The meaning of creativity in primary English education. *Primary English Education, 19*(2), 49–69.

Park, J., & Kim, H.-R. (2022). An action research for exploring the aspects of level-differentiated literacy learning based on picture books in primary English. *Primary English Education, 28*(3), 27–54.

Park, K.-J. (2022). Effects of smarlogue type reading activities using parody picture books on elementary school students' critical literacy. *Journal of Learner-Centered Curriculum and Instruction, 22*(18), 393–412.

Park, K.-J., & Kim, H.-R. (2019). Enhancing productive skills and critical thinking ability through critical literacy activities in primary English lessons. *Studies in English Education, 21*(4), 175–205.

Park, K.-J., & Kim, H.-R. (2023). Effects of utilizing postmodern picturebooks with metafictive devices on elementary school students' English communicative competence. *Primary English Education, 29*(4), 157–178.

Richards, D., & Renandya, A. (2002). *Methodology in language teaching: An anthology of current practice.* Cambridge University Press.

Rosenblatt, L. M. (1994). The transactional theory of reading and writing. In R. B. Ruddell, M. R. Ruddell, & H. Singer (Eds.), *Theoretical models and processes of reading* (pp. 1057–1092). International Reading Association.

Shin, H.-R., & Kim, H.-R. (2018). Teaching primary English using alphabet picture books: Focusing on improving vocabulary and developing creativity. *Primary English Education, 24*(2), 5–30.

Song, K., Chang, K., Kwon, H., & Choi, B. (2013). A case study of extensive reading using a blended English library system at a primary school. *Primary English Education, 19*(1), 147–167.

Yoon, S., Kim, H.-R., & Lee, N. (2018). Teaching primary English through cooperative learning-based activities using dialogue pattern poetry. *Primary English Education, 24*(1), 5–27.

Yoon, Y. B. (2023). Analysis of phonics in primary English textbooks in line with changes to the national curriculum. *English Language and Literature, 28*(2), 123–146.

## Children's Literature Cited

Dr. Seuss. (1963). *Hop on pop*. Random House.
Lobel, A., & Lobel, A. (1981). *On market street*. Greenwillow Books.
Scieszka, J., & Smith, L. (1989). *The true story of the 3 little pigs*. Viking Kestrel.
Silverstein, S. (1974). *Where the sidewalk ends: The poems & drawings of Shel Silverstein*. Harper & Row.

# 3

# Transforming Language Education Through AI: Artificial Intelligence Digital Textbook (AIDT)

Sangmin-Michelle Lee and Junseong Bang

## Introduction

The Korean Ministry of Education announced that a suite of digital textbooks, referred to as the AI Digital Textbook, or AIDT, will be used in primary and secondary schools across the country starting in 2025. AIDT, according to Korea Education and Research Information Service (KERIS) (2024), comprises software that uses learner profiling and learning analytics to facilitate personalized adaptive learning, but it also refers to textbooks for public schools. The initial rollout will focus on English, mathematics, and informatics, with plans to expand to other subjects in subsequent years. This initiative aims to address a critical challenge in education in Korea: the stark divide between public and private

---

S.-M. Lee (✉)
Kyung Hee University, Yongin, South Korea
e-mail: sangminlee@khu.ac.kr

J. Bang
Ymatics Corp., Seoul, South Korea

education. The disparity is particularly evident in English education, where affluent families have access to personalized instruction through private tutoring and education that is unavailable to others.

The appeal of private English education lies in its ability to provide personalized, small-group instruction tailored to individual student needs and proficiency levels. While the benefits of such personalized approaches are clear, implementing them in traditional public school classrooms, which typically follow a one-to-many teaching model, has proven impractical. Previous attempts at differentiated instruction in public schools have fallen short due to various classroom constraints, further widening the achievement gap between students with and without access to private education. Especially in English, there are large differences in the levels of knowledge of students in the classroom (Han & Ahn, 2023; Nam & Lee, 2022). In this situation, AIDT is expected to be an alternative solution to alleviate educational inequality and inequity in Korea. By providing personalized learning experiences for each student within the public school system, it has the potential to democratize access to learning opportunities regardless of socioeconomic background. The OECD (2024) refers to this educational transformation in Korea as a "paradigm shift" toward achieving educational equity.

As the first country to implement AI-enhanced personalized learning on a national scale, Korea's experience will provide crucial insights into the future of education. AIDT has the potential to improve student learning, increase educational equity, and enhance teacher practice, but at the same time, this ambitious initiative may face several challenges as it will create significant changes in the classroom. These include adapting to new roles for students and teachers, addressing gaps in digital literacy, fostering student agency, and ensuring that algorithmic biases do not inadvertently create new forms of educational inequality. This chapter explores three critical aspects of this transformation: the architecture and features of AIDT, the evolving roles of students and teachers in AI-enhanced personalized learning environments, and the considerations necessary for developing an AI-driven learning ecosystem.

# Architecture and Features of AIDT

## Definition and Architecture of AIDT

AIDT is defined as software that integrates various learning materials and supports functions using intelligent information technologies, including AI, to provide personalized learning opportunities tailored to each student's abilities and levels (KERIS, 2024). It involves students, teachers and parents as the three main stakeholders and aims to enable students to learn through optimized personalized learning content, teachers to design instruction based on data, and parents to receive comprehensive information about their children's learning activities. A dashboard is provided for each stakeholder, and users can access the dashboard to see how students are doing (Fig. 3.1). As shown in Fig. 3.2, AIDT's architecture is built around a central data hub that supports various AI-powered features across subject areas, including diagnostic assessments, learning materials, question banks, and interactive activities. AIDT is a combination of several different AI systems and agents, including what Baker and Smith (2019) categorized as three different types: learner-facing, teacher-facing, and system-facing AI tools. In addition to the AI-powered Learning Management System (LMS) (system-facing), AIDT includes specialized learner-facing and teacher-facing AI components: an AI tutor that provides personalized guidance to students, and an AI assistant that helps teachers plan and deliver instruction. In addition, private-sector partnerships play a critical role in the AIDT ecosystem, contributing to collection, training and analysis of data, as well as providing a variety of learning content.

## Features and Characteristics of AIDT

AIDT has three distinguishing features: AI-driven learning analytics, adaptive learning, and human-centered design. For students, AIDT offers a comprehensive suite of personalized learning services, providing differentiated and customized learning. For example, it enables remediation for slower learners and advanced learning for faster learners based

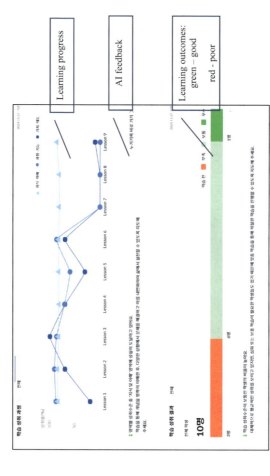

**Fig. 3.1** Middle school English AIDT, Teacher's view (Lee et al., 2025)

3 Transforming Language Education Through AI ... 53

**Fig. 3.2** The architecture of AIDT (KERIS, 2024, p. 21, translated into English)

on analytics results. Especially for slower learners, it can recommend basic concept-oriented content appropriate to the student's learning level to fill learning gaps. At its core, the system performs continuous diagnostic assessments, conducts detailed learning analytics, and delivers customized content recommendations. This dynamic process creates an optimized learning path that continually adapts to each student's progress, learning style, and instructional needs. As such, learning analytics plays a central role in AIDT's adaptive learning capabilities.

AIDT's adaptive learning system operates on two fundamental sets of data: learner profiles and learning content. To build comprehensive learner profiles, AIDT tracks and analyzes various aspects of student behavior, including participation rates, learning outcomes, progress patterns, and socio-emotional factors. At the same time, AIDT organizes learning content through knowledge-based mapping, systematically categorizing materials by difficulty level, topic, and other relevant parameters. Through sophisticated analysis of learner profiles, the AIDT algorithm matches each student with the most appropriate content.

To enhance student learning, AIDT features an AI tutor that provides instant feedback, answers student questions, and guides personalized learning. This feature is particularly valuable in English classes, where it serves as a conversation partner. Korean English-as-a-Foreign Language (EFL) students typically have limited opportunities for speaking practice both in the classroom and in everyday life (Lee & Ahn, 2024). In addition, they often experience high levels of speaking anxiety in traditional English classrooms (Ahn & Lee, 2016; Lee & Ahn, 2024). The AI tutor addresses these challenges by providing a ubiquitous conversation partner in an emotionally safe environment. Developed in line with the Korean National English Curriculum, the AI tutor is more constrained than general-purpose AI, but functions as an advanced peer to support students' language development in their zone of proximal development (ZPD), the optimal space between what a learner can do independently and what they can achieve with guidance (Vygotsky, 1978). As they learn, students can monitor their learning progress and results through an interactive dashboard that provides detailed feedback on their performance to reflect their learning progress.

Another key feature of AIDT is its Universal Design for Learning (UDL), an educational framework that aims to make learning accessible and effective for all students by providing flexible methods of instruction, engagement, and assessment (Meyer et al., 2014) from a user-centered design perspective. AIDT addresses diverse learning needs by providing multiple means of engagement through different media formats—including text, voice, and images. This multimodal approach allows students to access content through their preferred learning channels, making education more accessible and effective for learners with different needs and preferences. In addition, multi-language translation services are embedded to ensure learning for students with different language backgrounds, taking into account Korea's recently increasingly diverse population.

AIDT also offers several key features for teachers. The system provides comprehensive dashboards for tracking individual student and class-wide learning progress, including real-time monitoring during lessons and automatic alerts for underachieving students. These features allow for timely instructional intervention. Teachers can also customize and reorganize learning content to meet specific instructional goals and student needs, going beyond pre-designed curricula to create customized learning experiences. During this process, an AI assistant helps teachers plan lessons, organize learning materials, and answer pedagogical questions.

# Changing Roles of Students and Teachers with AIDT

## AI-Driven Personalized Adaptive Learning Systems

Unlike traditional "one-size-fits-all" models, personalized learning allows the pace, content, and instructional methods to be tailored to students' abilities and learning styles (Eduvate Rohde Island, 2017; Patricket al., 2013). Personalized learning allows learners to actively engage in their learning and have a greater sense of ownership and agency over their learning (Bray & McClaskey, 2014), thereby improving learning outcomes (Alamri et al., 2020; Bray & McClaskey, 2016). According to

Bloom (1984), students who received one-on-one personalized tutoring outperformed their peers in traditional classrooms by approximately two standard deviations. However, despite its remarkable effectiveness, the resource-intensive and costly nature of personalized tutoring makes it impractical for widespread implementation in educational systems (Bloom's 2-sigma problem), and most classrooms "are not able to realistically scale group instruction this way" (Khan, 2024, p. 35), limiting its application to specific specialized teaching contexts, such as high-cost private tutoring (Bernacki et al., 2021; Wu, 2015).

Recently, AI has emerged as a promising solution to the challenge of Bloom's 2-sigma problem, offering a scalable approach to personalized learning in traditional classroom settings. AI learning systems can continuously analyze students' learning progress, material interactions, and learning outcomes in real time, identify knowledge gaps, and deliver tailored educational resources. This capability enables personalized adaptive learning, which Peng et al. (2019) define as "a technology-empowered effective pedagogy which can adaptively adjust teaching strategies timely based on real-time monitored (enabled by smart technology) learners' differences and changes in individual characteristics, individual performance, and personal development" (p. 1). AI-enhanced personalized adaptive learning systems operate through data-informed and data-driven stages to optimize three critical aspects of the learning process: determining "what to learn" based on individual characteristics, determining "how to learn" based on individual performance, and evaluating "how well to learn" while predicting the likelihood of students achieving learning goals (Peng et al., 2019).

Two fundamental models play a central role in AI learning systems: the learner model and the knowledge model (Chen et al., 2020). The learner model is constructed by systematically collecting and analyzing behavioral data from students' learning processes. This model enables AI learning systems to evaluate learners' knowledge mastery levels and explore the complex relationships between learning outcomes and various factors, including teaching methods and environmental conditions. The knowledge model, which complements the learner model, develops comprehensive knowledge structure maps that describe learning content in detail. These maps serve as essential tools for identifying learners' misconceptions and systematic errors in their understanding (Chen et al., 2020).

Based on the data collected from the learner and knowledge models, learning analytics orchestrates pedagogical methods to meet the needs of individual students and facilitate learning through timely interventions and feedback. The pedagogical decision-making processes in these AI learning systems typically employ one of two methodologies: rule-based approaches that use predetermined decision trees or data-driven methods, depending on the local situation (Peng et al., 2019). A prime example of this technology in action can be found in AI-powered LMSs, such as ALEKS and Knewton. Another type of example is Intelligent Tutoring Systems (ITS), such as Khanmigo and MaTHia, which adapt to different student proficiency levels while continuously monitoring their performance. These ITS effectively function as educational assistants or pedagogical collaborators that help students complete tasks (Chen et al., 2020). According to Khan (2024), AI tutors are particularly effective at meeting learners' needs within their ZPD (Vygotsky, 1978).

AI has transformative potential in education, offering significant benefits from both the learner and teacher perspectives (Avella et al., 2016; Bryan et al., 2020; Channa et al., 2021). From the learner's perspective, AI technology effectively democratizes educational opportunities by removing traditional barriers to accessing learning opportunities while providing sophisticated, personalized learning experiences tailored to individual strengths and weaknesses (Chassignol et al., 2018; Chen et al., 2020). Khan (2024) argued that AI learning systems can democratize access to high-quality, personalized education by transcending socioeconomic boundaries that have historically limited educational opportunities. In other words, AI learning systems can take another step toward equity in education by providing more resources to students with more needs. In addition, through real-time analytics and adaptive learning algorithms, AI learning systems enable timely, targeted interventions that optimize the learning experience by ensuring that content and methodology are precisely aligned with learners' abilities and progress (Gibson et al., 2023; Khan, 2024).

From the teacher's perspective, AI technology serves as a powerful pedagogical tool that enhances teaching effectiveness in multiple dimensions. It enables teachers to optimize curriculum design through data-driven insights, make evidence-based pedagogical decisions, and continuously refine their teaching strategies based on objective and scientific data (Celik et al., 2022; Luckin & Cukurova, 2019). This systematic approach to instructional improvement allows teachers to improve their professional practice while providing more effective instruction tailored to individual student needs (Avella et al., 2016). A McKinsey report found that teachers spend less than half of their 50 hours per week interacting directly with students, with much of the rest spent on preparation and assessment (Bryan et al., 2020). AI is expected to ease the burden on teachers by helping them prepare lessons and assess student work, and by doing so, AI will allow teachers to have more meaningful interactions with students (idem).

## Changing Roles of Students: Student Agency and Self-Directed Learning

While AI learning systems offer personalized content, customized learning paths and adaptive feedback, they do not automatically guarantee successful learning outcomes. Instead, effective learning with AIDT, or any AI system, requires strong student agency and well-developed self-directed learning skills. Student agency, the ability to act independently, make decisions and take responsibility for one's own learning, is particularly important in this context. This agency promotes autonomy, ownership and self-directed learning (Collier, 2022; Kalaja & Ruohotie-Lyhty, 2022). Bandura (2001) characterizes agency through three key components: intentionality, self-processing and self-reflection, which emphasize the student's active role in educational engagement and autonomous decision making. Student agency enables learners to set and pursue goals, navigate their learning processes in alignment with these goals, and critically reflect on their progress (Stenalt & Lassesen, 2022). In AI-enhanced learning environments, students' ability to construct their own knowledge becomes even more critical than in traditional classroom settings with human teachers. As Jääskelä et al. (2021) note, students need "the ability and capacity to set goals, make choices, and act on those choices during learning" (p. 792) in AI learning systems because learning with AI learning systems requires students' agency and self-directed learning strategies, including planning, monitoring, and controlling their learning (Oxford, 2017).

While student agency and self-directed learning are critical to learning with AI systems, these skills cannot develop naturally in students, but must be intentionally cultivated during learning (Vaughn, 2019). Agency is dynamic and contextually situated and can develop through the interplay of personal dispositions, teacher involvement, and contextual factors (Jääskelä et al., 2021; Vaughn, 2019). According to Klemenčič (2017), agency is shaped in a specific context of action and varies depending on the context. Therefore, the AI learning system, as a learning context, is important in shaping students' agency. For example, AI learning systems can provide strategic features such as epistemic questioning, constructive feedback, and intentionally structured learning processes (Channa et al., 2021). Such design elements can trigger active knowledge construction and develop students' agency and capacity for self-directed learning. In this way, AI learning systems should serve not only to deliver educational content, but also to systematically foster more fundamental learning skills that students need to play active and independent roles.

## Changing Roles of Teachers: Transformative Multiple Roles

Teachers play multiple roles in teaching with AI systems. First, in the case of AIDT, because it allows teachers to reorganize learning content, teachers can take on the role of curriculum designer. This role is particularly important for orchestrating learning content and methods and maximizing student learning outcomes in personalized adaptive learning systems (Hong et al., 2024). While AIDT can provide personalized learning pathways, teachers retain the critical responsibility of curating and sequencing content and activities for individual students. The flexibility of AIDT allows for unprecedented customization, potentially creating what KERIS (2024) describes as "5 million textbooks for 5 million students." This level of personalization means that instructional practices can be infinitely varied, with teachers making informed decisions about how to use AI capabilities to best meet the unique needs of their students.

As shown in Fig. 3.3, teachers and AIDT will serve distinct but complementary roles within Bloom's Taxonomy. While AIDT effectively supports students in developing lower-order thinking skills, such as remembering and understanding basic concepts, teachers can focus on cultivating higher-order thinking skills, such as evaluation and creativity, that AI alone cannot adequately develop. This strategic partnership represents a balanced "High Touch and High Tech" model, where AI and humans work in synergy to enhance the overall learning experience. In this model, High Tech represents adaptive learning provided by AIDT, and High Touch represents more interactive learning with human teachers and peers, provided by teachers. By distributing teaching responsibilities according to their respective strengths, this approach maximizes the potential of both AI technology and human teaching expertise.

Second, teachers serve as facilitators of personalized learning, interpreting student data, analyzing individual strengths and weaknesses, and making pedagogical decisions to optimize learning outcomes. This role requires teachers to develop multifaceted competencies, particularly in Technological Pedagogical Content Knowledge (TPACK), the different

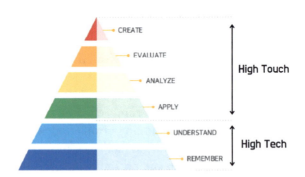

Fig. 3.3 Bloom's Taxonomy (1956) and the High Touch and High Tech model (Adapted from KERIS [2024, p. 16])

types of knowledge required of teachers when technology integration occurs in the classroom (Koehler & Mishra, 2006). Moreover, as AI integration raises concerns about AI ethics, overreliance on technology, and bias and inequality in data access and use (Chen et al., 2020; Holmes, 2023), teachers must also develop Technological Pedagogical Content Ethical Knowledge (TPCEK) (Deng & Zhang, 2023). Furthermore, maneuvering through these complicated dynamics of learning and teaching with AIDT requires teachers' agency, which is critical in driving and shaping their actions in dealing with available resources, including AI tools (Damşa et al., 2021). More specifically, as Reinders et al. (2024) argue in *Humanizing Technology*, teachers need to become digitally literate, develop digital well-being, humanize students' learning experiences, and use data in positive ways.

Third, teachers take on the role of social and emotional supporters. Numerous studies have confirmed that learning is a social practice, in which meaningful interactions and collaboration are critical to knowledge acquisition (Zawacki-Richter et al., 2019). As emphasized by Channa et al. (2021), "emotions can influence cognitive behaviors such as attentional focus, decision making, reasoning, and memory retrieval. They are influential factors in learning and achievement" (p. 3205). While AI learning systems may excel at content delivery, they cannot replicate the social and emotional support that teachers provide through engaging social activities and responsive emotional guidance.

Niemi (2024) notes that AI will not only impact student learning, but also transform the entire educational ecosystem. AI learning systems, including AIDT, are fundamentally reshaping the relationships between students, teachers, and learning materials, while redefining traditional educational roles. The relationship dynamics between humans (teachers and students) and AI systems can be fluid, ranging from AI-directed (learner-as-recipient) to AI-supported (learner-as-collaborator) to AI-enhanced (learner-as-leader) (Ouyang & Jiao, 2021). Because younger learners typically lack the experience to optimize their interaction with AI learning systems such as AIDT, including positioning themselves within the AI learning system, teachers must strategically determine and guide the roles of both AI and students within each learning context to benefit student learning and personal growth.

# Future Issues and Discussions

## Learning Gap Issues

While AIDT's primary strength lies in its ability to personalize learning, educators must carefully consider several challenges when implementing it in the classroom. First, contrary to expectations, AIDT's personalized approach may actually exacerbate the learning gap between advanced and struggling students. As mentioned above, simply providing individualized content does not ensure effective learning outcomes. As AIDT continues to adapt to the rapid progress of advanced learners, it risks widening existing achievement gaps between students. To address these challenges, educators and practitioners must develop strategies to mitigate potential learning disparities in the implementation of AIDT. For instance, as Khan (2024) suggests, rather than continually moving high-achieving students to new content levels, AIDT can promote deeper conceptual understanding by providing more comprehensive, in-depth material on current topics. This strategy promotes mastery learning while helping to maintain classroom cohesion.

Similarly, AIDT can serve as a powerful educational infrastructure for highly motivated students, enabling them to take ownership of their learning. These students can effectively use AIDT to set personal learning goals and manage their progress. However, this potential remains largely untapped for students who lack the intrinsic motivation or confidence to make autonomous learning decisions. That is, students with lower levels of motivation, self-direction and agency may struggle to complete AIDT-assigned tasks while their more self-motivated peers thrive in this environment. In addition, less motivated students may consistently select easier tasks from the content pool and avoid more challenging and complex tasks (performance-avoidance strategy) (Elliot & McGregor, 2001). To support less-motivated students, teachers must actively use the learner data collected by AIDT to identify individual strengths and weaknesses and provide targeted feedback and intervention where needed. In addition, because AIDT cannot fully account for students' emotional states and social interactions, students who need emotional support may be less responsive to AI systems, and there is a risk that their motivation and academic performance may suffer. As student well-being and social-emotional learning have become increasingly important (Reinders et al., 2024), teachers should consider students' social-emotional states during learning. "Viewing well-being as something that can be proactively developed" (Reinders et al., 2024, p. 14), it is important to understand how AIDT can be designed to inherently support students' learning process, especially in contexts where direct teacher supervision is not present.

Finally, AIDT's ability to provide immediate feedback, while seemingly beneficial, may inadvertently hinder deeper learning processes. Although AI tutors can respond immediately to students' questions and queries, this immediacy may deprive students of crucial time for cognitive processing and reflection, and the development of patience. When students solve problems and learn, they engage in complex cognitive strategies, as outlined in Bloom's Taxonomy (1984), that require time. Instant feedback, while efficient, may short-circuit these essential thinking processes. To effectively foster students' cognitive development, AIDT should incorporate strategic delays and scaffolded feedback mechanisms. One possible approach is the implementation of graded feedback, which guides students through the thinking process in measured steps, allowing time for reflection and deeper understanding at each stage.

## Data Management

In AIDT, proper data management is critical, and accordingly, a comprehensive data management policy must be established to ensure data stability, reliability, and security, especially with respect to students' personal information (KERIS, 2024). This policy framework encompasses several critical aspects of data handling and protection. When collecting and storing learner data generated by AIDT, it is important to follow international standards, such as Caliper Analytics and xAPI. These standards provide a robust framework for managing learning analytics and effectively tracking learning activities. Security measures must be implemented through role-based access control, which assigns different levels of permissions to administrators, teachers, students and parents to ensure appropriate data access based on user status.

Prior to using a student's learner data, explicit consent must be obtained from both the student and the student's parents. This consent should clearly outline the purpose, scope, and duration of the data use. When delivering personalized content, the system should adhere to the principles of data minimization—collecting and using only essential information while eliminating unnecessary data points. Regular audits of data access and usage patterns are critical to verify that data handling remains secure and within acceptable parameters.

Protecting student privacy requires that any learner data that may contain personally identifiable information undergo thorough anonymization and de-identification processes. Throughout the system lifecycle, regular monitoring and assessment of data management practices should ensure ongoing compliance with privacy regulations and maintain the effectiveness of the AIDT system. This includes periodic reviews of access controls, data usage patterns, and model performance metrics to support continuous improvement of both the system and its data management policies. Last, in the first year of using AIDT, the system will rely on training data rather than data collected from the students who will actually use AIDT, and this may result in lower prediction accuracy. It is imperative to recognize that learner data characteristics evolve over time, and AI models trained on the characteristics of past learner data will be less accurate in predicting current learner behavior. Therefore, it will be important to rapidly collect and incorporate new data into AIDT.

## AI Divide and Inequity

While AIDT promises to promote educational equality and equity through personalized resource allocation, as the OECD (2024) warns, AI learning systems may paradoxically create new forms of inequality—particularly through the "AI divide"—and potentially undermine its equity goals. This divide manifests itself in several ways. First, some students may lack access to essential infrastructure, such as devices or reliable Internet connectivity, preventing them from taking full advantage of AIDT resources. Second, AIDT recommendation algorithms may inherently favor certain groups, particularly high-achieving students, while disadvantaging those with lower achievement levels or special learning needs. As Stray (2023) notes, because AI (and AIDT) bases its decisions on students' past learning outcomes and behavioral patterns to guide future learning, this bias can create a self-reinforcing feedback loop that widens existing learning gaps. In addition, students' varying initial learning levels, influenced by their environmental and socioeconomic backgrounds, may make AI predictions and recommendations inappropriate for some learners. Bang and Lee (2024) also argue that recent AI applications in education have shifted the focus from equality to equity, potentially creating new forms of educational inequality (Fig. 3.4).

The following technical issues should also be considered to ensure educational equity and fairness with AIDT.

- **Bridging the digital divide:** Developing accessible, complementary technologies for all learning environments is essential. This includes the development of AI models optimized for low-bandwidth connections and lightweight solutions compatible with basic devices. Such innovations will ensure that technological limitations do not prevent access to quality educational resources.
- **Ensuring algorithmic fairness:** The development of fair learning recommendation algorithms is critical. To this end, it is important to find ways to eliminate data and algorithmic bias by implementing non-discriminatory, fairness-conscious modeling and data processing techniques, so that they can effectively serve students from diverse backgrounds, avoiding preferential treatment of certain groups while maintaining the benefits of personalization.
- **Implementing dynamic learning analytics:** Future AIDT should incorporate dynamic learning analytics that look beyond student achievement data. By taking into account past and current learning contexts and various environmental factors, AIDT can better support students from disadvantaged backgrounds and help them achieve progressive learning growth.

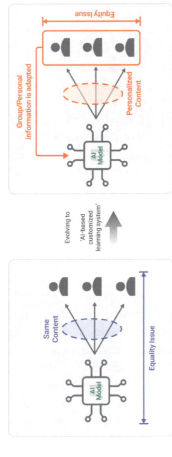

**Fig. 3.4** Transition from Equality to Equity in the AI-driven Learning Systems (Bang & Lee, 2024)

- **Integrating social-emotional intelligence:** Given the inherently human nature of education, AIDT should be developed with robust social and emotional considerations for students. It must recognize and respond appropriately to students, emotional states and social circumstances, and provide targeted support that goes beyond mere academic feedback.

## Conclusion

The introduction of AIDT is an important step in the transformation of education in Korea, which aims to improve the quality of public education through personalized learning experiences. By providing learning content tailored to students' abilities and learning styles, it will help individual students follow their optimal learning path. This innovative approach has the potential not only to improve the overall quality of public education, but also to narrow achievement gaps between students and promote educational equity in Korea. The implementation of AIDT is catalyzing a fundamental shift in educational roles. As AI systems support the development of lower-order thinking skills, teachers can shift their focus to cultivating higher-order cognitive skills. This evolution presents an opportunity to explore the optimal balance between "High Touch and High Tech" to provide the best learning experience for students.

However, the successful implementation of AIDT faces several critical challenges that require immediate attention. Technical solutions must be developed to address three primary concerns: data security, fairness, and algorithmic bias. The learning recommendation system must accurately reflect individual learner characteristics and needs, while ensuring that no demographic group is disadvantaged. In addition, complementary technologies must be developed to bridge digital accessibility gaps and enhance social-emotional support for students. These technical challenges intersect with deeper concerns about the increasing commercialization of education, particularly with respect to datafication and learnification processes that risk reducing complex educational experiences to quantifiable metrics and potentially turning education into what Knox et al. (2019) call "machine behaviorism."

As AIDT evolves, it must maintain a delicate balance between meeting emerging educational needs and maintaining ethical responsibilities while pursuing the dual goals of personalization and equity. The path forward requires not only the identification of implementation challenges, but also the development of AI technologies to mitigate those challenges. Ultimately, success depends on achieving a synergy between continued technological advancement and meaningful engagement of teachers and students. Only through this comprehensive, balanced approach can we fully realize the transformative potential of AI-based education and ensure that it serves its intended purpose of enhancing the learning experience while preserving educational integrity.

# References

Ahn, T., & Lee, S.-M. (2016). User experience of a mobile speaking application with automatic speech recognition for EFL learners. *British Journal of Educational Technology, 47*(4), 778–786.

Alamri, H., Lowell, V., Watson, W., & Watson, S. (2020). Using personalized learning as an instructional approach to motivate learners in online higher education: Learner self-determination and intrinsic motivation. *Journal of Research on Technology in Education, 52*(3), 322–352.

Avella, J., Kebritchi, M., Nunn, S., & Kanai, T. (2016). Learning analytics methods, benefits, and challenges in higher education: A systematic literature review. *Online Learning, 20*(2), 13–29.

Baker, T., & Smith, L. (2019). *Educ-AI-tion rebooted? Exploring the future of artificial intelligence in schools and colleges.* Nesta. https://media.nesta.org.uk/documents/Future_of_AI_and_education_v5_WEB.pdf

Bandura, A. (2001). Social cognitive theory: An agentic perspective. *Annual Review of Psychology, 52*, 1–26.

Bang, J., & Lee, S-M. (2024). Addressing bias for equity in AI-driven customized learning systems. *Multimedia-Assisted Language Learning, 27*(4), 70–86.

Bernacki, M. L., Greene, M. J., & Lobczowski, N. (2021). A systematic review of research on personalized learning: Personalized by whom, to what, how, and for what purpose(s)? *Educational Psychology Review, 33*, 1675–1715.
Bloom, B. (1956). *Taxonomy of educational objectives, handbook: The cognitive domain.* David McKay.
Bloom, B. (1984). The 2-sigma problem: The search for methods of group instruction as effective as one-to-one tutoring. *Educational Researcher, 13*(6), 4–16.
Bray, B., & McClaskey, K. (2014). *Make learning personal: The what, who, wow, where, and why.* Corwin Press.
Bray, B., & McClaskey, K. (2016). *How to personalize learning: A practical guide for getting started and going deeper.* Corwin Press.
Bryan, J., Heitz, C., Shanghvi, S., & Wagle, D. (2020). *How artificial intelligence will impact K-12 teachers.* McKinsey & Company. https://www.mckinsey.com/industries/education/our-insights/how-artificial-intelligence-will-impact-k-12-teachers
Channa, F., Sarhandi, P., Bugti, F., & Brohi, I. (2021). Supporting self-regulated learning by affect detection and responding in AI-driven learning systems. *Elementary Education Online, 20*(5), 3205–3211.
Chassignol, M., Khoroshavin, A., Klimova, A., & Bilyatdinova, A. (2018). Artificial intelligence trends in education: A narrative overview. *Procedia of Computer Science, 136*, 16–24.
Celik, I., Dindar, M., Muukkonen, H., & Järvelä, S. (2022). The promises and challenges of artificial intelligence for teachers: A systematic review of research. *TechTrends, 66*, 616–630.
Chen, L., Chen, P., & Lin, Z. (2020). Artificial intelligence in education: A review. *IEEE Access, 8*, 75284–75278.
Collier, C. (2022). Becoming an autonomous learner: Building the skills of self-directed learning. *Journal of Transformative Learning, 9*(1), 111–120.
Damşa, C., Langford, M., Uehara, D., & Scherer, R. (2021). Teachers' agency and online education in times of crisis. *Computers in Human Behavior, 121*, 106793.
Deng, G., & Zhang, J. (2023). Technological pedagogical content ethical knowledge (TPCEK): The development of an assessment instrument for pre-service teachers. *Computers & Education, 197*, 10740.
Eduvate Rhode Island. (2017). *Creating a shared understanding of personalized learning for Rhode Island.* Educate RI. http://eduvateri.org/projects/personalized/personalizedlearningpaper/

Elliot, A. J., & McGregor, H. A. (2001). A 2 x 2 achievement goal framework. *Journal of Personality and Social Psychology, 80*(3), 501–519.

Gibson, D., Kovanovic, V., Ifenthaler, D., Dexter, S., & Feng, S. (2023). Learning theories for artificial intelligence promoting learning processes. *British Journal of Educational Technology, 54*, 1125–1146.

Han, E., & Ahn, K. (2023). Exploring Korean elementary teachers' perceptions, experiences, and related factors of teaching written English for 3rd and 4th graders. *Korean Journal of English Language and Linguistics, 23*, 587–609.

Holmes, W. (2023). *The unintended consequences of artificial intelligence and education.* Education International. https://www.ei-ie.org/en/item/28115:the-unintended-consequences-of-artificial-intelligence-and-education

Hong, S., Hwang, Y., Park, Y., & Lee, S.-M. (2024). Expectations and concerns about adopting AI digital textbooks: Based on investigation of teachers' use of AI and digital tools. *The Modern Linguistic Society of Korea, 40*(1), 7–20.

Jääskelä, P., Heilala, V., Kärkkäinen, T., & Häkkinen, P. (2021). Student agency analytics: Learning analytics as a tool for analysing student agency in higher education. *Behaviour & Information Technology, 40*(8), 790–808.

Kalaja, P., & Ruohotie-Lyhty, M. (2022). Autonomy and agency. In T. Gregersen & S. Mercer (Eds.), *The Routledge handbook of the psychology of language learning and teaching* (pp. 245–259). Routledge.

KERIS. (2024). *Guidelines for AI Digital development.* Korea Education and Research Information Service.

Khan, S. (2024). *Brave new words: How AI will revolutionize education.* Viking

Klemenčič, M. (2017). From student engagement to student agency: Conceptual considerations of European policies on student-centered learning in higher education. *Higher Education Policy, 30*, 69–85.

Koehler, M. J., & Mishra, P. (2006). Technological pedagogical content knowledge: A framework for teacher knowledge. *Teachers College Record, 108*(6), 1017–1054.

Knox, J., Williamson, B., & Bayne, S. (2019). Machine behaviourism: Future visions of 'learnification' and 'datafication' across humans and digital technologies. *Learning, Media and Technology, 45*(1), 31–45.

Lee, S-M., & Ahn, T. (2024). L2 learner experiences in a playful constructivist metaverse space. *ReCALL.* FirstView. https://doi.org/10.1017/S0958344024000235

Lee, B., Lee, S-M., Koh, M., Kang, S., & Kim, C. (2025). *Middle school English AIDT.* Dong-Ah.

Luckin, R., & Cukurova, M. (2019). Designing educational technologies in the age of AI: A learning sciences-driven approach. *British Journal of Educational Technology, 50*(6), 2824–2838.

Meyer, A., Rose, D.H., & Gordon, D. (2014). *Universal design for learning: Theory and practice.* CAST Professional Publishing.

Nam, I., & Lee, A. (2022). The effects of within-school achievement gap on student engagement and affective outcomes. *Korean Journal of Educational Administration, 40*(1), 459–487.

Niemi, H. (2024). AI in education and learning: Perspectives on the education ecosystem. In M. Streit-Bianchi & V. Gorini. (Eds) *New frontiers in science in the era of AI* (pp. 169–194). Springer.

OECD. (2024). *The potential impact of artificial intelligence equity and inclusion in education.* OECD publishing.

Ouyang, F., & Jiao, P. (2021). Artificial intelligence in education: The three paradigms. *Computers and Education: Artificial Intelligence, 2,* 100020.

Oxford, R. L. (2017). *Teaching and researching language learning strategies: Self-regulation in context.* Routledge.

Patrick, S., Kennedy, K., & Powell, A. (2013). Mean what you say: Defining and integrating personalized, blended and competency education. *International Association for K-12 Online Learning.* https://eric.ed.gov/?id=ED561301

Peng, H., Ma, S., & Spector, J. (2019). Personalized adaptive learning: An emerging pedagogical approach enabled by a smart learning environment. *Learning Environments, 6,* 1–14.

Reinders, H., Wilson, A., & Kukulska-Hulme, A. (2024). *Humanising technology in language learning and teaching.* Oxford University Press.

Stray, J. (2023). The AI learns to lie to please you: Preventing biased feedback loops in machine-assisted intelligence analysis. *Analytics, 2*(2), 350–358.

Stenalt, M., & Lassesen, B. (2022). Does student agency benefit student learning? A systematic review of higher education research. *Assessment & Evaluation in Higher Education, 47*(5), 653–669.

Vaughn, M. (2019). What is student agency and why is it needed now more than ever? *Theory into Practice, 59*(2), 109–118.

Vygotsky, L. S. (1978). *Mind in society: The development of higher psychological processes.* Harvard University Press.

Wu, G. (2015). Personalized education in globalization era. *Nanjing J. Soc. Sci., 7,* 104–110.

Zawacki-Richter, O., Marín, V., Bond, M., & Gouverneur, F. (2019). Systematic review of research on artificial intelligence applications in higher education—Where are the educators? *International Journal of Educational Technology in Higher Education, 16*, 39.

# 4

# Integrating Informal Digital Learning of English (IDLE) into Korean Middle School Contexts

Joohyun Bae

## Area of Innovation: The IDLE Approach

Based on the literature on IDLE, this section examines why adopting the IDLE approach as a new teaching method can be pedagogically innovative by explaining some of the critical benefits of IDLE. The IDLE approach represents a novel method for enhancing language acquisition among Korean middle learners by engaging students in English through various digital platforms outside the formal classroom setting. In Computer-assisted Language Learning (CALL), IDLE has established itself as a noteworthy subfield. The concept of IDLE is based on Benson's (2011) four dimensions of out-of-class second language (L2)

---

This chapter incorporated the author's previous research findings (Bae, 2024) and interview research.

---

J. Bae (✉)
Korea University, Seoul, South Korea
e-mail: skskaa12@korea.ac.kr

© The Author(s), under exclusive license to Springer Nature Switzerland AG 2025
H. Reinders et al. (eds.), *Innovation in Language Learning and Teaching*, New Language Learning and Teaching Environments,
https://doi.org/10.1007/978-3-031-83561-2_4

learning: location, formality, pedagogy, and locus of control. The location dimension includes learning inside and outside the classroom and in extracurricular or extramural settings. Formality refers to the spectrum of teaching and learning methods ranging from formal to informal. Pedagogy covers self-directed and naturalistic learning methods, while locus of control focuses on who makes critical decisions in the learning process, highlighting the importance of learner autonomy.

With this framework, IDLE can be described as a self-directed, unstructured, and naturalistic English learning activity in extramural digital environments (J. Lee et al., 2022a). There are two types of IDLE: receptive and productive. Receptive IDLE activities include watching English videos, movies, and TV shows on platforms like YouTube and Netflix. These activities help students improve their listening skills and expose them to various accents and vocabulary. Productive IDLE activities involve active participation in online communities, such as commenting on social media posts, engaging in discussions on forums, and communicating with peers through instant messaging apps. Such activities encourage students to use English in real time, enhancing their speaking and writing skills (Zhang et al., 2021). Systematic reviews have shown that many young EFL students participate in IDLE activities, and there is increasing evidence that IDLE benefits language learning (Soyoof, 2022; Zhang et al., 2021). This approach capitalizes on the extensive availability of online English content and students' widespread use of digital devices.

There are numerous linguistic benefits of IDLE. Increased exposure to the language is one of its primary advantages, as IDLE provides students with abundant opportunities to engage with English in various contexts, which is essential for developing comprehensive language skills. In addition, by allowing students to choose content that interests them, IDLE fosters greater learner autonomy and intrinsic motivation. Students are more likely to engage in language when they align with their interests. The informal nature of IDLE activities helps reduce foreign language anxiety often associated with classroom contexts, allowing students to practice English at their pace and in a comfortable environment (Lai et al., 2015). Previous research has shown that participating in IDLE activities can positively impact students' WTC in various EFL contexts, such as Iran (Soyoof, 2022), Hong Kong (J. Lee et al., 2022a), Indonesia (J. Lee & Drajati, 2019), China (Zhang & Liu, 2022), and Korea (J. Lee & Sylvén, 2021; J. Lee et al., 2022b). As students become more proficient in the language, they become more confident and more likely to engage in conversations. By incorporating social media, video streaming services, and online forums into its approach, it offers interactive and engaging environments for language practice. For example, one study found that IDLE activities significantly correlate with increased L2 WTC among Korean middle school and university students (J. Lee et al., 2022b). The study found that IDLE had a more emotional impact on middle school students by alleviating the stress from high-stakes exams and increased enjoyment. It seems imperative for them to experience positive emotions through IDLE activities. Also, students who frequently engage in receptive and productive IDLE activities exhibit higher confidence levels and are more WTC in English.

Additionally, recent studies found a relationship between IDLE, EIL, and L2 WTC in various contexts. Due to the increased use of digital technologies, EIL studies have expanded into various digital contexts, utilizing resources like videoconferencing and emailing to enhance cross-cultural communication skills (J. Ke & Cahyani, 2014; Lee et al., 2017). Informal settings such as social media and digital games have shown that engaging in IDLE activities can improve learners' perceptions of various English varieties and strategies for multicultural communication (J. Lee & K. Lee, 2019b). This enhanced perception of EIL positively impacts learners' L2 WTC in English. Research indicates that adequate exposure to diverse English forms through IDLE activities fosters favorable attitudes towards EIL, thereby increasing learners' readiness to communicate English (J. Lee et al., 2022b; Zarrinabadi & Khodarahmi, 2017).

In summary, the IDLE approach offers a transformative way to address the limitations of traditional English-language teaching in Korea. By incorporating informal digital learning into students' daily lives, this approach not only improves language proficiency but also fosters a more positive and proactive attitude towards learning English.

## Impetus for the Innovation: Challenges in Korean Pedagogy

This section will introduce a brief history of National Curriculums and then identify some critical pedagogical issues in Korea. The 6th (Ministry of Education, 1992) and 7th National Curriculums (Ministry of Education, 1997) introduced significant changes to English education. From 1992 to 1997, the 6th National Curriculum shifted to a communicative approach based on notional-functional syllabuses, emphasizing the practical use of English in everyday contexts. The 7th National Curriculum (1997–2006) made English compulsory from Grade 3 and introduced a level-differentiated approach, allowing students to choose courses based on proficiency. These changes aimed to enhance communicative competence and cater to diverse academic abilities. However, traditional methods focused on exam preparation persisted, limiting the development of productive language skills like speaking and writing. Despite these curriculum advancements, the NEAT[1] aimed at assessing productive skills, was not incorporated as a major test for university entrance (Park, 2013). The partially revised 7th curriculum (2006–2009) continued supporting level-differentiated plans. This policy aimed to provide equal opportunities for all children to learn English, improve teaching methods traditionally based on grammar-translation in secondary schools, and enhance Korea's competitiveness in the global economy (K. Lee, 2009).

The impetus for adopting the IDLE approach in Korean middle school education arises from several critical issues within the existing pedagogy. Traditionally, Korean students learn English with a strong emphasis on grammar and receptive skills, such as reading and listening, often neglecting productive skills like speaking, which are crucial for real-world communication. This approach is deeply ingrained in the education system, particularly in secondary schools, making it challenging

---

[1] The National English Ability Test (NEAT) aimed to assess all four language skills to enhance communicative competence in Korean students. However, it faced challenges such as misalignment with the College Scholastic Ability Test (CSAT), insufficient teacher training, and resource constraints, limiting its adoption and impact. Future improvements may need better integration with existing exams and enhanced teacher training (Y. Lee, 2015).

to replace with more communicative approaches (Li, 1998). Although the English curriculum emphasizes communicative competence, implementing Communicative Language Teaching (CLT) in Korea faces significant challenges. CLT was originally designed for small, well-equipped classrooms in Western contexts and may not suit overcrowded Korean classrooms with different educational traditions (McKay, 2003). Many teachers misunderstand CLT, equating it with focusing solely on fluency and neglecting accuracy. This misunderstanding stems from insufficient training in CLT's theoretical and practical aspects (Butler, 2005; Littlewood, 2007).

There is often a disconnect between pedagogic policy and classroom practice. Teachers tend to adopt weak forms of CLT, adjusting the methods to fit their local contexts rather than fully adopting them (Mitchell & Lee, 2003). Teachers in various studies reported using communicative activities such as games, songs, and role plays as prescribed by their governments, yet many were unclear about the objectives of these activities (Butler, 2005). Teachers frequently adapt the recommended communicative approaches to focus on discrete language items, blending traditional and communicative methods. This gap between policy and practice, combined with the traditional emphasis on grammar and receptive skills, hinders the development of productive language skills like speaking and writing among Korean students. The CSAT prioritizes listening and reading comprehension over communicative competence, misaligning with CLT goals (Jeon & Lee, 2017). Despite recognizing CLT's importance, teachers predominantly use text-only textbooks for instruction. Textbooks are the most frequently used materials. The main obstacles to implementing CLT include exam-oriented teaching norms, lack of English exposure, and traditional grammar-based instruction. These challenges are primarily dictated by the educational system's focus on CSAT results, limiting teachers' ability to employ CLT effectively in their classrooms (Jin & Yoo, 2019).

The IDLE approach offers a promising solution to these challenges by providing opportunities for students to practice English in informal and low-pressure settings (Sundqvist & Wikström, 2015). Engaging in IDLE activities helps students develop positive attitudes towards

EIL, which enhances their WTC. This approach encourages exposure to various English accents and diverse communication strategies, supporting the development of intercultural competence and preparing students for global interactions. Research by J. Lee and K. Lee (2019b) has shown that the practice of IDLE significantly improves Korean university students' perceptions of EIL. Additionally, IDLE activities positively influenced TOEIC scores, which include British, Canadian, and Australian English accents (J. Lee, 2020).

Changing perceptions among students and teachers is essential for successfully implementing the IDLE approach. A recent study by Shin and Walkinshaw (2023) explored the perceptions of middle and high school teachers regarding World Englishes[2] (WE). The study found that while teachers viewed English as a global communication tool, they often considered 'native' English varieties more prestigious than others. Despite recognizing the importance of integrating a WE-informed approach into Korea's English education system, they predominantly supported English varieties from Anglophone countries. It is crucial to broaden teachers' perspectives and acceptance of diverse English varieties. Educators should be encouraged to appreciate the diversity inherent in English and move beyond idealizing accents from Anglophone countries. This shift in mindset will enable teachers to better support their students in developing comprehensive English language skills necessary for effective global communication.

Researchers have proposed a Three-stage Continuum Model for integrating IDLE into formal contexts (J. Lee et al., 2018; J. Lee & Drajati, 2019). The first stage, In-class CALL, entails instructors incorporating technology in the classroom. This may include using blogs to practice writing in a computer lab setting and integrating traditional textbook instruction with computer-based essay writing to enhance accuracy, fluency, and complexity (J. Lee & K. Lee, 2010). The second stage, Extracurricular CALL, involves semi-structured, self-directed digital

---

[2] English as an International Language (EIL), World Englishes (WE), and English as a Lingua Franca (ELF) are frameworks that challenge the traditional distinction between native and non-native English speakers. These concepts also reject the unquestioned acceptance of notions like *the Queen's English* or *General American English* as the only legitimate forms of English (Marlina, 2017).

learning activities linked to the formal curriculum. For example, students use online communities, YouTube tutorials, Wikipedia, online chats, machine translation tools, and digital games to complete assigned tasks, which teachers later assess. J. Lee et al. (2018) demonstrated this with a videoconference-embedded classroom program where students engaged in pre-task reading, in-class presentations, and synchronous discussions with international peers. The third stage, Extramural CALL, allows students to control their learning entirely through independent and naturalistic digital learning outside the classroom. This stage can be semistructured or entirely unstructured, with minimal teacher guidance. For instance, Kusyk (2017) tracked non-English majors in France engaging in leisure activities in English online, showing significant time spent in out-of-class digital settings. This stage aims to develop learner autonomy, helping students choose appropriate resources, organize activities, and critically evaluate their learning processes independently.

As J. Lee (2021) stated, the main objective of the IDLE method is to empower students to establish their IDLE environment and actively participate without relying on teacher guidance or intervention. Students can build confidence and proficiency in speaking by incorporating activities that encourage the practical use of English, such as games, discussions, and interactive projects. These activities help mitigate the anxiety associated with speaking in formal settings by providing a supportive environment where students can practice without the pressure of grades or exams. In summary, adopting the IDLE approach in Korean middle school education seeks to bridge the gap between formal instruction and real-world language use. It addresses the limitations of traditional English language teaching by fostering a more effective and enjoyable learning experience for students. This approach enhances students' WTC in English and equips them with the skills and confidence needed for successful global interactions. The IDLE approach represents a transformative step in improving English education in Korea by shifting student and teacher perceptions towards a more inclusive view of English.

## Context of Implementation

This chapter is grounded in survey research findings and integrated insights from educators to further elucidate the practical application of the IDLE approach. For survey research, 209 students from a girls' middle school in a suburban region of Korea participated. The participants, aged 15 to 16, included 60.8% second and 39.2% third graders, all receiving 51 to 68 hours of compulsory English instruction per semester. The average self-assessed proficiency score was 2.24 out of 4.00, with approximately 25% of participants rating their proficiency as low, 67% as intermediate, and 7.5% as high. Over 70% of participants began learning English by age 10. After screening the data, 206 valid responses were analyzed. The research utilized three main scales: the IDLE activities scale, the EIL perception scale, and the L2 WTC scale.

First, the IDLE scale assessed the frequency of receptive and productive IDLE activities (adopted from J. Lee, 2022) during the past month based on the participants' interests. Receptive IDLE activities, centered on understanding English content, included tasks such as reading and listening. Items in this study included 'I watch YouTube videos, movies, television shows, and YouTube Shorts or Instagram Reels'. They covered all forms of English-language content voluntarily watched online by learners. Productive IDLE activities focused on production and communication, such as speaking and writing, with examples including 'I communicate with English speakers on social media platforms like YouTube, Instagram, and Kakao Talk.' The study utilized a 5-point Likert scale to measure the frequency of IDLE activities (1 = never, 2 = once per week, 3 = two to three times per week, 4 = daily, 5 = multiple times per day).

Second, empirical testing in Korea and Indonesia has demonstrated the robust scale properties of the EIL perception scale (adapted from J. Lee & K. Lee, 2019a). EIL perception was measured using three constructs: Current Status of English (CSE), Varieties of English (VE), and Strategies for Multilingual/Multicultural Communication (SMC). Examples of items include 'Many non-native English-speaking countries employ English as their official or working language' (CSE), 'Different varieties of English, including Hong Kong English, Indian, and Singaporean English, are accepted' (VE), and 'I can effectively communicate my own cultural and customary practices in English to individuals from diverse backgrounds' (SMC).

Third, the L2 WTC scale (adopted from J. Lee & Drajati, 2019) includes 7 items, with examples like 'I am willing to discuss with a small group of class' and 'I feel the willingness to communicate in English in front of the class in an English class.' The EIL perception and L2 WTC scales are rated using a 5-point Likert scale from 1 = (strongly disagree) to 5 = (strongly agree). The survey was conducted online, and all items were translated from English into Korean to ensure comprehension.

For data analysis, regression and mediation analyses were employed to examine the relationships among these variables. IDLE was entered as the independent variable and L2 WTC as the dependent variable, positioning EIL perceptions as the mediating variable and finally employing IDLE and EIL perceptions as co-predictors for L2 WTC.

Additionally, this chapter conducted interviews with three English teachers in Korea to incorporate their insights into existing survey results. The interviews, conducted in a semi-structured format for 60 minutes with each teacher, involved educators with over ten years of teaching experience and expertise in digitalized classrooms, such as using Padlet, Google Classroom, and electronic boards to practice In-class CALL. They shared their interpretations of survey results and lesson plans for a Three-stage Continuum Model for integrating IDLE into formal contexts based on their teaching experiences.

## Results and Discussion

### Survey Results

This section presents the survey findings (Table 4.1) and discusses implications alongside insights from middle school English teachers. Data from 206 participants were analyzed for statistical purposes. As seen in Fig. 4.1, in IDLE activities, item 3 (watching memes on YouTube Shorts or Instagram Reels) had the highest mean value ($M = 3.00$), while item 5 (talking with foreign friends on social media) had the lowest mean value ($M = 1.32$). The results indicate that middle school students prefer receptive activities over productive ones and favor short videos over watching dramas or movies (item 2, $M = 1.36$) or instructional videos like TED Talks in English (item 4, $M = 1.79$). Semi-structured interviews with English teachers provided further context to the survey findings. The teachers highlighted several reasons for the low engagement in IDLE activities. They noted that receptive skills, such as listening and reading, are more passive than productive skills, like speaking and writing. They observed that IDLE activities, especially short-form video content, are more engaging and less intimidating for students. One of the teachers observed that middle school students find it challenging to watch videos longer than 20 minutes. This might be because many students are more familiar with short-form videos on social media. Teachers emphasized the importance of motivation in language learning. They recommended incorporating IDLE activities that align with students' interests, such as popular challenges on YouTube or TikTok, to boost engagement and reduce language anxiety.

In EIL perception, item 2 measuring CSE (English as the language of business, culture, and education globally, $M = 4.11$) had the highest mean value. In contrast, item 3 measuring VE (acceptance of varieties such as Indonesian, Taiwanese, and Japanese English as equal to American or British English, $M = 2.87$) had the lowest. Interestingly, item 6 (acceptance of Korean-accented English and other English accents) received the highest score among VE items compared to the acceptance of Hong Kong or Singapore-accented English. The results indicate that English is widely recognized as a global language in business, culture, and education. However, there is less acceptance of different English varieties being equal to American or British English, though Korean-accented

Table 4.1 Descriptive statistics

|  | Mean | SD | Skewness | Kurtosis |
| --- | --- | --- | --- | --- |
| IDLE | 1.83 | 0.66 | 0.73 | −0.18 |
| EIL perceptions | 3.56 | 0.78 | −0.44 | 0.60 |
| L2 WTC | 2.70 | 1.05 | 0.23 | −0.62 |

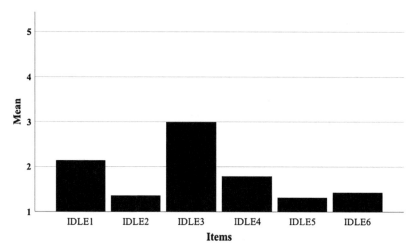

Fig. 4.1 Mean scores of IDLE activities (*Note* IDLE1 = watching YouTube, IDLE2 = watching movies/drama, IDLE3 = watching memes, IDLE4 = watching instructional videos, IDLE5 = talking on social media, IDLE6 = writing comments)

English is more accepted than other non-native accents. The teachers agreed on the importance of exposing students to different English accents and emphasized that students should perceive these differences as part of the diversity of English rather than something strange or incorrect. They acknowledged that Korean students are more familiar with American and British accents due to their prevalence in popular media and education systems. However, they stressed the importance of exposing students to various English accents to prepare them for global interactions. Teachers also highlighted that their preference for American and British English could influence their students' attitudes, suggesting a need for teachers to broaden their perspectives and accept diverse English varieties.

For L2 WTC, item 5 (desire to have playful conversations with friends in English, $M = 3.43$) had the highest mean score, while item 7 (willingness to discuss in large groups of more than ten people in English, $M = 2.09$) had the lowest. Participants were most eager for casual conversations with friends in English and less willing to engage in large group discussions. Teachers noted that students tend to shy away from speaking in English because they fear being judged by their peers for making mistakes. Moreover, middle school students find speaking and writing activities challenging, requiring more active participation than receptive activities. They recommended engaging English content, such as popular YouTube channels or social media accounts related to students' interests, to increase engagement in English activities outside the classroom. Teachers' support seems crucial in boosting students' involvement in English-related activities.

Following Plonsky and Oswald (2014), the survey found that students who frequently engaged in IDLE activities had more positive perceptions of EIL and higher L2 WTC, with effect sizes considered small to medium ($r = 0.380$, $p < 0.01$) and ($r = 0.234$, $p < 0.01$), respectively. This suggests that regular engagement in informal English learning can help students feel more comfortable and willing to use English in real-life situations. There was also a significant positive correlation between EIL perceptions and L2 WTC with a small-to-medium effect ($r = 0.437$, $p < 0.01$). The study explored the mediating effect of students' perceptions of EIL on the relationship between IDLE activities and L2 WTC. In the mediation model, IDLE served as the antecedent variable (X), WTC as the consequent variable (Y), and EIL as the mediating variable (M). To test the mediation model, multiple regression analysis was executed, and it revealed the following results:

1. The frequency of IDLE activities positively and significantly predicted L2 WTC ($\beta = 0.380$, $p < 0.001$).
2. The frequency of IDLE activities significantly predicted EIL perceptions ($\beta = 0.234$, $p < 0.001$).
3. In a model including both IDLE and EIL perceptions, EIL significantly predicted L2 WTC ($\beta = 0.368$, $p < 0.001$), and the predictive influence of IDLE on L2 WTC remained significant ($\beta = 0.294$, $p < 0.001$).

The results presented in Table 4.2 explain how engaging in IDLE activities influences students' L2 WTC and how their perceptions of EIL play a role in this process. The table shows the direct influence of IDLE on L2 WTC, the indirect effect mediated by EIL perceptions, and the combined total effect. The direct effect of IDLE on L2 WTC has a coefficient of 0.500, accounting for 82.51% of the total effect. This means that IDLE activities alone have a significant positive impact on students' L2 WTC. The indirect effect, mediated by perception of EIL, has a coefficient of 0.109, accounting for 17.49% of the total effect. IDLE activities also influence L2 WTC by changing students' EIL perceptions. The total effect of IDLE on L2 WTC is 0.606, combining both direct and indirect effects. The analysis indicates that the direct effect of IDLE on L2 WTC is substantial, with a significant proportion of this effect being mediated by EIL perceptions. A thorough examination of the data reveals that the 95% confidence intervals for direct and indirect effects do not include zero. This confidently asserts that perceived EIL mediates the impact of IDLE on L2 WTC. The mediation model is illustrated in Fig. 4.2.

Table 4.2 Analysis of the mediation model

| Pathway | Coefficient | SE | Confidence interval 95% | | Percentage of effect |
|---|---|---|---|---|---|
| | | | Boot LLCL | Boot ULCL | |
| Direct effect | 0.500 | 0.100 | 0.300 | 0.700 | 82.51% |
| Indirect effect | 0.109 | 0.049 | 0.026 | 0.200 | 17.49% |
| Total effect | 0.606 | 0.104 | 0.398 | 0.815 | 100% |

*Note* Coefficient = the strength and direction of the effect, SE = standard error, LLCL = Lower Limit Confidence Level, ULCL = Upper Limit Confidence Level

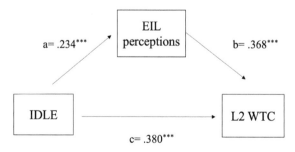

Fig. 4.2 Mediation model ***$p < 0.001$

The combined analysis of the survey study revealed intricate connections among the variables. Initially, IDLE positively correlated with perceived EIL and L2 WTC, suggesting that consistent involvement in out-of-class learning encourages favorable attitudes towards different English accents. This outcome aligns with earlier research, proving that IDLE activities significantly improve EFL students' views on English as a global language (J. Lee & K. Lee, 2019a, 2019b; J. Lee, 2022). Moreover, participants with more positive attitudes towards EIL also exhibited higher levels of WTC in the classroom. It can be deduced that learners participating in informal online English activities are likely to cultivate positive attitudes towards various English accents, thus enhancing their readiness to communicate in English. Both multiple regression and mediation analyses offered comprehensive insights. IDLE directly, positively, and significantly impacted learners' WTC, explaining roughly 14% of the variance. Perceptions of EIL mediated this influence. The regression analysis revealed that IDLE activities significantly predicted learners' perceived EIL, accounting for about 6% of the variance. Mediation analysis further showed that EIL perceptions contributed to 17.49% of the total mediating effect of IDLE on WTC. The findings indicate that learners' willingness to communicate is closely linked to a supportive environment for English communication. Participating in receptive and productive IDLE activities is essential for developing learners' EIL perceptions, including various English varieties and multicultural communication. The findings align with previous research, emphasizing the interconnectedness of learners' autonomy, attitudes, and WTC within the broader scope of SLA.

Teachers observed that some students who accepted a variety of English were more willing to participate in English classrooms because they viewed their accents as part of the diversity of the English language. Teachers suggested practical ways to use these findings to improve student engagement, such as incorporating more IDLE activities into the curriculum and creating a supportive environment that reduces the anxiety associated with speaking English in formal settings. One teacher noted that as students learn English in their daily lives outside of school, they will likely be exposed to various forms of English, primarily through platforms like YouTube, English-language games, and social media, to improve engagement and communication skills. This exposure could positively affect their perceptions of EIL. Additionally, increased exposure to different forms of English in daily life could boost students' confidence and L2 WTC. Practical suggestions included studying English lyrics of popular Korean songs, watching Indian movies to familiarize students with various accents, and creating dub or short films. Schools could also run programs or campaigns to promote these activities.

The integration of IDLE has addressed the problem of low WTC to a significant extent. First, the preference for receptive IDLE activities suggests that students are willing to engage with English in informal and receptive ways with friends. This engagement is a critical first step towards building confidence and willingness to use English in more formal and productive ways. Second, by frequently participating in IDLE activities, students developed more positive attitudes towards EIL. These positive perceptions are crucial for enhancing WTC, as students favored Korean-accented English over other varieties of English. By accepting their accent as legitimate English, they will engage more in speaking English. Lastly, teachers reported that IDLE activities could effectively supplement traditional teaching methods, providing a low-pressure environment for students to practice English. This approach helps bridge the gap between classroom learning and real-world language use, fostering a more holistic language learning experience.

## Implications for Practice: Action Plans for Korean EFL Teachers

1. Action plans for integrating IDLE

Based on the findings and discussion, this section outlines practical implications for Korean EFL teachers. It provides step-by-step action plans to tackle the problem of low WTC through the integration of IDLE (Table 4.3).

Integrating IDLE into Korean middle school education offers a practical solution to enhancing students' WTC in English. By following

Table 4.3 Action plans for IDLE integration

| Targeted domains of improvement | Goals | Major action plans |
|---|---|---|
| 1. Teacher training | • Equip teachers with the skills and knowledge to effectively integrate IDLE into their teaching practices | • Organize workshops and training sessions focused on IDLE, like the one conducted in Hong Kong. Include tasks such as group work, blog reflections, and lesson planning<br>• Encourage teachers to pursue certifications, such as the Google Educator Certification, and provide financial support if necessary<br>• Facilitate regular seminars and collaborative networks among teachers to share successful IDLE integration cases and provide mutual feedback |
| 2. Curriculum integration | • Seamlessly integrate IDLE activities into the existing English curriculum | • Adopt a Flipped Learning approach, where students watch engaging English videos at home and participate in related activities in class<br>• Select videos that align with the class topic<br>• Conduct discussions, group activities, or role-playing based on the video content<br>• Assign reflective blog posts or online discussions as homework |

(continued)

**Table 4.3** (continued)

| Targeted domains of improvement | Goals | Major action plans |
|---|---|---|
| 3. Student engagement | • Encourage students to participate in IDLE activities outside the classroom actively<br>• Enhance EIL perceptions through IDLE activities | • Develop engaging and relevant digital content that appeals to students' interests<br>• Implement reward systems to recognize and encourage participation in IDLE activities<br>• Create social learning environments where students can share their experiences and progress with peers<br>• Pair students with foreign peers in language exchange programs to foster real-life communication |
| 4. Assessment | • Regularly assess the effectiveness of IDLE integration and make necessary adjustments | • Collect feedback from students and teachers on the effectiveness of IDLE activities<br>• Monitor changes in students' WTC and EIL perceptions through regular assessments<br>• Adjust the curriculum and training programs based on feedback and assessment results |

these step-by-step action plans, Korean EFL teachers can create a more engaging and effective learning environment that bridges the gap between formal instruction and real-world language use. This approach improves language proficiency and fosters a more positive and proactive attitude towards learning English, ultimately preparing students for successful global communication. Additionally, teachers provided specific examples of how IDLE activities can be integrated into the formal setting, as seen in Table 4.4.

2. Remaining problems to consider

The teachers identified several obstacles to implementing the Three-stage Continuum Model of integrating IDLE approach in Korean middle schools. One significant challenge is device availability. Despite efforts to promote electronic devices, not all students have their own devices, making it challenging to conduct full-fledged lessons. Some students are also unfamiliar with creating online accounts. Additionally, there are doubts about the effectiveness of online learning. When students use online resources, they sometimes rely on translators, completing assignments without critical thinking. It raises concerns about the effectiveness of in-class CALL activities. Another challenge is the negative perception of assignments. Students often view assignments negatively, which can decrease their interest and motivation to learn English. Moreover, selecting and developing appropriate content can be difficult. The abundance of video resources can make it challenging for teachers to select and develop the right content for each stage of the IDLE approach.

Table 4.4 Lesson plans for three-stage continuum model of integrating IDLE

| IDLE stage | Lesson plans |
| --- | --- |
| In-class CALL | • Recommend YouTube channels and have students watch videos and post links to their Padlet<br>• Use class time to watch videos together and introduce useful expressions<br>• Using digital tools, engage students in discussions, group mind mapping, and role-playing activities |
| Extracurricular CALL | • Assign students to watch English videos and attach related expressions and links to Padlet<br>• Use interactive quizzes and reading assignments to reinforce learning |
| Extramural CALL | • Encourage students to keep a reflective journal about what they have learned from English videos or online conversations<br>• Set up online discussion forums and creative projects to continue learning outside the classroom |

To address these issues, they suggested incorporating IDLE into actual assessments, running motivational programs that allow students to set learning goals, and rewarding students based on learning outcomes. These strategies aim to make learning more engaging and motivate students to participate in IDLE activities.

## Conclusion

This chapter provided a comprehensive analysis based on previous research findings regarding the intricate relationships among IDLE, perceptions of EIL, and learners' WTC, incorporating insights from practitioners within the context of Korean middle schools. The survey examined the multifaceted nature of learners' perceptions and communication readiness through the perspectives of digital learning environments. The findings contribute to theoretical understanding and pedagogical implications in SLA research. The results corroborated existing theories, reaffirming the central role of L2 WTC in language learning and highlighting its significance as a psychological precursor to actual L2 use. Exploring various factors influencing L2 WTC, including learner autonomy and positive attitudes, enriched the understanding of the trait-like and state-like variables that shape learners' communicative dispositions.

Furthermore, the findings imply potential impacts on educational policies, highlighting the importance of recognizing and supporting students' engagement in out-of-class language learning experiences. The research enriches the ongoing discourse in L2 WTC studies by connecting digital learning with EIL perceptions. This chapter demonstrates that IDLE can significantly enhance students' WTC in English by fostering positive attitudes towards the language. By incorporating these activities into the educational curriculum, teachers can help bridge the gap between formal instruction and practical language use. The findings suggest that integrating IDLE into the classroom can foster a positive classroom environment for L2 communication, ultimately enhancing students' confidence and willingness to use English in diverse contexts.

In future studies, detailed investigations into specific IDLE activities, considering how different IDLE activities influence learners' cognitive and affective states, would provide more nuanced insights. Longitudinal studies are needed to observe changes in WTC and EIL perceptions over time and to identify the long-term impacts of IDLE activities. Employing qualitative research methods, such as interviews and focus groups of students, will gain deeper insights into their experiences and perceptions of IDLE. By addressing these areas, future research can provide a more comprehensive understanding of the role of IDLE in language learning and contribute to the development of viable language education strategies.

## References

Bae, J. (2024). Informal digital learning of English and L2 willingness to communicate of Korean middle school learners: The mediating role of English as an international language. *Secondary English Education, 17*(1), 87–115.

Benson, P. (2011). Language learning and teaching beyond the classroom: An introduction to the field. In P. Benson & H. Reinders (Eds.), *Beyond the language classroom* (pp. 7–16). Palgrave Macmillan.

Butler, Y. G. (2005). Comparative perspectives towards communicative activities among elementary school teachers in South Korea, Japan and Taiwan. *Language Teaching Research, 9*(4), 423–446.

Jeon, J., & Lee, H. (2017). Secondary teachers' perception on English education policies in Korea. *The Journal of Asia TEFL, 14*(1), 47–63.

Jin, Y. J., & Yoo, I. W. (2019). Why communicative language teaching has yet to work in Korea: Exploring teachers' viewpoints. *Journal of Asia TEFL, 16*(4), 1332.

Ke, I., & Cahyani, H. (2014). Learning to become users of English as a lingua franca (ELF): How ELF online communication affects Taiwanese learners' beliefs of English. *System, 46*, 28–38.

Kusyk, M. (2017). The development of complexity, accuracy and fluency in L2 written production through informal participation in online activities. *CALICO Journal, 34*(1), 75–96.

Lai, C., Zhu, W., & Gong, G. (2015). Understanding the quality of out-of-class English learning. *TESOL Quarterly, 49*(2), 278–308.

Lee, J. S. (2020). The role of informal digital learning of English and a high-stakes English test on perceptions of English as an international language. *Australian Journal of Educational Technology, 36*(2), 155–168.

Lee, J. S. (2021). *Informal digital learning of English: Research to practice.* Routledge.

Lee, J. S. (2022). The role of grit and classroom enjoyment in EFL learners' willingness to communicate. *Journal of Multilingual and Multicultural Development, 43*(5), 452–468.

Lee, J. S., & Drajati, N. (2019). Affective variables and informal digital learning of English: Keys to willingness to communicate in a second language. *Australian Journal of Educational Technology, 35*(5), 168–182.

Lee, J. S., & Lee, K. (2010). Corrective feedback through computer-mediated communication in EFL college level. *English Language Teaching, 22*(1), 171–193.

Lee, J. S., & Lee, K. (2019a). Informal digital learning of English and English as an international language: The path less traveled. *British Journal of Educational Technology, 50*(3), 1447–1461.

Lee, J. S., & Lee, K. (2019b). Perceptions of English as an international language by Korean English-major and non-English-major students. *Journal of Multilingual and Multicultural Development, 40*(1), 76–89.

Lee, J. S., & Sylvén, L. K. (2021). The role of informal digital learning of English in Korean and Swedish EFL learners' communication behaviour. *British Journal of Educational Technology, 52*(3), 1279–1296.

Lee, J. S., Lee, K., & Chen Hsieh, J. (2022a). Understanding willingness to communicate in L2 between Korean and Taiwanese students. *Language Teaching Research, 26*(3), 455–476.

Lee, J. S., Nakamura, Y., & Sadler, R. (2017). Effects of videoconference-embedded classrooms (VEC) on learners' perceptions toward English as an international language (EIL). *ReCALL, 30*(3), 1–18.

Lee, J. S., Nakamura, Y., & Sadler, R. (2018). Effects of videoconference-embedded classrooms (VEC) on learners' perceptions towards English as an international language (EIL). *ReCALL, 30*(3), 1–18.

Lee, J. S., Sylvén, L. K., & Lee, K. (2021). Cross-cultural insights into Korean and Swedish secondary school students' willingness to communicate in a second language. *Journal of Multilingual and Multicultural Development, 42*(6), 522–536.

Lee, J. S., Xie, Q., & Lee, K. (2021). Informal digital learning of English and L2 willingness to communicate: Roles of emotions, gender, and educational stage. *Journal of Multilingual and Multicultural Development*. https://doi.org/10.1080/01434632.2021.1918699

Lee, J. S., Yeung, N. M., & Osburn, M. B. (2022b). Foreign language enjoyment as a mediator between informal digital learning of english and willingness to communicate: A sample of Hong Kong EFL secondary students. *Journal of Multilingual and Multicultural Development, 45*(9), 3613–3631.

Lee, K. (2009) Exploring in service teacher education in Korea. In Y.H. Choi and B. Spolsky (Eds.), *English language teacher education in Asia*. Asia TEFL Book Series (pp. 49–70). Asia TEFL.

Lee, Y. S. (2015). Innovating secondary English education in Korea. In B. Spolsky & K. Sung (Eds.), *Secondary school English education in Asia* (pp. 47–64). Routledge.

Li, D. F. (1998). 'It's always more difficult than you plan and imagine': Teachers' perceived difficulties in introducing the communicative approach in South Korea. *TESOL Quarterly, 32*(4), 677–703.

Littlewood, W. (2007). Communicative and task-based language teaching in East Asian classrooms. *Language Teaching, 40*(3), 243–249.

Marlina, R. (2017). Practices of teaching Englishes for international communication. In A. Matsuda (Ed.), *Preparing teachers to teach English as an international language* (pp. 100–113). Multilingual Matters.

McKay, S. (2003). Teaching English as an international language: The Chilean context. *ELT Journal, 57*(2), 139–148.

Ministry of Education. (1992). *Explaining the 6th national curriculum of English*. Daehan Textbook Publishing Co.

Ministry of Education. (1997). *The 7th national curriculum of English*. MOE.

Mitchell, R., & Lee, J.H.-W. (2003). Sameness and difference in classroom learning cultures: Interpretations of communicative pedagogy in the UK and Korea. *Language Teaching Research, 7*(1), 35–63.

Park, B.-R. (2013, December 12). *The current status of English education: From the perspective of classroom teaching at schools* [Conference session]. Korea Association of Teachers of English: Commemorating 130 years of English education in Korea. Hankuk University of Foreign Studies, Seoul, Korea.

Plonsky, L., & Oswald, F. L. (2014). How big is 'big'? Interpreting effect sizes in L2 research. *Language Learning, 64*, 878–912.

Shin, S. Y., & Walkinshaw, I. (2023). Incorporating world Englishes into middle and high schools in Korea: Teachers' awareness and attitudes. *RELC Journal*. https://doi.org/10.1177/00336882231214304

Soyoof, A. (2022). Iranian EFL students' perception of willingness to communicate in an extramural digital context. *Interactive Learning Environments, 31*(9), 1–18.

Sundqvist, P., & Wikström, P. (2015). Out-of-school digital gameplay and in-school L2 English vocabulary outcomes. *System, 51*, 65–76.

Zarrinabadi, N., & Khodarahmi, E. (2017). L2 willingness to communicate and perceived accent strength: A qualitative inquiry. *Journal of Intercultural Communication Research, 46*(2), 173–187.

Zhang, R., Zou, D., Cheng, G., Xie, H., Wang, F. L., & Au, O. (2021). Target languages, types of activities, engagement, and effectiveness of extramural language learning. *PLoS ONE, 16*(6), e0253431.

Zhang, Y., & Liu, G. (2022). Revisiting informal digital learning of English (IDLE): A structural equation modeling approach in a university EFL context. *Computer Assisted Language Learning*, 1–33.

# 5

# Artificial Intelligence in Enhancing Korean High School Students' English Skills

Rakhun Kim

## Area of Innovation

Artificial Intelligence (AI) stands at the forefront of an innovative transition in educational contexts worldwide, with Korea notably advocating for its expansive integration (Lee & Lee, 2023; Willige, 2024). This chapter explores the substantial potential of AI to transform traditional teaching methodologies, particularly aiming to reinforce educational efficiencies. Specifically, it examines the integration of AI technologies within the context of English education in Korean secondary schools, providing a critical review of how these AI tools innovate teaching and learning practices in Korean English as a Foreign Language (EFL) context.

---

R. Kim (✉)
Hongik University, Seoul, South Korea
e-mail: kimrhee02@hongik.ac.kr

The integration of AI aims to overcome traditional limitations in Korean educational contexts such as large class sizes and limited teacher-student interactions (Byun, 2023; Jung, 2024). This integration of AI technology into the Korean educational framework is a coordinated effort involving various stakeholders, including policymakers, educators, and technologists (Lee & Lee, 2024). By using AI technology, Korean educational authorities, such as Korean Ministry of Education (MOE), seek to foster an educational ecosystem where personalized learning becomes the norm, rather than the exception, thereby significantly enhancing both the educational experience and accessibility (Choi, 2024; Kim & Kwon, 2023).

Korea has adopted various AI technologies for personalized learning, including AI-powered digital textbooks (AIDTs), AI chatbots for language learning, and learning management systems (LMSs) (Kwon, 2024; Seo, 2023; Seo & Kim, 2023; So et al., 2023). These tools are designed to provide learners with adaptive learning experiences, making education more interactive and effective. In this respect, EdTech, which refers to AI technology in educational contexts, facilitates an innovative transition to a more interactive and personalized learning process in Korean EFL learning contexts.

For example, the implementation of AIDT represents a significant advancement in digital educational transformation in Korean educational context. These AIDTs will be introduced for subjects such as Mathematics, English, and Information Technology in 2025, with plans to expand to other subjects by 2028 (Ministry of Education, 2023). The primary objective of AIDT is to provide "personalized" learning experiences tailored to individual student data. To ensure successful integration, the MOE is initiating the teacher training programs and the customized teaching and learning methods appropriate for the use of AIDT. The basic framework of AIDT is illustrated in Fig. 5.1.

As demonstrated in Fig. 5.1, the MOE has fostered collaboration between traditional textbook publishing companies experienced in textbook development and Edtech companies equipped with advanced technologies. This collaboration aims to develop high-quality AI Digital Textbooks that align with the 2022 revised national curriculum (Ministry of Education, 2022, 2023).

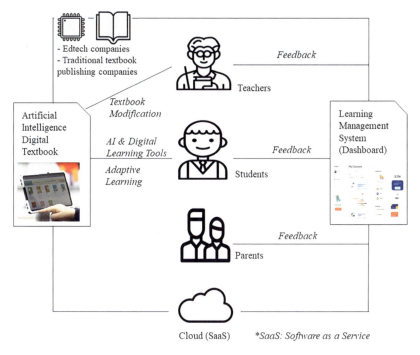

Fig. 5.1 The basic framework of AI Digital Textbook (AIDT)

This implementation of the AIDT system, guided by established pedagogical principles, is essential for the personalized educational practices. Specifically, learners will engage with various artificial intelligence and digital learning tools provided by the AI Digital Textbook (AIDT), with their learning data stored in the Software as a Service (SaaS) cloud. This cloud-stored data will be used to recommend and deliver optimal learning materials tailored to each learner. Teachers can also utilize AIDT to reorganize textbooks and monitor students' learning status via the Learning Management System (LMS) dashboard, enabling them to design lessons that best fit each student's needs. Furthermore, parents can use the LMS dashboard to support their children's learning at home, making the educational process more cohesive and integrated across different environments.

To further advance digital transformation within educational settings in Korea, MOE has established a robust hardware infrastructure specifically designed for classroom use (Ministry of Education, 2024). This strategic initiative encompasses the provision of Personal Digital Devices (PDDs) to each student. These devices are interconnected through Wi-Fi Access Points (APs), which facilitate seamless connectivity between the PDDs and interactive whiteboards. This system conceptually empowers learners to access a variety of internet-based language learning resources, including Artificial Intelligence-Driven Tools (AIDTs), AI chatbots, and Learning Management Systems (LMS) on their PDDs. Additionally, it supports collaborative group activities and enables the presentation of group project outcomes on digital whiteboards. The holistic integration of these digital tools, as depicted in Fig. 5.2, is strategically designed to enhance interactive learning experiences and foster a dynamic classroom environment.

## Impetus for the Innovation

With the substantial governmental supports for educational technology (Edtech) in Korea, there has been a continuous internal drive within the Korean English educational community to use AI technology or computer-assisted language learning (CALL) tools to address pedagogical challenges within Korean EFL contexts (Kim, 2018; Yarrow et al., 2022). This drive has been grounded in the critical insight that traditional practices of English education in Korean EFL settings have generally failed to provide learners with personalized learning experiences (Byun, 2023; Kim, 2022b). In fact, advancements in AI technology have now evolved to a point where they can replicate pedagogical practices of human teachers, such as discriminating between correct and incorrect sentence constructions and providing personalized corrective feedback (Kong & Yang, 2024).

However, previous attempts to incorporate AI technologies in Korean EFL contexts have often overemphasized the technological aspects, neglecting the necessary integration of insights from linguistics and English education pedagogy (Kim, 2018; Lee & Lee, 2024). In this

# 5 Artificial Intelligence in Enhancing Korean High ...

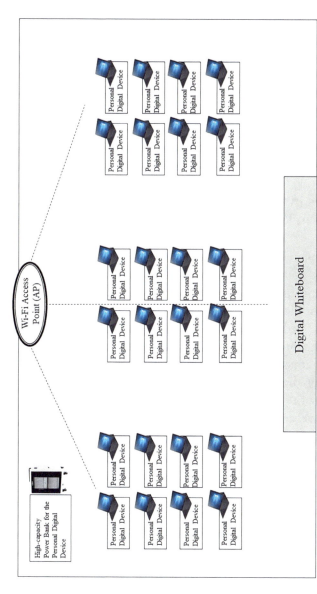

**Fig. 5.2** Hardware infrastructure supporting digital transformation in Korean educational settings

respect, there is a crucial demand for developing AI-based foreign language learning frameworks that incorporate not only technological considerations but also pedagogical and linguistic insights (Kim, 2022a, 2022b; Lee & Lee, 2024). Such AI-based English language learning and teaching frameworks should be capable of delivering personalized feedback that accurately addresses the specific challenges faced by learners, thereby enhancing the overall efficiency of English education in Korea, including both receptive and productive skills (Seo & Kim, 2023).

## Specific Context of Implementation

### Challenges in the Digital Transformation of English Education in Korea

In the ongoing discourse surrounding digital transformation in the Korean EFL context, one of the primary challenges is the absence of a coherent instructional English language learning and teaching model specifically targeted for AI-based digital environments (Cardona et al., 2023). Traditional English learning and teaching procedures often struggle to adapt efficiently to digital environments, highlighting the necessity for innovative pedagogic models that fully utilize the distinct advantages of digital tools. This adaptation requires a comprehensive reevaluation of teaching strategies to ensure that the new model exploits the interactive and personalized potential of AI technology, particularly to promote individualized learning experiences in the Korean EFL context (Barrot, 2023; Bonner et al., 2023; Chan & Hu, 2023; Hang et al., 2024).

Additionally, there is a considerable lack of empirical evidence supporting the effectiveness of new EFL programs that utilize advanced digital technologies. The rapid adoption of AI tools such as AI chatbots and generative AI technologies in Korean EFL practices has outpaced the research needed to substantiate their educational value (Rahman & Watanobe, 2023; Tlili et al., 2023). This deficiency in rigorous, evidence-based studies on the educational impacts of new technologies leads to uncertainties regarding their role in promoting English language learning in Korean EFL contexts (Escueta et al., 2017).

To address these challenges, it is crucial for the academic community to prioritize research that evaluates the effectiveness of digital tools in Korean EFL contexts. Such studies should aim to establish evidence-based practices that can specify the development of digital instructional models and ensure that technological advancements contribute positively to educational outcomes. Furthermore, collaboration between technologists, second language acquisition (SLA) practitioners, and linguists is essential to create a comprehensive and adaptable educational framework that is both innovative and grounded in evidence-based educational principles (Ellis & Bogart, 2007).

## Case Studies

### Case Study (1): Use of Generative AI for the Development of English Receptive Skills of Korean High School EFL Learners (Kim, 2024a)

This case study aims to address the limitations identified in previous research and assess the effectiveness of using ChatGPT to facilitate learners' higher-order cognitive processing, specifically top-down processing (Kim, 2024a). Prior studies have shown that EFL learners often rely on bottom-up processing when using ChatGPT without instructional support from a human teacher (Chan & Hu, 2023; Jeon & Lee, 2023; Kim, 2023). This reliance leads learners to focus solely on lexical details and linguistic grammaticality, neglecting the advanced cognitive skills required to understand overall meanings and contexts.

To resolve this issue, this case study presents an instructional methodology that combines the complementary roles of ChatGPT and human teachers (Barrot, 2023; Chan & Hu, 2023; Mohamed, 2024). This study investigates how this integrated approach can enhance Korean EFL learners' ability to engage in top-down processing. By using ChatGPT, the case study aims to encourage Korean EFL learners to analyze texts more strategically and critically, thereby enabling them to identify main ideas. This helps learners move from merely 'decoding' text to truly 'comprehending' it (Goodman, 1998).

Thus, the purpose of this case study is to empirically demonstrate how the integration of ChatGPT with human teacher guidance can enhance learners' top-down English reading skills. Specifically, by focusing on this higher-order cognitive process, this case study aims to effectively incorporate AI technology into traditional educational methods for English reading in Korean EFL contexts. To achieve this, this case study considers several key factors, including technological components, linguistic insights, and pedagogical strategies.

*Technological Considerations:*

Generative and Transformative Capabilities: ChatGPT demonstrates advanced capabilities in understanding and generating human-like responses (Goodfellow et al., 2016; Krizhevsky et al., 2017). These technological advancements allow it to function effectively as an educational tool, providing interactive, real-time assistance similar to human tutor (Jeon & Lee, 2023; Kohnke et al., 2023; Shaikh et al., 2023).

*Linguistic Considerations:*

Top-Down and Bottom-Up Processing: Balancing top-down and bottom-up processing strategies is crucial for effective language acquisition especially for reading comprehension in Korean EFL context (Carrell, 1998; Chamot & O'Malley, 1994; Chong & Kim, 2023; Park, 2018). ChatGPT supports both processes by assisting with with vocabulary and grammar (e.g., bottom-up processing) and engaging EFL learners in discussions about text structure and meaning (e.g., top-down processing).

*Pedagogical Considerations:*

Hypothesis Testing and Confirmation: This case study highlights the importance of hypothesis testing in reading comprehension, a cognitive process where learners predict their hypothesis for the text, and confirm such idea based on their existing knowledge (Goodman, 1998; Urquhart & Weir, 1998). ChatGPT serves as an interlocutor in this process, helping Korean EFL learners test their hypotheses by providing instant feedback on their predictions for the text, thereby facilitating a deeper understanding through active learning strategies.

*Participants*

To investigate the instructional effects of ChatGPT on English reading skill development using top-down processing, students were divided into two groups. The one was control group ($n = 20$) and the other was instructional group ($n = 20$). Before the instruction, both groups were found to have homogeneous reading comprehension capabilities, without any statistical differences in their pre-test scores.

*Procedure and Material*

The control group received traditional instructional methods for English reading comprehension tasks, while the experimental group received ChatGPT-based English reading comprehension instruction. As outlined in Table 5.1, the experimental group participants actively used ChatGPT during their learning sessions, whereas the control group relied solely on conventional strategies without the assistance of ChatGPT.

Pre-task

Both groups were provided with the same reading comprehension tasks from the K-CSAT (Korean-College Scholastic Aptitude Test), aimed at developing English reading skills such as finding main ideas (FMI) through top-down processing, retrieving factual information through bottom-up processing, and making inferences through interactive processing (Yi et al., 2023). A variety of reading comprehension tasks were employed across the two groups, encompassing diverse genres, including narrative, expository, and argumentative texts.

Additionally, the human teacher introduced the concept of identifying main idea sentences using discourse markers: All participants, in both the control and experimental groups, received explicit instruction from a human teacher, emphasizing the activation of top-down processing through the use of discourse markers. As is outlined in Table 5.2, all the participants were exposed to the same instructional treatments that included the implementation of a top-down reading strategy, with a

Table 5.1 Procedure of the instruction

| Instructional Phase |
|---|
| **[Pre-task: Instructional Treatments Commonly Provided to Both Groups]**<br>(1) Instruction on top-down processing by human English teacher: Table 5.2<br>  – Instructional Material: English reading comprehension tasks from K-CSAT<br>(2) Self-reading Phase<br>  – Read and provide their own answer based upon the instruction for the FMI tasks |
| **[While-task]**<br><Control Group><br>– Quick answer check on the reference book<br>– Using AI translator for L1–L2 translation and vocabulary consultation<br><br><Experimental Group><br>– Interaction with ChatGPT to find out the reasons for their choice of the tasks<br>– Using ChatGPT as a linguistic resource for L1–L2 translation and vocabulary consultation |
| **[Post-task]**<br>(1) Whole Class instruction & final check-up by human English teacher<br>  – Specification and reason for the thesis statement of the passage<br>  – Form Focused Instruction (FFI) for the relative clause<br>(2) Wrap-up |

*Note* Adapted from "Effects of ChatGPT on Korean EFL Learners' Main-Idea Reading Comprehension via Top-Down Processing," by R. Kim, 2024a, *Language Research*, *60*(1), p. 89 (https://doi.org/https://doi.org/10.30961/lr.2024.60.1.83). Copyright 2024 by Language Education Institute, Seoul National University

particular emphasis on discourse markers, specifically targeting keywords for FMI tasks.

After the instruction, the participants were asked to independently read the English reading comprehension tasks for 20 minutes.

## While-Task: Key Distinctions Between the Two Groups and Platform Overview

The fundamental distinction between the experimental and control groups was access to ChatGPT. Only participants in the experimental group were permitted to use ChatGPT through a platform called *GPT to*

**Table 5.2** Instructional material shared across the two groups: list of discourse markers for Finding Main Idea (FMI) tasks

| Discourse structure | Discourse marker |
|---|---|
| Thesis Statement & Example | Thesis statement is placed prior to the discourse markers indicating list of examples (e.g., *For example, According to* ...) |
| Deontic Modality Auxiliary | Thesis statement usually incorporates deontic modality auxiliary (e.g., *Should, have to*...) |
| Adversative Transition | Thesis statement usually incorporates adversative transitional words (e.g., *However, but* ...) |
| Causal Transition | Thesis statement usually incorporates causal transitional words (e.g., *Consequently, to sum up* ...) |

*Note* Adapted from "Effects of ChatGPT on Korean EFL Learners' Main-Idea Reading Comprehension via Top-Down Processing," by R. Kim, 2024a, *Language Research, 60*(1), p. 90 (https://doi.org/https://doi.org/10.30961/lr.2024.60.1.83). Copyright 2024 by Language Education Institute, Seoul National University

*Excel* (Yim & Kim, 2023), as illustrated in Fig. 5.3. This web-based platform was specifically developed to automate the collection of interactions between the experimental group participants and ChatGPT, channeling these interactional data into an Excel file for analytical purposes by the researcher.

To construct this system, prompts from the users were submitted to GPT-3 Turbo via OpenAI API. Responses from GPT were then displayed in a chat format to the users. Concurrently, user information, time stamps, question content, and response content were systematically recorded in an Excel file. Upon request by the administrator, a comprehensive Excel file containing all the recorded data was made available, ensuring that all interactions could be scrutinized by the researcher as necessary.

The experimental group was taught how to use this ChatGPT system to elaborate on the reasoning behind their identification of main idea. During this stage, all the learners' utterances to ChatGPT were monitored on the GPT to Excel server system, and immediate questions regarding bottom-up processing were strictly prohibited. Prompts to ChatGPT were given in the students' native language, Korean, with a

**Fig. 5.3** GPT to EXCEL and User Log

specific focus on identifying the most informative sentence ("*Show me the most informative sentences.*"). The phrase "thesis statement" was avoided since ChatGPT typically highlighted the first sentence of a paragraph as the thesis statement of the paragraph, when responding to such queries.

Students actively engaged with ChatGPT to explore why certain sentences were considered more informative than others and to critically assess ChatGPT's analysis against their own interpretations. This interaction was dynamic; experimental group participants persisted in their inquiries, if ChatGPT's explanations did not align with their expectations. Depending on the responses, ChatGPT might alter its viewpoint or maintain its initial stance. This engagement served as a crucial foundation for deeper discussions between students and AI, marking a significant phase in developing critical analytical skills through AI-assisted learning. Subsequently, the experimental group participants were allowed to inquire ChatGPT about linguistic details, such as vocabulary and grammar, facilitating bottom-up processing.

On the other hand, the control group participants employed a traditional learning approach, which enabled them to independently verify their responses. Initially, similar to the experimental group, they were prohibited from using digital tools for accessing linguistic details such as vocabulary or grammatical information. Instead, they were instructed to read passages and independently identify the main idea based on instructions from the human teacher. Subsequently, they quickly checked their answers using a reference book. After completing this verification, they were permitted to use an AI translator for L1–L2 translation and vocabulary consultation.

## Post-task: Key Distinctions Between the Two Groups and Platform Overview

In the latter part of the instruction, the human teacher played a critical role in consolidating the learning process and ensuring a deep understanding of the reading text. This phase was characterized as whole-class instruction and a final check-up led by the human English teacher. During this session, the teacher specifically addressed the thesis statement of the passage, providing the reasoning behind it. This clarification helped solidify all the participants' understanding of the main idea and addressed any potential misunderstandings that may have arisen from interactions with ChatGPT, such as the hallucination effect where incorrect information is generated by the generative AI agent.

Additionally, this instructional phase included Form Focused Instruction (FFI) on a specific grammatical item (e.g., relative clause). This component of the instruction aimed to enhance the learners' grammatical accuracy, focusing specifically on how the target grammar point was used within the context of the reading passage. The FFI not only reinforced grammar rules but also tied these structures back to the main reading passage, ensuring that learners could apply grammatical knowledge to promote the comprehension of the text.

By integrating these elements, the human teacher ensured that all students left the instructional session with a clear understanding of the key concepts and the linguistic tools necessary to analyze the reading passage. This approach not only addressed immediate learning needs but also reinforced students' critical thinking and linguistic skills.

*Test and Findings*

Students' progress was monitored through a series of assessments designed to evaluate English reading comprehension, specifically focusing on main idea identification. These included pre-, immediate post-, and delayed-post tests, aimed at measuring the effectiveness of ChatGPT-assisted learning compared to traditional methods. The results from these assessments quantitatively demonstrated the impact of ChatGPT on students' reading comprehension skills.

To complement the quantitative data, qualitative analysis was conducted through post-session reflections where students shared their experiences of learning with ChatGPT. This qualitative analysis was crucial for collecting insights into the perceived benefits and challenges of integrating ChatGPT in reading comprehension tasks.

The findings of the case study demonstrated a statistically significant improvement in the top-down processing skills of the experimental group. Additionally, the qualitative analysis from interviews with learners and the evaluation of ChatGPT and human interaction data highlighted the potential benefits and challenges of using ChatGPT for English reading comprehension. These insights underline the importance of a balanced approach to integrating technology with traditional pedagogical practices to optimize learning experiences in Korean EFL contexts.

## Case Study (2): Use of AI Chatbot for the Development of English Productive Skills by Korean High School EFL Learners (Kim, 2024b)

The case study aimed to assess the impact of using an AI chatbot to enhance the productive English skills of Korean high school EFL learners, specifically focusing on their ability to use English caused-motion constructions (e.g., *Jane sneezed the tissue off the table.*) (Goldberg, 1995).

Previous studies have generally demonstrated that the significant challenges faced by Korean learners of English primarily stems from the substantial linguistic differences between the Korean and English (Croft, 1998; Folli & Harley, 2006; Matsumoto, 1996; Talmy, 1985). Specifically, Korean, being a verb-framed language, integrates the manner and result of motion directly within two verbs, whereas English, a satellite-framed language, often uses separate elements like prepositions or particles to express manner of motion and relies on a single verb as a result of the motion (Choi, 2020; Choi & Bowerman, 1991; Folli & Harley, 2006; Lee & Kim, 2011; Shibatani & Pardeshi, 2002; Sung, 2019; Talmy, 1985; Zubizarreta & Oh, 2007). This typological divergence results in persistent difficulties for Korean learners to adapt to the English way of formulating sentences that convey manner and result of motion. Such crosslinguistic interference frequently leads to incorrect or awkward sentence constructions when speaking English by Korean EFL learners.

To account for the difficulties stemming from the crosslinguistic differences, a corrective recast has been suggested. Corrective recast has been defined as a persistent provision of corrective feedback, which may enhance the noticeability of the corrective feedbacks to account for the language learning difficulties to overcome these persistent linguistic barriers (Chen et al., 2017; Choi, 2019; Chowdhary, 2020; Deng & Liu, 2018; Hirschberg & Manning, 2015; Wang & Petrina, 2013). To do so, the following linguistic, pedagogical and technological issues were considered.

## Linguistic Considerations

The study addressed significant syntactic and semantic differences between Korean and English, particularly concerning the English caused-motion construction, which does not have a direct equivalent in Korean (Croft, 1998; Folli & Harley, 2006; Matsumoto, 1996; Talmy, 1985). By focusing on this construction, the study aimed to provide targeted linguistic support to overcome crosslinguistic interference, which is crucial for effective language acquisition.

## Pedagogical Considerations

The study specifically explored the impact of corrective recasts—a form of corrective feedback where the correct form is provided after an error is made (Ellis et al., 2006). This method helps in highlighting errors implicitly and providing the correct linguistic forms explicitly, which is shown to be crucial for learning. The AI chatbots were programmed to deliver the corrective recasts, including (i) repetition & clarification request, (ii) elicitation, and (iii) recast (Doughty & Varela, 1998).

## Technological Considerations

AI chatbots were implemented to deliver consistent and individualized corrective feedback (CF), which is otherwise labor-intensive for human instructors (Semke, 1984). The natural language processing (NLP) engine embedded in the AI chatbot allows for intelligent computer-assisted language learning (ICALL), enabling more optimal and naturalistic corrective feedback that can adapt to individual learner responses (Heift, 2004; Petersen, 2010; Wilske, 2015).

## Participants

This case study involved 69 high school students, divided into three distinct groups. One group interacted with an AI chatbot that provided corrective feedback ($n = 23$), a second group received traditional grammar instruction without interactive feedback ($n = 23$), and a third, the control group, received no specific instruction ($n = 23$).

Experimental group participants engaged in communicative tasks designed to elicit the use of English caused-motion constructions. The AI chatbot employed in the present case study was hand-coded by the researcher via Chatfuel, which is a code-free chatbot development platform for text-based facebook messenger chatbot, and its primary objective was to provide a series of immediate corrective recast. Corrective recast draws learners' attention to the erroneous part in their utterance to implicitly encourage self-correction (i.e., prompt) and explicitly provides a correct linguistic exemplar to model the input (i.e., reformulation; Doughty & Varela, 1998). Although providing corrective recast may help Korean EFL learners' language learning processes, it is practically impossible for human instructors to provide corrective feedback in a consistent manner for every erroneous utterance within communicative contexts (Semke, 1984; Truscott, 1999; Valero et al., 2008).

*Material: AI Chatbot Overview*

To deal with for such practicality issue, AI chatbots has been introduced into foreign language environments (Heift, 2004). Figure 5.4 depicts the systematic application of corrective recasts by the text-based AI chatbot across all learners in the experimental group. When an initial mistake was identified (e.g., "Amy's mom take a rub."), the chatbot initiated a corrective feedback (CF) sequence using implicit techniques such as repetition & clarification request ("[Repetition] Amy's mom take a rub??? [Clarification Request] Excuse me? Could you repeat that?"). However, the learner's subsequent response, "I don't know," indicated a continued misunderstanding. In response, the AI chatbot escalated its feedback to more explicit elicitation, focusing only on the subject and verb necessary for correct expression ("Hmm… Could you try saying, 'Amy's mom rubbed…'?"). This prompted a partial correction from the learner ("Amy's mom rubbed lotion."), although it still lacked the necessary prepositional phrase. To account for the persistent errors, the chatbot then provided a recast, clearly modeling the correct structure ("Oh! 'Amy's mom rubbed the lotion on Amy's back.' Correct?"), despite a minor spelling error ("lotio"), which the NLP system recognized as correct. This corrective recast sequence enabled the learner to successfully repair their linguistic mistakes ("Amy's mom rubbed lotion on Amy's back.").

*Test and Findings*

Assessment of the learners' proficiency was conducted using the Elicited Writing Task (EWT), which measured their understanding of the target constructions before and after the instructional period through both immediate and delayed posttests. This evaluation strategy was chosen to gauge both the short-term and long-term effects of the instructional interventions.

Results from the Elicited Writing Tasks (EWT) demonstrated that participants in the experimental group showed statistically significant improvements in both the immediate and delayed posttests, specifically in their ability to produce English caused-motion construction. Additionally, there was a positive correlation between the learners' ability to successfully correct errors following the AI chatbots' corrective recasts and their learning advancements in the two EWT posttests. These results emphasize the importance of the noticeability of corrective feedback from AI chatbots in the context of learning foreign languages.

# Findings

## What Worked

### Case Study (1): Receptive Skill

(1) *Dynamic AI Integration with Traditional English Reading Class*: The incorporation of ChatGPT into the English reading curriculum went beyond its mere use as a digital tool; it involved a strategic

5 Artificial Intelligence in Enhancing Korean High ... 115

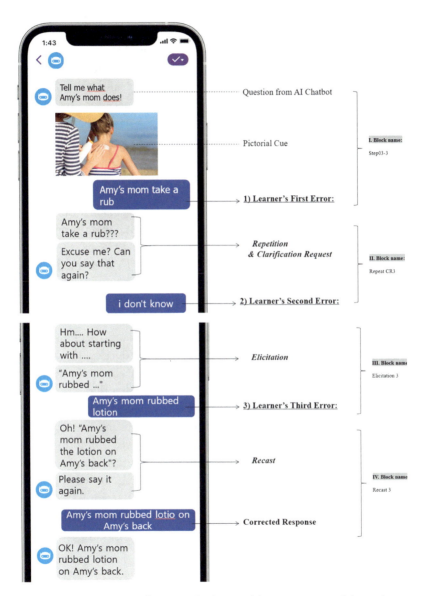

**Fig. 5.4** Corrective recast from AI Chatbot and learner's successful repair

blend with dynamic teaching methodologies. The interactions facilitated by ChatGPT were designed to stimulate deeper cognitive engagement, allowing students to actively explore text interpretations. This method enhanced engagement and stimulated the development of higher-order cognitive skills necessary for effective top-down processing.

(2) *Adaptive and Personalized Feedback by ChatGPT:* ChatGPT's role in providing real-time, tailored responses to students' inputs was crucial. This adaptive feedback mechanism ensured that students received individualized support, catering to their specific needs and queries during the reading process. This personalization helps students progress at their own pace, which is vital in accommodating diverse learning speeds and styles within the classroom.

(3) *Active Engagement in Learning via ChatGPT*: The methodology used in this case study facilitated active engagement with the top-down reading processes, moving students beyond passive reading. By encouraging students to actively responding to the ChatGPT, they questioned, and analyzed the texts with ChatGPT. This instructional model was essential in helping students develop the necessary skills for top-down processing, such as identifying main ideas and making inferences based on broader context rather than just focusing on discrete lexical or grammatical details.

(4) *Indispensable Role of Human Instructors:* Despite the advanced capabilities of ChatGPT, human instructors played an indispensable role. Teachers were pivotal in monitoring the interactions between students and ChatGPT, especially in addressing and correcting the inaccuracies or misunderstandings that arose from AI responses. Teachers used these inaccuracies as opportunities to deepen students' understanding of the texts, focusing on higher-level cognitive skills like main idea identification.

## Case Study (2): Productive Skill

(1) *Interactive Language Learning Experience*: The use of AI chatbots creates a continuous loop of interaction and feedback, which was

essential for keeping students actively engaged with their learning experiences. This persistent interaction on AI chatbots was not just repetitive; it was a dynamic process that adjusted to the student's learning pace and style, encouraging deeper involvement to the acquisition of English caused-motion construction. Such an interactive AI chatbot system helped in reinforcing new linguistic construction and ensured that learning was not a passive activity but an engaging dialogue that enhanced students' ability to apply what they learned in real-world interaction.

(2) *Real-Time, Personalized Corrective Feedback*: The AI chatbots were particularly effective due to their ability to immediately identify and respond to errors during language learning sessions. This immediacy ensured that students could understand and rectify mistakes as they occurred, significantly enhancing the learning process. Furthermore, the feedback was tailored to each student's specific linguistic needs, making it highly relevant and more likely to improve individual learning outcomes. This approach supported the pedagogical benefits of immediate provision of corrective feedback in dealing with persistent linguistic errors frequently faced by Korean EFL learners due to L1–L2 linguistic variation (Talmy, 1985).

(3) *Graduated Corrective Feedback Loop with High Noticeability*: The successful deployment of AI chatbots particularly for Korean high school EFL learners introduced a sophisticated corrective feedback mechanism that significantly enhanced the learning of complex English grammatical structures such as the caused-motion constructions. This innovative approach highlighted the dynamic and interactive capabilities of AI to provide a continuous loop of corrective feedback, crucial for navigating the linguistic disparities between Korean and English. The sequence of corrective feedback initiated by the chatbot started with the identification of errors in real-time, followed by immediate, personalized responses that catered to the specific linguistic needs of each student. This method of feedback was strategic, moving from implicit hints (i.e., repetition & clarification requests) to explicit corrections (i.e., recast), thereby scaffolding the learning process in step-wise manner. Noticeability was key in this feedback loop. Providing learners with a sequence of corrective

feedback loop ensured that feedback was not only noticed but also processed by the learners, aligning with SLA theories that emphasize the significance of immediate and noticeable feedback (Kartchava & Ammar, 2014).

(4) *Enlightened Use of AI Technology to Address Linguistic and Pedagogical Challenges*

The implementation of the AI chatbot was primarily motivated by significant linguistic challenges faced by Korean EFL learners, particularly the complex grammatical structure of English caused-motion constructions, which have no direct translation equivalents in the Korean language (Choi & Bowerman, 1991; Kim, 2022b). Korean learners must not only learn these new structures but also unlearn their native linguistic patterns, which is a significantly challenging process due to the foundational differences between the two languages. Thus, the focus on these structures in the AI chatbot's design underscores an "enlightened" approach to a linguistic issue that is critical to develop English productive skills by Korean EFL learners (Ellis & Bogart, 2007).

In fact, traditional teaching methods (e.g., explicit instruction) significantly struggled to address the deep linguistic barriers encountered by Korean learners, particularly with complex grammatical structures such as English caused-motion constructions, which have no direct translation equivalents in Korean. The profound differences between the two languages require more active instructional practices that go far beyond the capabilities of conventional strategies. This requires for dynamic and interactive instruction. However, due to practicality issue, human teachers alone cannot consistently perform such an interactive interaction. This is where AI-powered systems come into play, equipped to offer graduated corrective feedback that is crucial for the unlearning of ingrained L1 properties and the acquisition of challenging L2 constructions. The limitations inherent in traditional EFL practices, particularly the inconsistency and infrequency of personalized feedback, necessitated the integration of AI technologies. By integrating AI into the educational framework, we could ensure a level of engagement and precision in feedback that human teachers, due to constraints in time, resources, and individual attention capacities, were unable to achieve on their own.

This shift to AI-enhanced methods was not just an improvement but a critical need in the face of the unique educational challenges presented by the linguistic complexity facing Korean EFL learners.

To sum up, this case study demonstrated that the strategic use of AI in this educational framework was a deliberate choice, driven by the urgent need to address specific linguistic and pedagogical challenges in Korean EFL context. This approach emphasizes that the deployment of AI technologies is not about following educational trends but about practically using advanced tools to address practical issues in language education. By focusing on these targeted needs, AI transcends its role as a novel technology and becomes an essential element in the linguistic and educational advancement of Korean EFL learners.

## What Didn't Work

### Case Study (1): Receptive Skill

The first case study examining the integration of ChatGPT into English reading comprehension presents several noteworthy limitations. First, Students predominantly utilized ChatGPT to assist with understanding and responding to reading comprehension tasks, focusing primarily on lower-level cognitive skills (e.g., bottom-up processing) like vocabulary recognition and comprehension of factual information. This misguided reliance could potentially diminish the activation of higher-order reading skills. Second, while the feedback provided by ChatGPT was useful for certain learning outcomes, it often lacked the cognitive engagement in which students enhance their skills with active support from peer interactions and teacher guidance.

To address these shortcomings, future studies should consider more sophisticated applications of ChatGPT that more effectively support the development of higher-order cognitive skills. This might involve integrating AI tools with traditional pedagogical practices, ensuring a balanced approach that capitalizes on the strengths of both AI and human instructional methodologies. In dealing with these limitations, future research could explore more sophisticated integrations of

ChatGPT that better support the development of higher-order cognitive skills.

**Case Study (2): Productive Skill**

One of the prominent limitations highlighted in the second case study concerning the AI chatbot's technology was its inconsistency in accurately distinguishing between grammatical and ungrammatical formulations (Kim, 2022a, 2024b). This limitation was particularly critical in language learning environments where the correct modeling of grammatical structures was essential for learners to acquire productive language skills accurately.

The chatbot, primarily designed to process and respond based on pattern recognition and predefined scripts, occasionally miscategorized the learner's input, leading to incorrect judgments for the grammaticality of the learners' utterances. This issue is exacerbated when learners produce sentences that are structurally complex or contain prepositional expressions.

This inaccuracy can hinder learners' ability to develop a reliable sense of grammatical judgement, crucial for their progression to advanced levels of language proficiency. Thus, it is imperative that further refinements be made to enhance the chatbot's algorithmic capabilities, particularly in parsing and analyzing complex sentence structures. Such improvements are essential to ensure that the AI chatbot not only recognizes patterns more accurately but also adapts to the nuances of language that are critical for effective learning. This would enable the chatbot to provide more reliable and precise feedback, thereby supporting learners more effectively as they work towards achieving higher proficiency in language use.

## Lessons Learned Though the Programs

The integration of Artificial Intelligence (AI) into the curriculum for Korean high school EFL learners has demonstrated substantial improvements in English comprehension and production skills. This subsection elucidates the lessons derived from employing AI in educational settings.

### Comprehension Skills

The deployment of ChatGPT significantly enhanced students' comprehension abilities via top-down processing, which moved Korean EFL learners beyond mere decoding of English texts. Hypothesis testing and interactive dialogues with ChatGPT allowed Korean EFL students to actively construct and refine their understanding of the material. Importantly, the role of human instructors was critical; they ensured that AI tools were used effectively, guiding students in applying feedback to foster a deeper comprehension and retention of content.

### Production Skills

AI chatbot technologies proved instrumental in enhancing the accuracy and complexity of students' linguistic output. AI chatbot's immediate and structured corrective feedback significantly improved students' ability to construct grammatically correct sentences, particularly with complex grammatical structures such as English caused-motion construction. The graduated noticeability in the corrective feedback sequence employed by the AI—ranging from implicit prompts to more explicit recast—allowed for real-time correction and nuanced understanding of errors. This continuous and immediate feedback loop facilitated a dynamic learning environment where students could experiment with and refine their language use, thereby accelerating their linguistic development.

Overall, the implementation of AI technology in Korean EFL context has promoted personalized and interactive learning experiences that are essential for enhancing students' English language learning experiences.

These results demonstrate the considerable potential of AI to improve language instruction by merging adaptive technologies with traditional teaching methods. Future efforts should continue to explore how AI tools can be seamlessly combined with established pedagogical techniques to optimize language learning outcomes. Additionally, there is a pressing need to develop a generalizable and coherent instructional model that can be effectively applied to both the comprehension and production aspects of English language education.

# References

Barrot, J. S. (2023). Using ChatGPT for second language writing: Pitfalls and potentials. *Assessing Writing, 57*, 1000745.

Bonner, E., Lege, R., & Frazier, E. (2023). Large language model-based artificial intelligence in the language classroom: Practical ideas for teaching. *Teaching English with Technology, 23*(1), 23–41.

Byun, J. (2023, November 1). More schools, students brace for AI-driven classrooms. *The Korea Times*. https://www.koreatimes.co.kr/www/nation/2024/06/113_362278.html

Cardona, M. A., Rodríguez, R. J., & Ishmael, K. (2023). *Artificial intelligence and the future of teaching and learning: Insights and recommendations*. U.S Department of Education. https://policycommons.net/artifacts/3854312/ai-report/4660267/

Carrell, P. L. (1998). Can reading strategies be successfully taught? *Australian Review of Applied Linguistics, 21*(1), 1–20.

Chamot, A. U., & O'malley, J. M. (1994). *The CALLA handbook: Implementing the cognitive academic language learning approach*. Longman.

Chan, C. K. Y., & Hu, W. (2023). Students' voices on generative AI: Perceptions, benefits, and challenges in higher education. *International Journal of Educational Technology in Higher Education, 20*(43).

Chen, H., Liu, X., Yin, D., & Tang, J. (2017). A survey on dialogue systems: Recent advances and new frontiers. *ACM SIGKDD Explorations Newsletter, 19*(2), 25–35.

Choi, I. C. (2019). Exploring the potential of a computerized corrective feedback system based on a process-oriented qualitative error analysis. *Journal of English Teaching Through Movies and Media, 20*(1), 89–117.

Choi, J. (2024, May 14). S. Korea to inject $70m into AI-powered public education. *The Korea Herald*. https://www.koreaherald.com/view.php?ud=20240514050619

Choi, S. (2020). Development of clause chaining in Korean. *Frontiers in Psychology, 11*, Article 256.

Choi, S., & Bowerman, M. (1991). Learning to express motion events in English and Korean: The influence of language-specific lexicalization patterns. *Cognition, 41*(1), 83–121.

Chong, I., & Kim, H. (2023). Effects of explicit reading strategy instruction on high and low English proficiency learners. *Journal of Learner-Centered Curriculum and Instruction, 23*(4), 715–731.

Chowdhary, K. R. (2020). *Fundamentals of Artificial Intelligence*. Springer.

Croft, W. (1998). Linguistic evidence and mental representations. *Cognitive Linguistics, 9*(2), 151–174.

Deng, L., & Liu, Y. (2018). *Deep learning in natural language processing*. Springer.

Doughty, C., & Varela, E. (1998). Communicative focus on form. In C. Doughty & J. Williams (Eds.), *Focus on form in classroom second language acquisition* (pp. 114–138). Cambridge University Press.

Escueta, M., Quan, V., Nickow, A. J., & Oreopoulos, P. (2017). *Education technology: An evidence-based review*. https://ssrn.com/abstract=3031695

Ellis, N. C., & Bogart, P. S. (2007). Speech and language technology in education: the perspective from SLA research and practice. In *Proceedings of the SLaTE Workshop on Speech and Language Technology in Education* (pp. 1–8). Carnegie Mellon University and ISCA Archive.

Ellis, R., Loewen, S., & Erlam, R. (2006). Implicit and explicit corrective feedback and the acquisition of L2 grammar. *Studies in Second Language Acquisition, 28*(2), 339–368.

Folli, R., & Harley, H. (2006). On the licensing of causatives of directed motion: Waltzing Matilda all over. *Studia Linguistica, 60*(2), 121–155.

Goldberg, A. E. (1995). *Constructions: A construction grammar approach to argument structure*. University of Chicago Press.

Goodfellow, I., Bengio, Y., & Courville, A. (2016). *Deep learning*. MIT Press.

Goodman, K. (1998). The reading process. In P. Carrell, J. Devine, & D. Eskey (Eds.), *Interactive approaches to second language reading* (pp. 11–21). Cambridge University Press.

Hang, Y., Khan, S., Alharbi, A., & Nazir, S. (2024). Assessing English teaching linguistic and artificial intelligence for efficient learning using analytical hierarchy process and Technique for Order of Preference by Similarity to Ideal Solution. *Journal of Software: Evolution and Process, 36*(2), e2462.

Heift, T. (2004). Corrective feedback and learner uptake in CALL. *ReCALL, 16*(2), 416–431.

Hirschberg, J., & Manning, C. D. (2015). Advances in natural language processing. *Science, 349*(6245), 261–266.

Jeon, J., & Lee, S. (2023). Large language models in education: A focus on the complementary relationship between human teachers and ChatGPT. *Education and Information Technologies*, 1–20.

Jung, S. (2024, May 15). South Korea's $70 million investment in AI-powered learning. *Korea Tech Today*. https://www.koreatechtoday.com/south-koreas-70-million-investment-in-ai-powered-learning/

Kartchava, E., & Ammar, A. (2014). The noticeability and effectiveness of corrective feedback in relation to target type. *Language Teaching Research, 18*(4), 428–452.

Kim, K., & Kwon, K. (2023). Exploring the AI competencies of elementary school teachers in South Korea. *Computers and Education: Artificial Intelligence, 4*, 100137.

Kim, R. (2018). A critical review of the impact of the fourth industrial revolution on the development of the basic communicative competence of Korean EFL learners. *Multimedia-Assisted Language Learning, 21*(3), 115–148.

Kim, R. (2022a). Effects of data augmentation on the accuracy of response in AI chatbot for L2 English learning and the learners' satisfaction level. *Multimedia-Assisted Language Learning, 25*(2), 152–181.

Kim, R. (2022b). *Effects of AI Chatbot-based instruction on the learning of English adjectival transitive resultative construction by Korean high school students* (Doctoral Thesis, Seoul National University). https://s-space.snu.ac.kr/handle/10371/181242

Kim, R. (2023). Effects of ChatGPT on the cognitive processing of K-CSAT English reading tasks by Korean high school learners: A preliminary study. *Secondary English Education, 16*(2), 179–205.

Kim, R. (2024a). Effects of ChatGPT on Korean EFL learners' main-idea reading comprehension via top-down processing. *Language Research, 60*(1), 83–106.

Kim, R. (2024b). Effects of learner uptake following automatic corrective recast from Artificial Intelligence chatbots on the learning of English caused-motion construction. *Language Learning & Technology, 28*(2), 109–133.

Kohnke, L., Moorhouse, B. L., & Zou, D. (2023). ChatGPT for language teaching and learning. *RELC Journal, 54*(2), 537–550.

Kong, S. C., & Yang, Y. (2024). A human-centred learning and teaching framework using generative artificial intelligence for self-regulated learning development through domain knowledge learning in K–12 settings. *IEEE Transactions on Learning Technologies, 17*, 1588–1599.

Krizhevsky, A., Sutskever, I., & Hinton, G. E. (2017). Imagenet classification with deep convolutional neural networks. *Communications of the ACM, 60*(6), 84–90.

Kwon, E. (2024). Analysis of trends in domestic mobile-assisted language learning in English education: Using text mining. *Korean Journal of English Language and Linguistics, 24*, 325–347.

Lee, H., & Lee, J. H. (2024). The effects of AI-Guided individualized language learning: A meta-analysis. *Language Learning & Technology, 28*(2), 131–159.

Lee, J.-H., & Kim, H. M. (2011). The L2 developmental sequence of English constructions and underlying factors. *Korean Journal of English Language and Linguistics, 11*(3), 577–600.

Lee, S. & Lee, E. (2023, October 4). New AI services dominate Korea's education technology industry. *Pulse by Maeil Business News Korea*. https://pulse.mk.co.kr/news/english/10841783

Matsumoto, Y. (1996). *Complex predicates in Japanese: A syntactic and semantic study of the notion 'word'*. CSLI Publications.

Ministry of Education. (2022). *Announcement of the Revised National Curriculum 2022*. https://www.moe.go.kr/boardCnts/viewRenew.do?boardID=294&lev=0&statusYN=W&s=moe&m=020402&opType=N&boardSeq=93459

Ministry of Education. (2023). *Announcement of the AI Digital Textbook (AIDT)*. https://www.moe.go.kr/boardCnts/viewRenew.do?boardID=294&boardSeq=96172&lev=0&searchType=null&statusYN=W&page=1&s=moe&m=020402&opType=N

Ministry of Education. (2024). *Efforts are being made to qualitatively improve secondary school digital infrastructure in preparation for the full introduction of AI digital textbooks*. https://www.moe.go.kr/boardCnts/viewRenew.do?boardID=294&lev=0&statusYN=W&s=moe&m=020402&opType=N&boardSeq=98896

Mohamed, A. M. (2024). Exploring the potential of an AI-based Chatbot (ChatGPT) in enhancing English as a Foreign Language (EFL) teaching: Perceptions of EFL Faculty Members. *Education and Information Technologies, 29*(3), 3195–3217.

Park, J. (2018). The impact of EFL students' English proficiency on reading strategies and usage of annotation tools. *English Language Assessment, 13*, 85–120.

Petersen, K. A. (2010). *Implicit corrective feedback in computer-guided interaction: Does mode matter?* (Unpublished doctoral dissertation). Georgetown University. http://hdl.handle.net/10822/553155

Rahman, M. M., & Watanobe, Y. (2023). ChatGPT for education and research: Opportunities, threats, and strategies. *Applied Sciences, 13*(9), 5783.

Semke, H. D. (1984). Effects of the red pen. *Foreign Language Annals, 17*(3), 195–202.

Seo, J. (2023). *Digital transformation of education: The case of South Korea.* UNESCO. https://unesdoc.unesco.org/ark:/48223/pf0000387833

Seo, S., & Kim, J.-R. (2023). A meta-analysis on the effects of using AI chatbots in Korean English education. *Foreign Languages Education, 30*(3), 25–42.

Shaikh, S., Yayilgan, S. Y., Klimova, B., & Pikhart, M. (2023). Assessing the usability of ChatGPT for formal English language learning. *European Journal of Investigation in Health, Psychology and Education, 13*(9), 1937–1960.

Shibatani, M., & Pardeshi, P. (2002). The causative continuum. In M. Shibatani (Ed.), *The grammar of causation and interpersonal manipulation* (pp. 85–126). John Benjamins.

So, H-J., Jang, H., & Kim, M. (2023). Trends and issues of digital learning in Korea. In Lee, Y-F., & Lee, L-S (Eds.), *Trends and issues of promoting digital learning in high-digital-competitiveness countries: Country reports and international comparison* (pp. 269–310). Technological and Vocational Education Research Center (TVERC).

Sung, H. (2019). Korean EFL learners' processing of English caused-motion construction. *English Teaching, 74*(1), 49–73.

Talmy, L. (1985). Lexicalization patterns: Semantic structure in lexical forms. In T. Shopen (Ed.), *Language typology and semantic description: Grammatical categories and the lexicon* (Vol. 3, pp. 36–149). Cambridge University Press.

Tlili, A., Shehata, B., Adarkwah, M. A., Bozkurt, A., Hickey, D. T., Huang, R., & Agyemang, B. (2023). What if the devil is my guardian angel: ChatGPT as a case study of using chatbots in education. *Smart Learning Environments, 10*(15), 1–24.

Truscott, J. (1999). The case for "The case against grammar correction in L2 writing classes": A response to Ferris. *Journal of Second Language Writing, 8*(2), 111–122.

Urquhart, A. H., & Weir, C. (1998). *Reading in a second language: Process, product and practice.* Longman.

Valero, A. L., Fernandez, E. E., Iseni, A., & Clarkson, C. P. (2008). Teachers' attitudes towards correcting students' written errors and mistakes. *Porta Linguarum, 10*(1), 21–30.

Wang, Y. F., & Petrina, S. (2013). Using learning analytics to understand the design of an intelligent language tutor–Chatbot Lucy. *International Journal of Advanced Computer Science and Applications, 4*(11), 124–131.

Willige, A. (2024, May 10). *From virtual tutors to accessible textbooks: 5 ways AI is transforming education.* Word Economic Forum. https://www.weforum.org/agenda/2024/05/ways-ai-can-benefit-education/

Wilske, S. (2015). *Form and meaning in dialog-based computer-assisted language learning* (Unpublished doctoral dissertation). Saarland University. https://d-nb.info/1077007051/34

Yarrow, N. B., Kim, H., Yoo, J., & Pfutze, T. (2022). *EdTech in COVID Korea: Learning with inequality.* https://thedocs.worldbank.org/en/doc/286e9d2e22dd4122f15249083ca84772-0200022022/original/EdTech-paper-4-29.pdf

Yi, M., Lee, Y., Chou, H., & Choi, I.-C. (2023). Predicting the difficulty of college scholastic ability test based on ChatGPT and corpus linguistic features. *Multimedia-Assisted Language Learning, 26*(4), 29–50.

Yim, H. & Kim, R. (2023*). GPT to Excel (version 1.0) [Computer software].*

Zubizarreta, M., & Oh, E. (2007). *On the syntactic composition of manner and motion.* MIT Press.

# 6

## An Innovative In-Service English Teacher Education Program: Toward a Closer Coupling of Knowledge and Practice

Eun-kyoung Jang, Ahn S.-H. Gyemyong, and Mun Woo Lee

## In-Service English Teacher Education

As (language) teaching, learning, and their contexts were understood better in international academia, the goal of the language teacher education (LTE) has been elaborated into teachers' competencies that consist of their *knowledge* of, their *attitudes* toward, and their *skills* related to content areas, students as learners, teaching practices, and social contexts; and of their awareness of the three components (Ahn et al., 2022,

---

E. Jang
Doonchon High School, Seoul, South Korea

A. S.-H. Gyemyong
Department of English Education, College of Education, Hanyang University, Seoul, South Korea

M. W. Lee (✉)
Department of English Language and Literature, Yonsei University, Seoul, South Korea
e-mail: munwoo@yonsei.ac.kr

Table 1; Bartlett, 1990; Freeman, 1989; Freeman & Johnson, 1998; Kumaravadivelu, 2012; Tarone & Allwright, 2005).

This elaboration was accompanied by the gradual distinction between *training* and *development* (Freeman, 1989), of types of supervision (Gebhard, 1990), and of supervisor roles (Roberts, 1998) in teacher education. If training is mainly for knowledge and skills, development is for attitudes and awareness; accordingly, supervision can be collaborative, nondirective, creative and/or even explorative while supervisors playing appropriate different roles. Furthermore, ideas on LTE programs could be constellated into different *models*: based on knowledge sources, craft, applied science, reflective, and experiential ones (Deirich & Stunnel, 2014; Wallace, 1991); based on outcomes, gestalt-, schema-, and theory-level ones (Korthagen, 2010).

All these changes correlated in one way or another with at least four transitions in the approaches to LTE summarized by Crandall (2000) at the turn of the millennium. A first transition was from transmission-orientedness to process-orientedness. This was a shift to valuing the (social) construction of knowledge (Berger & Luckman, 1966). Instead of the top-down approach presenting the best practice for teachers to imitate, this new perspective took a bottom-up approach in which knowledge is constructed by teachers via inquiry, research and reflection. If an existential transformation is added, this transition is in line with a transition from banking-type education to *problem-posing* education advocated in Freire (2000), whose pedagogical tenets were translated, for instance, into 25 principles of curricular organization (Crawford-Lange, 1981).

A second transition was due to the realization that traditional LTE programs were unable to equip the participants with capabilities to cope with the "multidimensionality and unpredictability" (Crandall, 2000, p. 35) of their own classrooms. This was due to the *decontextualized* nature of abstract knowledge. When the classroom situation was not understood sufficiently, "far transfer" (Wiggins & McTighe, 2005, p. 79) would not be easy to make. The shift came to appreciate the *situatedness* of teacher cognition (Lave & Wenger, 1991), to emphasize a closer *coupling* between theory and practice, and to promote a partnership between the LTE program and schools to improve chances of contextualization of the educational content.

A third transition was based on the recognition that, when participating in an LTE program, teachers carry with them strong preconceptions they had formed through their previous experiences in school and society. Under a *sociocultural* perspective, it was revealed that such, frequently implicit, teacher beliefs exercise significant influences on teacher decisions made during classes (Johnson, 2009). Thus, LTE programs came to urge participants to self-observe and reflect on their own teaching practices.

A fourth transition was that teaching came to be viewed as a profession (Coombe, 2018), which meant that teachers were expected to develop theories of practice and to determine the directions of "their own professional development through collaborative observation, teacher research and inquiry, and sustained in-service programs" (Crandall, 2000, p. 36).

Domestically in Korea, those four transitions were clearly witnessed in practical analyses and theoretical discussions of existent LTE programs.[1] B. E. Park (2006), for example, surveyed 253 English teachers who were in or had finished LTE programs for primary English education. Her findings included that there was a correlation between participants' levels of English fluency and motivation, on the one hand, and improved results in actual classes, on the other. This implied that the success of English LTE program would be dependent on the recruitment of highly motivated and English-fluent participants. Motivation is a basic requirement for successful learning. Hence, well-motivated participants would have a higher chance for objective attainment (Chapman & Vagle, 2015; Keller, 2009); they would also function as a *near peer role model* to contribute to a successful learning of their colleagues (Murphey, 1998). Y.-O. Kim et al. (2008) surveyed 484 English teachers who finished their first-level training programs and found out that the respondents felt the transmitted knowledge in their programs was so theoretical that it was difficult to translate into actual classes. These survey results among others

---

[1] In Korea, there has been a fifth significant transition in English LTE. At the beginning of the twenty-first century, the Korean government supported intensive English LTE programs extensively to remote teaching English through English.

are in accord with the international realization that triggered the second transition: The LTE programs in Korea couldn't equip the participants with competencies to couple theory and practice closely.

K. Chang (2007), in this vein, urged more generally that an LTE program should shift its focus from knowledge transmission to supporting participants so that they could develop teaching competencies, critically reflect on theories and their teaching practices, and learn more actively by teaching in class. This reflects the first, second and fourth international transitions emphasizing the constructivism in knowledge production, the situatedness of teacher learning, and teacher professionalism. Jung and Chang (2009) suggested that English LTE programs be based on schools so that they would help participants gain a *sense of plausibility* (Prabhu, 1987) more easily. This was in line with the second international transition that came to emphasize the situated learning of teaching. Evaluating on-line English LTE programs, further, J. Y. Kim et al. (2015) problematized their "worn-out" facets. For a more effective remote program, then, they recommended "bottom-up access to curriculum development, establishment of a community of practice (DuFour, 2004; Hord, 2008) for teacher development sustainability, and reflective teacher learning to link teacher education to field practices" (Ahn et al., 2022, p. 506). Their recommendations were close to urges to pay attention to the four international transitions mentioned above.

These domestic needs were at least partially satisfied by programs like the Cambridge ESOL ICELT (In-service Certificate in English Language Training), a six-month program (Lee, 2010). It started out to improve participants' English skills and pedagogical competencies, the second of which were more emphasized to satisfy the participants' needs.

## Impetus for the Innovation

The idea for the 2015 innovation in English LTE had, in fact, been engendered a long time before in Ms. Eun-kyoung Jang's dissatisfaction. Since her first year of teaching in 1992, she had wanted to practice a proper English education that would allow students to read the world and express their voices. She believed that a good school English education should not only equip students with the skills and confidence they need to succeed in school but also give them opportunities to use their English skills in real-world situations. However, she found the mandated textbooks inadequate for achieving these goals. Being crafted for appropriate language levels, the textbooks contained dull content and awkwardly forced dialogues, hindering genuine learning.

To address these issues, Ms. Jang began creating her own teaching materials. In 2002, a decade into her teaching career, she recognized the potential value of movies with their visual appeal and cultural authenticity; she thought that they could effectively engage learners providing rich discussion and writing content and thus becoming powerful English learning tools. She developed a series of movie-based lesson plans and supplementary materials to overcome the limitations of textbooks. Her English classes were received rapturously by her students and readily adopted by her colleagues in the same school. Word of this series of lesson plans spread to neighboring schools. In 2007, eventually, she was invited into the Seoul Metropolitan Office of Education's Teaching Improvement Support Team (TIST).

TIST was a group of outstanding teachers who offered general teachers some necessary guidance and support with their instructional planning. They also held monthly meetings and shared their teaching experiences, discussed contemporary teaching methodologies, assessed the lessons of their fellow teachers, offered seminars and workshops for the public, and worked towards building their professional capacities.

Ms. Jang's experiences in TIST instigated her keen interest in teacher education. She and her colleagues also taught at teacher education programs, and the participants responded enthusiastically. In the early stages of her role as a teacher training instructor, she found great satisfaction in researching and sharing effective teaching practices. However, a turning point came from a comment of a trainee. She expressed, "Your lecture turned my fear and anxiety about returning from parental leave into anticipation and enthusiasm." The feedback came to her as enlightenment on the significance of teacher education. She imagined that a good impact would ripple from one teacher to countless students.

This solidified her belief in the need for a systematic teacher education framework in Korea.

In 2012, Korea introduced a master teacher system to prioritize experienced educators, as specified in Article 20 of the Elementary and Secondary Education Act (Korean Law Translation Center, 2023). This initiative aimed to elevate teaching standards and to shift the educational focus from administration to teaching practice itself. The system divided teacher qualifications into administrative specialists (principals and vice principals) and teaching specialists (master teachers), reshaping school culture. Master teachers were to nurture students and aid fellow teachers in refining teaching methods, enhancing instructional proficiency (Department of Secondary Education, 2019). Ms. Jang chose to go through a rigorous selection process which evaluated applicants' subject expertise, teaching skills, and curriculum development and presentation abilities, and through in-depth interviews. That year, she became the youngest inaugural master teacher.

As a master teacher, Ms. Jang significantly widened her scope of teaching, consulting, and mentoring; she worked as an expert in various fields such as teacher education, curriculum design, and policy advisory. Interacting with teachers in a variety of contexts across the nation and accumulating data from various cases, she recognized acutely the constraints of the prevailing top-down teacher education paradigm, which generally stopped short at the dissemination of instructional techniques. The clearly noticeable gap between theory and practice led her to imagine more dynamic and adaptable approaches to teacher education.

Grounded in interviews conducted with teachers across diverse training programs and consultation sessions, Ms. Jang identified several factors contributing to the disconnect between teacher training and its application in the classroom. Firstly, many teachers grasped the educational trajectory during their training and acquired valuable lesson concepts. However, upon their return to school, they were confronted with a multitude of responsibilities, encompassing both homeroom class duties and administrative tasks. These tasks yielded immediate, observable outcomes, while the exploration of lesson development often took a lower priority due to its lack of immediate, tangible results. This dynamic could breed complacency and disrupt the seamless flow of professional growth and development.

Secondly, even if teachers learned how to teach well through training and had the will to implement it, simple imitation was unlikely to succeed in a situation where teachers' unique abilities, their instructional contexts, and the subjects and levels they had to handle varied significantly. In other words, just like student learning, teachers' instructional practices necessitated targeted feedback on their real-time performance to facilitate growth. Regrettably, however, schools frequently lacked experienced seniors or mentors who could provide such guidance.

Thirdly, teacher training frequently comprised a single, brief course, primarily focused on input sessions devoid of a connection to practical implementation. Without a subsequent phase involving verification, reflection, and enhancement of diverse output methods derived from the input, the efficacy of the initial input remained unsubstantiated.

Based on this analysis, Ms. Jang made a proposal to the Seoul Education Training Institute (SETI) that they need a new English LTE program with the following features:

- **Personalized, self-directed, and research-focused**: To establish a strong correlation between training and classroom application, it is imperative for the program to provide teacher participants with personalized training that caters to their distinct requirements. Instead of passively absorbing trainers' best practices and implementing them, the participants should be empowered to take charge of their learning process. This involves identifying their specific needs within their unique contexts, defining their learning objectives, and utilizing these as research topics. Subsequently, teachers will delve into them, study them thoroughly, and then integrate their findings into their classroom practices.
- **Collaborative, supportive, and sustainable**: Groups of participants must investigate shared themes and topics and unite as collaborative research peers. This arrangement will facilitate mutual learning and interdependence among teachers, fortifying their resolve to persevere and resist premature discouragement. It is also crucial to maintain an ongoing loop of feedback from peers and professional mentors during

practical implementation. This will require not only scheduled face-to-face sessions, but also an online network that allows for continuous and immediate feedback and create a dynamic and supportive learning environment.
- **Practical, hands-on, and reflective**: The program must center on real-world application, practice, and careful reflection. This requires that it include steps to apply and implement in a real-world school environment, which naturally leads to long-term training.

This proposal was accepted seriously, in 2014, by the educational administrator Y (pseudonym) in SETI, who had collaborated with Ms. Jang in a policy research project to enhance teacher training models, where they realized a pressing requirement for a novel and alternative training paradigm. Subsequently in 2015, Ms. Y with Ms. Jang launched at SETI an English LTE program called Snowball: Professional Development Program for Secondary English Teachers.

This new program was to be relevant to the pressure on English teachers by the drastic innovation that happened in the 2015 Revised National Curriculum, which introduced as educational goals student competencies in self-management, knowledge information processing, creative thinking, aesthetic sensitivity, communication, and community competence. Naturally, this curricular change led to increased teacher interest, among others, in project-based learning and process-oriented assessment.

## Information About the Specific Context

### Goals, Codes of Conduct, and Overview of the Snowball Program

The Secondary English Teachers Snowball Job Training Course was a long-term, field-based, self-directed LTE program that aimed to (1) enhance teaching competence through a professional and systematic lesson reflection process; (2) develop and expand specific and practical lesson models that can be applied in the field; and (3) foster professional teacher educators and competent instructional consultants (Jang, 2018).

To achieve these goals, Snowball was underpinned by the following codes of conduct:

- Apply and implement all your learning here. As with your students, you learn best by doing.
- Never stay silent or passive. Share in one another's trials and errors. Work with other teachers sharing ideas and experiences, reflecting and getting constructive feedback on your own practice.
- Share the resulting growth in your learning journey with colleagues beyond Snowball.

It was evident that the program valued learning, doing, caring, and sharing.

In the first four years, participants were selected based on their self-introductions and teaching portfolios. In 2020, however, SETI shifted its policy to embrace the entire applicants. A total of 74 teachers successfully completed the program in the first four years: In 2015, 16 participants in the inaugural program; in 2016, 13 participants; in 2018, 24 participants; and in 2019, 21 participants. The 54 participants in 2020, regretfully, had to complete only the first half.[2]

## Program Course Details

Snowball was a hybrid of action research and learning communities where participants conducted research on their most troublesome issues and applied its results to their teaching. The challenge was to backwardly design and implement a full one-semester course of English education in their own schools: Firstly, its goals; secondly, how to evaluate their achievements; and thirdly and lastly, how to teach to ensure student success (Wiggins & McTighe, 2005). The participants shared their own

---

[2] Notably, the program was not offered in 2017 due to Ms. Jang's person unavailability, and the Covid-19 pandemic forced the 2020 program to be held only online and be unable to run its second half.

progresses in them over the course of the program, evolved them through collective and collaborative feedback, and then made them public. The program was structured as a year-long program, comprising 30 hours of the *foundational* course in the first half of the year and additional 30 hours of the *advanced* course in the second half.

1. The foundational course

The foundational course consisted of ten three-hour sessions. These sessions took place after regular school hours, typically from 17:30 to 20:30. While there were minor variations in the operational approaches based on specific conditions, the majority adhered to the following operational framework of participants' activities, as in Table 6.1.

In Session 1, participant groups were formed basically according to their common pedagogical interests. If the specific education themes that participants were interested in weren't clearly defined, however, the mentor took the initiative to propose essential areas of research. Subsequently, 4 or 5 individuals were allocated to each group based on urgent educational themes. The themes that participant groups decided on

Table 6.1 Activities of different sessions in the foundational course

| Sessions | Activities |
|---|---|
| 1 | (1) Reflecting on their own classroom practices to diagnose their strengths and weaknesses<br>(2) Presenting their teaching philosophy and their educational themes to explore<br>(3) Organizing research groups around the same or closely related themes |
| 2–4 | (1) Collaborating on research and learning<br>(2) Presenting what they had learned as groups<br>(3) Exchanging ideas and feedback |
| 5–10 | (1) Practically applying and executing learning content in real-world settings<br>(2) Developing and introducing instructional materials<br>(3) Exchanging practical case studies, receiving feedback from peers and experienced mentors<br>(4) Iterating through cycles of revision, supplementation, and repetition of this sequence |

Table 6.2 Theme groups of each program

| Program | Theme groups |
|---|---|
| 1 | Extensive Reading (ER), Flipped Learning, Slow Learner Teaching, Project Based Learning (PBL), Korean SAT Instruction, and Career Guidance in English Class |
| 2 | Assessment for Learning (AfL), Active Reading (AR), and Differentiated Instruction (DI) |
| 3 | Integrative Approach to Language Teaching (IAtLT), AR, DI, PBL, and AfL |
| 4 | DI, PBL, Effective Technology Use, ER, and AfL |
| 5 | DI, PBL, Effective Technology Use, ER, and AfL |

in each program were as in Table 6.2 (Seoul Education and Training Institute, ).

The theme of "Slow Learner Teaching", introduced in Program 1, evolved into DI from the second program on. The themes of DI, ER, and PBL were quite popular; AfL, however, enjoyed the strongest popularity and was selected in every program. Such popular themes were clearly shaped by the priorities outlined in the 2015 National Revised Curriculum centering on the concept of student competencies (Ministry of Education, 2015). As assessment that emphasized the learning process was strengthened, among others, teachers had to do research into assessment methods that allow students to reflect on their learning and use the assessment results to improve the quality of teaching and learning.

Because schooling exhibited strong interconnections across disciplines, all participants were deeply interested not only in their own group research, but also in the findings of other groups. Throughout the program, participants were prompted to attain expertise within their chosen domains, and they also benefited from indirect learning opportunities facilitated through the exchange with other groups of knowledge and practical applications.

Participants in each research group took initiative in selecting specific books and articles for in-depth study and research. Many groups began by studying a book together, as shown below in Table 6.3 (Seoul Education and Training Institute, 2016, 2018, 2019).

Other groups like Flipped Learning, Korean SAT Instruction, Career Guidance in English Class studied online articles and columns without

Table 6.3 Books & articles for study & research in different theme groups

| Theme Groups | Books for Study & Research |
|---|---|
| ER | *Extensive Reading in the Second Language Classroom* (Day & Bamford, 1998) |
| DI | *Differentiated Instruction: A Guide for World Language Teachers* (Blaz, 2016) |
| PBL | *Project Based Teaching: How to Create Rigorous and Engaging Learning Experiences* (Boss & Larmer, 2018) |
| AfL | *How to Create and Use Rubrics for Formative Assessment and Grading* (Brookhart, 2013) |
| AR | *Reading in a Second Language: Moving from Theory to Practice* (Grabe, 2008) |
| IAtLT | *Yungbokhapgyoyuk-ui Iron-gwa Silje* (Theory and Practice of *Yungbokhap* Education) (Cha et al., 2014) |

any special textbooks and learned by sharing classroom examples with each other; the Effective Technology Use group learned how to use diverse educational technology tools, applied them across various classroom scenarios, and presented the advantages and disadvantages of their implementations.

All the learning materials and activities from each group were documented and disseminated through an online platform closed to the public, named "English Education Snowball Classroom Specialist Training Program" (https://cafe.daum.net/englishsnowball). In addition, participants were encouraged to openly ask for help and exchange ideas at any time in the real time online chatting tool.

2. The advanced course

The advanced course also comprised ten three-hour sessions aimed at extending the learning outcomes and implementation from the basic course to regular schools beyond the LTE program. The program was organized as in Table 6.4.

Central to this process was the practice of class discussions, which did not only disassemble the notion of classroom observation as a mere assessment of teaching prowess but also positioned it as a tool for personal teaching development through shared insights.

Table 6.4 Activities of different sessions in the advanced course

| Sessions | Activities |
| --- | --- |
| 1 | (1) Scheduling units to cover and selecting a representative teacher for open class<br>(2) Collaboratively creating preliminary lesson plans |
| 2–5 | (1) Pre-consulting on class content and specific topics<br>(2) Developing teaching materials |
| 6–10 | [Open Classes & Conferences]<br>(1) [*Live classroom demonstration*] Conducting actual classes with students<br>(2) [*Topic lectures*] Presenting the group's research results, explaining theoretical principles, emphasizing the significance, and introducing additional activities or application methods not covered during open class<br>(3) [*Interactive class discussions*] Engaging Snowball participants and observers in class discussions |

In 2018, the third year of the Snowball program, the program's growing popularity had led to a surge in requests from teachers to attend the lesson-sharing conferences in Sessions 6–10. In line with the goal of disseminating the program's outcomes, Snowball orchestrated a conference on class-designing processes called "Snowball Concert" to be held on a Saturday in December. This event provided a platform for that year's participants to showcase their research and display the learning materials they had developed throughout the year. Notably, in that year, the event drew an audience of 110 attendees, and in 2019, more than 220 attendees.

## Program Outcomes

The completion of the Snowball program has notably elevated the teaching expertise of its participants, which manifested in tangible improvements within their educational beliefs and values and in instructional practices (Ahn et al., 2022). They now would *design* student-centered classes from a long-term perspective in view of ways of assessing students' genuine growth and interests; they came to care for their students heartily. They also shared valuable information and knowledge *with* their peer teachers taking initiatives in organizing in-school teacher learning communities (TLCs). They were unknowingly recognized and positioned as (in)formal leaders in their school communities.

Snowball empowered them to pursue their studies further: that is, to autonomously identify instructional challenges, undertake action research, voluntarily seek expert feedback, and subsequently implement refinements within their actual classrooms. The process involved gathering insights from their own class materials and student performance data, which they then analyzed and discussed collectively with other peers and/or active Snowball graduates. This iterative cycle led to modifications and enhancements.

Through the training program, crucially, participants came to understand that teaching isn't solely an individual pursuit, dependent on individual capabilities, but evolves through collaborative research, cooperation, and the spirit of sharing. This recognition fostered a greater willingness among teachers to open their classrooms to their colleagues. These enriching teaching experiences have been shared extensively through diverse mediums, including class results sharing, academic conferences, and educational district resources. The heightened competencies of the participants have propelled many to attain the prestigious role of national English teacher training instructors.

Recognizing this success, SETI extended the course's impact beyond English to encompass subjects such as Korean, Social Studies, Mathematics, and Science. This expansion took shape as programs for "becoming a teaching expert," from 2017. Furthermore, the influence of the Snowball program has traversed geographical boundaries, reaching beyond its initial scope of Seoul. This model has been integrated into the curricula for secondary English teachers in the Ulsan Metropolitan City and Gangwon Province, showcasing its adaptability and value in diverse educational contexts.

While the program has been closed since the pandemic in 2020, a group of Snowball alumni took the initiative to establish a professional learning community called "Snowballs on the Move," which convenes monthly in small breakout groups reminiscent of the program structure to engage in learning and best practice exchange. Research themes are created or dissolved to reflect the key educational issues in English education for the given year, but DI, AIED, POA, and ER have consistently been selected as research themes each year. In 2023, new themes such as 'Beautiful Failure' (focusing on social-emotional learning) and 'Critical Pedagogy' were added. As of 2024, eight research subgroups are currently operating: ER, AIED, International Baccalaureate (IB) Middle Years Programme (MYP), IB Diploma Programme (DP), Social Emotional Learning (SEL), Universal Design for Learning (UDL), Learning Science, and Teaching College Scholastic Ability Test.

Currently, the Snowball community has 111 members, including teachers, vice principals, and educational administrators from various regions including Seoul, Daegu, Gangwon, Ulsan, Mokpo, and Jeju. Given the broad scope and total number of members, most of the study groups meet only online, but the entire community is activated through in-person gatherings during summer and winter breaks. The community still inherits the Snowball spirit of rolling and changing the field by sharing class cases on its YouTube channel, Snowball on the Move (https://youtu.be/fC8-st3WVL8).

The entire outcomes could be represented in a diagram as in Fig. 6.1.

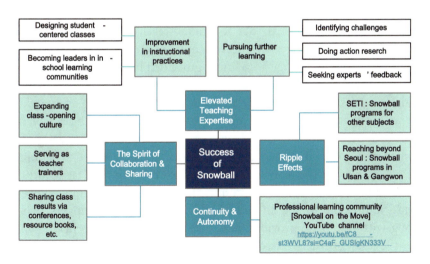

Fig. 6.1 Characteristics of the program outcomes

## What Worked

As reported by Ahn et al. (2022), the success of the Snowball program could be attributed to its four features: (1) *customized special interest groups (SIGs)*, (2) *long-term action research*, (3) *abundant sources of inspiration*, and (4) *a culture of sharing*. These features emerged in the coupling of participants' doing action research and their participation in learning communities in the framework of the official LTE program.

### Teachers' Continued Growth Through Long-Term Action Research

Snowball's success lay in its multiple contributions to the participants' growth through long-term action research. First, the participants unanimously reported that they had genuinely learned how to improve their teaching as groups because the Snowball program was based on their own interests and needs. It involved not only theoretical examinations of their themes, such as ER or AfL, but also practical aspects such as hands-on classroom activities and micro-teaching [*customized SIGs*]. While working on their own research topics as groups, they successfully learned teaching skills that were firmly grounded in theory, implemented them in their classrooms, and shared the results with other participants. This was possible because they could engage in their long-term action research projects, which lasted an *entire* academic year. In this *long-term* endeavor, they could also experience the entire process of class designing and implementation. When they happened to fail, further, they could try again; eventually achieving successes, they came to not fear failures.

The longevity of the program and the participant-screening process made it possible to recruit only highly motivated participants, who, along with Ms. Jang, provided near peer role models (Murphey, 1998), fresh ideas, constructive feedback [*abundant sources of inspiration*]. This was closely related to the *culture of sharing* that was promoted by the program's structure and codes of conduct, which urged every participant to share their entire knowledge and wisdom with one another. Many voluntarily participated in the next Snowball program as mentors because they felt that the program had changed their lives as teachers, and they wanted the same thing to happen to other teachers.

## Establishing Teachers' Learning Communities

Snowball's success was also due to the successful formation and maintenance of TLCs. In fact, during the program, all participants came to build up TLCs in the SIGs customized to their needs, which facilitated and supported their long-term action research projects. As mentioned above, they studied theoretical ideas and planned classes together as groups and shared their learning results and class plans with their group members for different ideas and/or constructive feedback. Such sharing was done with the entire class as well, which effectuated the whole class as another larger scale of TLC. For easier TLC communication, all SIGs opened their own online chatrooms, and the entire class, its own bigger one. Ms. Jang also set up an online club where all previous and current Snowball classes could archive and freely access teaching materials and other pedagogical resources.

Partaking in the two tiers of TLCs during the program, the Snowball participants found one another, along with the supervisor, constituting abundant sources of information and inspiration. They met together every week and spent considerable amounts of time working together; they shared their teaching needs and interests. The SIG and whole-class chatrooms enabled them to communicate with one another almost 24/7; they came to bond together very closely. Their TLCs, thus reinforced, became very strong and performed super productively.

When the program ended, however, the SIG and whole class TLCs frequently lost their livelihood due to the different situations of individual members. Crucially, Ms. Jang invited all Snowball graduates to *freely* join the Snowball Alumni TLC. Through its chatroom, the members now met and interacted with *life-long comrades* from the same or *different* classes who had the *same* concerns, passion, and vision. When a member put up a post, (s)he received almost immediate responses from other members: their own experiences, tips, evaluative opinions. (S)he and other members frequently attempted to create *novel* solutions together; (s)he was supported fully emotionally as well, regarding tough issues (s)he faced. Ms. Jang also coordinated occasional offline gatherings, which secured more human relationships among the TLC members. To many participants, in a sense, this TLC was an extended moderate version of Snowball itself.

In these ways, the Snowball Alumni TLC had been functioning to fully support its members intellectually, socially, and psychologically, giving its members a sense of camaraderie. It helped the members adhere adamantly to the *spirit of Snowball*. The members could/would persevere in diverse adverse sociocultural milieus, as under the COVID 19 pandemic, and take the next step in their careers, growing into the competent *educators* they had aspired to become. They have been creating ripple effects in their local schools and nationwide as lecturers in conventional teacher training programs and through their attendance at professional conferences. The Snowball Alumni TLC has evolved eventually into Snowball on the Move.

## What Didn't Work

As noted by Ms. Jang and previous works, general English LTE programs before Snowball could not bring forth systematic improvement of English classes. It didn't work when they focused only on the input of theoretical knowledge or *excellent* models of instruction and gave participants no sufficient chances to reflect on their own practices (Chang, 2007; Jung & Chang, 2009; Kim et al., 2008). It didn't work when participants came back to school and were allured to administrative and other non-pedagogical tasks to produce immediately visible results. It didn't work when participants back to work found no mentors or colleagues to support them with feedback and encouragement. These *problems* didn't arise with most Snowball graduates because they could establish desirable educational philosophy and more reflective practices, and because they could find themselves in supportive professional learning communities (Kim et al., 2015).

Since the Snowball program was such a big success overall with excellent outcomes, it is not easy to find what did not work with it. However, some issues arose as its limitations.

## Enormous Requirements on the Supervisor

A program like Snowball needs a supervisor who *really understands* the subject, teaching, teachers, and learners (Wiggins & McTighe, 2005) and who is equipped with appropriate educational philosophy. Such supervisors can come into being from sufficient experiences of *devoted* teaching, researching and reflection. When Snowball supervisees came to be at a stand, Ms. Jang was able to raise their ability to a higher level with critical feedback or, at least, suggest a direction to pursue.

A serious difficulty with the Snowball program, though, was that the supervisor had to do too much work. Ms. Jang reflected that she "needed to be a Superman" to ensure that the program operated smoothly. This teacher had to design and organize the overall program throughout the year. She had to be a leader, discussant, interventionist, and colleague at the same time. Most of all, she had to maintain an emotional rapport with the participants so that they could fully develop as teachers and discover their potential through the program.

Incidentally, however, when Ms. Jang was unable to engage in this program in 2017, there was no one to substitute her; hence, no Snowball was offered in that year. As mentioned above, further, with its great success, this teacher education model spread to other subjects such as Korean, Mathematics, Science, and Social Studies in Seoul. They, however, could not sustain more than two years, mainly because they could not find a supervisor who was competent enough to lead the program appropriately and who was able to continue his or her job for such an extended period of time because of the heavy workload. In a nutshell, Snowball was not easily transferable; when transferred, it was not highly sustainable.

## Enormous Demands on the Supervisees

The Snowball program was officially a 60-hour course, but the teacher supervisees had to invest a lot *more* time to complete it. From Program 1 (2015) through Program 3 (2018), the participants weren't recognized for the time they spent for group activities for discussing books, articles, and/or individual members' attempts to improve their classes. From Program 4, several hours were recognized for group meetings, but the SIG members still had to spend much more time than that. Whole-group meetings also tended to overflow. Officially, they typically lasted from 17:30 to 20:30; in actuality, however, they usually ended around 21:00; sometimes around 22:00 in the evening. The number and duration of the planned activities couldn't be bottled in the official 60 hours. When they persistently endured, though, the participants experienced *glorious* breakthroughs.

## Difficulty to Maintain the Policy for an Elite Minority

Snowball started out as a program which was intended for a small number of highly motivated *screened* teachers. This was because one of its goals was to foster professional teacher educators. This policy was maintained up to Program 4, whose competition rate rose up to 3:1, but SETI could not ignore the civil complaints from those applicants who had been refused participation repeatedly. As described before, eventually, SETI decided to accept all the 54 applicants for Program 5: 34 supervisees under the charge of Ms. Jang, and 20 under another master teacher. The policy to recruit a small number of elite participants couldn't be sustained.

## Lessons Learned Through the Snowball Program

The Snowball program has provided several valuable lessons for LTE. If it wants the participants to genuinely improve their English classes, firstly, an LTE program will take a bottom-up approach and be based on genuine teacher needs. Each Snowball program began with the question, "What problems do you have in mind regarding your classes?" This was in accord with the *situated* nature of teacher knowledge (Crandall, 2000; Kim et al., 2015) and the spirit of the *problem*-posing education that revolves around *existential* problems of learners (Freire, 2000). It was also an important way to motivate learners by means of high relevance (Chapman & Vagle, 2015; Keller, 2009).

An effective LTE program, secondly, will make full use of the social psychology of small groups (Borek & Abraham, 2018). It will have participants to form *small* groups according to their common interests and/or tasks and provide them with enough chances to interact (Davis et al., 1976). In each group the members need a sufficient length of time to accept and trust one another and open up themselves to the others. Only when they have developed a form of *group cohesion*, they share ideas openly and freely and learn from one another efficiently; they will eventually form a learning community as well (Chapman & Vagle, 2015; DeFour, 2004; Hord, 2008; Kim et al., 2015). All this happened in Snowball when the participants were divided into SIGs based on their common interests, and when each group was given a full year to accomplish a common task of designing and implementing a best solution to its common problem: a best set of lesson plans.

Related to the second facet, thirdly, an effective LTE program will respect participants' *autonomy* by requesting them to do *autonomous* research into the problems at the root of their practical needs. They will decide what resources to tap on, how to design classes for their own subject matters and unique groups of students. Snowball allowed its participants to do action research into their own problems found in their own educational situations. What the teacher participants did was in fact trying to make a sense of plausibility (Prabhu, 1987) and to build up their own theories of practice (Kumaravadivelu, 2012). This is in accord with the fourth transition of Crandall's (2000), and incidentally with Freire's (2000) critical approach to education, where it should be the learners who do research and construct best solutions to their own existential problems (Crawford-Lange, 1981).

An effective LTE program will, fourthly, foster participants' *competence* by having them experience the *entirety* of the process of applying a set of theoretical ideas to specific English classes. Crucially, this experience will include committing errors or mistakes, which will give them a better insight into the process itself and its potential dangers. Such an experience of the entirety will help the participants to construct a comprehensive *perspective* on the problem and its solution. This is an important facet of true understanding (Wiggins & McTighe, 2005). The second, third, and fourth facets of an effective English LTE program are together a way of valuing the insights from the *self-determination* theory (Deci & Ryan, 2000; Ryan & Deci, 2002) as well. Well-formed small groups satisfy the members' need for relatedness. A long-term action research into one's own problem will foster autonomy and competence. Consequently, it will encourage participants to increase inherent motivation to do the work.

This facet of motivation is in fact related to the next lesson. An effective LTE program, fifthly, will screen in well-motivated participants (Park, 2006). As described above, the LTE program itself will be designed to enhance participants' intrinsic motivation. If well-motivated teachers are recruited, the task of motivating will be relatively easier; the participants will function as near peer role models (Murphey, 1998) providing one another with more sources of inspiration. When they were asked to share in Snowball what they did in class, their teaching practices and attitudes toward students constituted valuable sources of inspiration for one another, which was a form of peer mentoring.

An effective LTE program, sixthly, will not only make the participants a learning community during the program but also help them partake in a TLC after graduation which will support them to sustain what they learned through the program. The TLC will provide them with reciprocal acceptance, group cohesion, sharing, caring, chances of contribution, and an object of commitment (DeFour, 2004; Hord, 2008; Kim et al., 2015). Snowball was successful in this matter and its alumni experienced tremendous usefulness of such communities when they came back to school and were teaching classes in more advanced ways or under more threatening situations such as Covid 19.

An effective LTE program, seventhly, will deal with participants' teaching *philosophy*. It will give participants chances to (re-)examine and (re-)establish their own pedagogical beliefs, attitudes toward students, and values. This is in accord with Crandall's (2000) third transition regarding teacher preconceptions, whose significance was well evaluated in sociocultural perspectives (Johnson, 2009). In Snowball, participants had plenty of challenges from the supervisor and near peer role models and chances to discuss them in formal and informal interactions with their group members. Their such experiences must have revealed their preconceptions inappropriate to more desirable practices of teaching. Their occasions of reflection must also have helped many participants un-learn and/or re-shape some of them so that they may become more appropriate to their renewed teaching practices.

An effective LTE program, eighthly, will need a creative, affectionate, and denoted leadership that will function as a reliable and respectable supervisor and become one with the participants to learn together. He or she will need to build up and maintain healthy relationships with participants and support them academically, practically, and affectively.

An effective LTE program, ninthly, will be a product of the collaboration of the people and the government. Its leader on the side of the people should have a good relationship with, and be able to persuade, the administrators who are in a position of decision maker and/or policy creator. The administrator should also be a knowledgeable person with a healthy vision to instigate such a worthwhile innovation.

Since Snowball takes up more than 60 hours of devotion, tenthly and lastly, it can better be developed into two 48-hour courses as part of a master's program (Mr. Jin Young Choi, July 30, 2023, personal communication to Ms. Jang). Further, instructional supervision needs to be delved into as part of a doctoral course as well.

These lessons can be captured with the following core concepts: the situatedness of teacher cognition, significance of small group psychology, action research uncovering the entire process, self-determination, screening participants, TLC, teaching philosophy, creative leadership, and people-government collaboration.

## Implications for Other Similar LTE Contexts

The Snowball program would constantly send ripples of inspiration to language (teacher) educators in overseas LTE contexts. Inspired language (teacher) educators would be able to begin by examining the ten lessons that have been reaped through this case study. They could determine which one would be applicable or urgently needed in their own sociocultural milieus of language education. They would be able to *experiment* the lessons one by one (or a subset by a subset) as a working hypothesis for a different scale of educational innovation.

As described above, a crucial feature of Snowball was that it was conceived by Ms. Jang, who had continuously pursued instructional and educational innovations as an English teacher at a classroom or school level and finally had chances as a master teacher to encounter at first hand a *fuller* reality of English education in Korea. When her idea for a drastic change in LTE was listened to and accepted by the policy makers at SETI, the innovation reported here could come into being and produced *amazing* outcomes as depicted in Fig. 5.1. If a Snowball-like innovation is seriously desired, in this sense, a so-called *teaching expert* track for a teacher to pursue should be most urgently arranged through which experts would turn up with a good body of practical experience and knowledge of language-teaching tasks and of their sociocultural contexts. Such near peer models only can, we believe, persuade and *lead* teachers to strive for higher goals persistently. Given this, then, a government-people collaboration can import Snowball altogether adjusting it to their unique needs.

If some countries are not ready yet for such an educational administrative innovation, they could perhaps learn from the "reduced Snowball programs" running at Ulsan City and Gangwon Province. With no master teachers available in the English subject, the two districts have imported the program and recruited a small number of teachers so that they could run the two courses in an academic year as a TLC. The districts are currently inviting special lecturers for the TLCs, providing them with conference spaces and supporting them financially as well. They hope that the TLC participants would develop into a sustainable network of experts and comrades. The point is that the participants must be allowed to address their own problems they are facing in their immediate teaching context; they must be allowed to systematically explore the *entire* process of teaching in their own classes during the official academic period such as a semester or a year; they must be able to *experience* the *iterative* cycle of planning, implementation, peer feedback, revision, implementation, peer feedback, and so on.

If the local educational bureau is not ready for introducing such an LTE innovation, it can be attempted by school administrators in overseas EFL contexts. It would be the best if they can encourage their teach staff to organize TLCs and implement a Snowball-like program inside their own schools; they need to support such TLCs administratively and financially. If that is impossible, they could encourage and support volitional teachers to "find one teaching buddy" (Kim, 2012) within their schools and/or join an outside TLC via an SNS network. Whether in a multi-member TLC or with a single teaching buddy, such motivated teachers can spend time together regularly, e.g., eating lunches, talking about their professional and/or personal problems. They can explore some of such books as in Table 6.3. School administrators will support such innovators and recognize them as good models for other teachers to follow.

Well, an educational innovation can occur from the ground up as well. The Snowball narrative delivered here can serve as a ripple of inspiration to an individual language teacher overseas as well. Once inspired, a *live* language teacher would begin by asking a similar question to Snowball's initial question: "What problem(s) do I have in the language class I teach?" A short brainstorming would produce a list of such troubles. Maybe, the lists of themes in Table 6.2 would confirm that (s)he is not alone in having such troubles. A *live* and *pioneering* teacher will ask further: "Which one can I deal with immediately by myself?" (S)he might have to muster all the competencies and courage (s)he possesses; with his/her success, however, (s)he sets a good example for other teachers as a near peer model. (S)he may go on to ask: "Which one do I need more professional knowledge to understand?" (S)he may find some help from Tables 6.2 and 6.3. (S)he can pursue professional development in person. If (s)he promotes a culture of sharing by willingly offering her peers what (s)he has learned, (s)he can surely constitute an instigator of a grass-root innovation in language education.

Many teachers know well that it is quite difficult, if not impossible, to pursue a *sustained* instructional innovation alone; hence, *live* and *pioneering* teachers may ask further the following question: "Which problem(s) do I need reliable comrades to solve together?" Two heads are better than one, and it is better if they lift a sheet of white paper together. When such teachers get together, they can form a TLC and change the educational practices and philosophy that need to improve in their immediate environments. It may require an arduous labor, but it will surely benefit the teacher participants themselves and, above all things, their *students*.

# References

Ahn, S.-H. G., Jang, E.-K., & Lee, M. W. (2022). Characteristics and substantial outcomes of "Snowball": A long-term English teacher professional development program in Seoul. *Korean Journal of English Language and Linguistics, 22*, 500–527. https://doi.org/10.15738/kjell.22..202206.500

Bartlett, L. (1990). Teacher development through reflective teaching. In J. C. Richards & D. Nunan (Eds.), *Second language teacher education* (pp. 202–214). Cambridge University Press.

Berger, P. L., & Luckman, T. (1966). *The social construction of reality*. Penguin Books.

Blaz, D. (2016). *Differentiated instruction: A guide for world language teachers*. Eye On Education.

Borek, A. J., & Abraham, C. (2018). How do small groups promote behaviour change? An integrative conceptual review of explanatory mechanisms. *Applied Psychology: Health and Well-Being, 10*(1), 30–61. https://doi.org/10.1111/aphw.12120

Boss, S. & Larmer, J. (2018). *Project based teaching: How to create rigorous and engaging learning experiences*. ASCD.

Brookhart, S. M. (2013). *How to create and use rubrics for formative assessment and grading.* ASCD.

Cha, Y., Kim, S., Kim, S.-j, Moon, J., Song, R., Park, Y., Park, J., Ahn, S. G., Lee, S., Lee, S.-k., Lee, E., Ju, M., Ham, S., & Hwang, S. (2014). *Theory and practice of* yungbokhap *education.* Hakjisa.

Chang, K. (2007). Evaluation of intensive in-service English teacher training programs. *Foreign Languages Education, 14*(3), 257–282.

Chapman, C., & Vagle, N. (2015). *Motivating students: 25 strategies to light the fire of engagement.* Solution tree Press.

Coombe, C. (2018). Professionalism and English language teaching. In J. I. Liontas (Ed.), *The TESOL encyclopedia of English language teaching* (pp. 1–8). John Wiley & Sons. https://doi.org/10.1002/9781118784235.eelt0936

Crandall, J. (2000). Language teacher education. *Annual Review of Applied Linguistics, 20*, 34–55.

Crawford-Lange, L. M. (1981). Redirecting second language curricula: Paulo Freire's contribution. *Foreign Language Annals, 14*(4), 257–268.

Davis, J. H., Laughlin, P., & Komorita, S. S. (1976). The social psychology of small groups: Cooperative and mixed-motive interaction. *Annual Rev. Psychol., 27*, 501–541.

Day, R. R., & Bamford, J. (1998). *Extensive reading in the second language classroom.* Cambridge University Press.

Deci, E. L., & Ryan, R. M. (2000). The "what" and "why" of goal pursuits: Human needs and the self-determination of behavior. *Psychological Inquiry, 11*(4), 227–268.

Deirich, M.-C., & Stunnel, K. (2014). Language teacher education models: New issues and challenges. In J. de Dios & M. Agudo (Eds.), *English as a foreign language teacher education: Current perspectives and challenges* (pp. 83–105). Rodipi.

Department of Secondary Education. (2019, October). *2020nyeon suseokgyosa seonbal unyeong gyehoek* (The 2020 head teacher selection and operation plan). Seoul Metropolitan Office of Education. https://buseo.sen.go.kr/buseo/bu12/user/bbs/BD_selectBbs.do?q_bbsSn=1266&q_bbsDocNo=20211022104652000

DuFour, R. (2004). What is a professional learning community? *Educational Leadership, 61*(8), 6–11.

Freeman, D. (1989). Teacher training, development and decision making: A model of teaching and related strategies for language teacher education. *TESOL Quarterly, 23*(1), 27–45.

Freeman, D., & Johnson, K. E. (1998). Reconceptualizing the knowledge-base of language teacher education. *TESOL Quarterly, 32*(3), 397–417.
Freire, P. (2000). *Pedagogy of the oppressed* (30th anniversary ed.). Bloomsbury.
Gebhard, J. G. (1990). Models of supervision: Choices. In J. C. Richards & D. Nunan (Eds.), *Second language teacher education* (pp. 156–166). Cambridge University Press. (Reprinted from "Models of supervision: Choices," 1984, *TESOL Quarterly, 18*(3), 501–514)
Grabe, W. (2008). *Reading in a second language: Moving from theory to practice*. Cambridge University Press.
Hord, S. M. (2008). Evolution of the professional learning communities. *Journal of Staff Development, 29*(3), 10–13.
Jang, E. (2018). Nunsongi-ga nundeongi-ro kheojinun heuimang: "Snowball" (A hope for snowflakes rolling into snowballs: "Snowball"). In Seoul Education and Training Institute (Ed.), *2018 Jungdeung Yeongeo sueop jeonmunga doegi: Snowball Sueop Concert jaryojip* (Becoming English Class Experts in Secondary School 2018: Source Book for Snowball Concert) (pp. i–ii). Seoul Metropolitan Office of Education.
Johnson, K. E. (2009). *Second language teacher education: A sociocultural perspective*. Routledge.
Jung, K., & Chang, K. (2009). A study on the current state of in-service English teacher training and teachers' needs. *Modern English Education, 10*(3), 267–292.
Keller, J. M. (2009). *Motivational design for learning and performance: The ARCS model approach*. Springer.
Kim, T. H. (2012). *Gyosa, sueop-eseo na-rul mannada* (Teacher meets "me" in class). Joheun Gyosa (Good Teacher).
Kim, J. Y., Lee, H., & Lim, C. (2015). A preliminary study on developing on-line in-service English teacher education. *Foreign Languages Education, 22*(3), 233–260. https://doi.org/10.15334/FLE.2015.22.3.233
Kim, Y.-O., Kahng, Y.-K., & Sohng, H. S. (2008). The study of trainees' satisfaction with in-service training for the qualification of 1st grade English teachers in a secondary school. *English Language & Literature Teaching, 14*(1), 97–122.
Korean Law Translation Center. (2023, May 19). *Elementary and secondary education act* [Act No. 18993, Oct. 18, 2022]. Korea Legislation Research Institute. https://elaw.klri.re.kr/kor_service/lawView.do?hseq=61414&lang=ENG

Korthagen, F. A. J. (2010). Situated learning theory and the pedagogy of teacher education: Towards an integrative view of teacher behavior and teacher learning. *Teaching and Teacher Education, 26*, 98–106.

Kumaravadivelu, B. (2012). *Language teacher education for a global society: A modular model for knowing, analyzing, recognizing, doing, and seeing*. Routledge.

Lave, J., & Wenger, E. (1991). *Situated learning: Legitimate peripheral participation*. Cambridge University Press.

Lee, H. (2010). Integrating on-school and off-school English language teacher education: A case study of Cambridge ICELT in Korea. *English Language & Literature Teaching, 16*(1), 259–281.

Ministry of Education. (2015, September 23). *The national curriculum for the primary and secondary schools*. The Republic of Korea (Proclamation of the Ministry of Education #2015-74, [Annex 1]). https://ncic.re.kr/english.kri.org.inventoryList.do;jsessionid=8A340D6E2F08F84479D135878959CF7E

Murphey, T. (1998). Motivating with near peer role models. In B. Visgatis (Ed.), *Proceedings of the JALT 1997 International Conference on Language Teaching and Learning* (pp. 205–209). Tokyo: JALT.

Park, B. E. (2006). The effect of elementary English teacher training. *Explorations into Future Education, 27*(1), 1–28.

Prabhu, N. S. (1987). *Second language pedagogy*. Oxford University Press.

Roberts, J. (1998). *Language teacher education: The reflective trainer*. Arnold.

Ryan, R. M., & Deci, E. L. (2002). Overview of self-determination theory: An organismic perspective. In E. L. Deci & R. M. Ryan (Eds.), *Handbook of self-determination research* (pp. 3–33). The University of Rochester Press.

Seoul Education and Training Institute. (Ed.). (2016). *2015-2016 Snowball yeonsu gyeolgwa bogoseo* (Report on outcomes of the *2015–2016* Snowball programs). Seoul Metropolitan Office of Education.

Seoul Education and Training Institute. (Ed.). (2018). *2018 Jungdeung Yeongeo sueop jeonmunga doegi: Snowball Sueop Concert jaryojip* (Becoming English class experts in secondary school 2018: Source book for Snowball Class Concert). Seoul Metropolitan Office of Education.

Seoul Education and Training Institute. (Ed.). (2019). *2019 Jungdeung Yeongeo sueop jeonmunga doegi: Snowball Sueop Concert jaryojip* (Becoming English class experts in secondary school 2019: Source book for Snowball Class Concert). Seoul Metropolitan Office of Education.

Tarone, E., & Allwright, D. (2005). Second language teacher learning and student second language learning: Shaping the knowledge base. In D. J.

Tedick (Ed.), *Second language teacher education: International perspectives* (pp. 5–24). Lawrence Erlbaum Associates.

Wallace, M. J. (1991). *Training foreign language teachers: A reflective approach.* Cambridge University Press.

Wiggins, G., & McTighe, J. (2005) *Understanding by design* (Expanded 2nd ed.). Pearson.

# 7
# English for Peacebuilding Purposes Writing Courses

## Jocelyn Wright

## Area of innovation

> Values permeate all aspects of ELT. (Hall, 2011, p. 49)

Peace is a pressing universal need. Fortunately, despite certain challenges, the potential contribution of education to peace is widely recognized. Due to their large number, spread across sectors and countries, and daily influence, English language teachers are also well-positioned to help learners reflect on, develop, and contribute to this need (Birch, 2022; Friedrich, 2007; Gomes de Matos, 2014; McInnis & Wells, 1994; Oxford et al., 2021).

With this motivation and an understanding that all education is political (Freire, 1970), I introduced English for Peacebuilding Purposes (EPP) courses into my local curriculum. This innovation is a values- or

---

J. Wright (✉)
Mokpo National University, Mokpo, South Korea
e-mail: jocelyn@mokpo.ac.kr

© The Author(s), under exclusive license to Springer Nature Switzerland AG 2025
H. Reinders et al. (eds.), *Innovation in Language Learning and Teaching*, New Language Learning and Teaching Environments,
https://doi.org/10.1007/978-3-031-83561-2_7

159

purpose-guided attempt to transform traditional English as an additional language writing skills courses at a university in the foreign language context of South Korea (hereinafter Korea), and is largely the result of learning about two concepts: comprehensive peace and education *about, through,* and *for* it (Fisk, 1998) as well as communicative peace. Both fit within the scope of peace linguistics (PL), "an interdisciplinary field guided by the goal of promoting comprehensive peace through systematic study, deliberate education, and conscious uses of language spoken, written, and signed" (adapted from Wright, 2021), and more specifically, the branch of peace language education (PLE).

At the heart of PLE is peace. As defined by a father of peace studies, Johan Galtung (1996), peace is response to or prevention of violence (all types of avoidable hurt or harm: direct, structural, and cultural). Peace can be made by reducing or eliminating violence and by nurturing and developing five basic needs (survival, wellbeing, identity/meaning, freedom, and ecological balance). These peacemaking and peacebuilding approaches are referred to as negative and positive peace, respectively. According to Galtung's view, combining these approaches at various levels (from micro to macro) and in different areas can lead to comprehensive peace.

PLE draws on peace education and PL in its attempts to further comprehensive peace while improving language proficiency and communication skills, so basic background about both can help contextualize the EPP courses. First, peace education (e.g. as developed by Betty Reardon and succinctly described by Tony Jenkins) and PL (e.g. as developed by Francisco Gomes de Matos and Patricia Friedrich) are values-guided and hopeful enterprises which see comprehensive peace as both a desirable process and possible outcome. Both aim to critically[1] and creatively transform individuals and their lives and, thereby, positively impact relationships and structures as well as cultural norms and institutions, taking into consideration lived experiences and the specificities of local contexts through the joint activities of research, education, and action.

---

[1] Here, critical refers to the Freirean sense as reflective, dialogic, problematizing, democratic, action-oriented, and emancipatory (1970) as well as constructive, hopeful, and caring (1997).

The purpose of peace education is to help learners "acquire the knowledge, develop the skills, nurture the attitudes, and build those capacities necessary for human well-being and flourishing and the achievement of a culture of peace" (Jenkins, 2019, p. 4). Peace education contributes contents and perspectives about peace as well as peace pedagogies to PLE. According to the same source, contents range from healing and reconciliation, to spirituality, to nonviolence, to cultural proficiency and global citizenship, to conflict transformation, mediation, and restorative justice, to democracy and civic engagement, to human rights and social justice, to disarmament and reconstruction, to sustainable development and peace economics, to environmental justice and more, transversing the various levels as well as areas. As for pedagogies, peace education tends to emphasize holistic and integrative learning that is student-centered as well as collaborative, inquiry-based, and oriented toward transformation through praxis.

Meanwhile, PL contributes the goal of communicative peace, "a new, thought-and-action-provoking way of humanizing communication" (Gomes de Matos, 2005, p. 211) that extends Dell Hymes' notion of communicative competence. Two beliefs support Gomes de Matos' (2014) ideas about communicative peace and relate to the outcome and process:

1. Life can be improved communicatively when language use is thought of - and implemented - as a peacebuilding force and
2. Life can be communicatively improved when language users are educated to learn to use languages peacefully for the good of persons, groups, Humankind. (p. 418)

The still little known disciplinary field of PL has been emerging since the 1980s (Gomes de Matos, 1987). Landmark events such as the 1987 Linguapax conference on "Teaching foreign languages for peace and understanding" began a movement, which, if the past few years are any indication, may be picking up speed. More numerous calls for a commitment to PLE in recent edited collections (e.g. Birch, 2022; Oxford et al., 2021) is perhaps recognition of its urgency and promise.

## Impetus for the Innovation

The development of EPP courses came about in part due to a personal interest in PL and peace education and calls for action in language education. Another impetus was a search for a critical response to the challenging higher education context in Korea and local circumstances, and this innovation was afforded by the relative freedom to develop curriculum in the humanities (cf. education, which is strictly monitored by the national Ministry of Education).

Current higher education reflects and is affected by demographic, socioeconomic, and exam pressures. First, overall enrolment rates are declining due to consistently low fertility rates. In 2022, the rate was just 0.78 as reported by the Korean Statistical Information Service (KOSIS, 2023), and Korea has had among the lowest rates in the world over the last two decades according to the Organisation for Economic Co-operation and Development (OECD, 2023).

Second, according to Kim's (2019) socioeconomic analysis, due to the general economic slowdown and the ability of the wealthy to monopolize access to top universities, usually in the Seoul/metropolitan area, Korean education serves as a mechanism for class reproduction, offering only limited opportunities for social mobility. Due to neoliberal government policies with funding related to performance (based on 'gamed' rankings), universities adopt a strategic market approach to recruitment, targeting "the wealthiest, best connected and most promising students" (p. 180) resulting in a "hyper-competitive" (p. 180) society. With political and economic power concentrated in the Seoul/metropolitan area, as well as universities with connections to these, and more various cultural opportunities, Seoul/metropolitan universities can increase selectivity, offer better guarantees of employability, and consequently gain access to funding "to finance reputation-increasing 'luxuries' such as research" (p. 179) which, in turn, affect rankings. Meanwhile, other regions confronting a student brain drain, struggle to recruit (strong) applicants, to secure needed funding, and to maintain competitive rankings. The result is increasing urban/regional educational disparity, with rural universities especially being forced to innovate and restructure or close.

In addition, there are the negative washback effects of the national College Scholastic Ability Test (CSAT),[2] unofficially referred to as the university entrance exam. Access to universities is largely determined by student performance on this test, a core component being English (proficiency and skills). Because the stakes are high and results decisive, students experience psychological and socioeconomic pressure (e.g. instrumental motivation, disorientation, anxiety, low confidence, and costly private education) to study and real consequences if they do not succeed (Kwon et al., 2017).

While certain students prefer to stay local or strategically enroll in regional national universities because they offer certain benefits (e.g. low tuition, scholarships, access to national programs, etc.) and are less competitive, others can feel relegated to them because they come from lower-income families and/or did not achieve high scores on their CSAT (Kim, 2019). If due to the English component, students may arrive at (English programs at) regional universities feeling demotivated, suffering from weak English language proficiency/communication skills, and having low confidence in English, or a combination of the above, which may, in turn, affect their academic expectations and/or performance if no changes in the learning environment or "investment value" is found to (internally and/or externally) remotivate them (Jung, 2011; Kim & Kim, 2016).

As mentioned, the EPP courses are a critical response to this challenging situation that affects students in Korea and at regional national universities in particular (Jung, 2011). Providing EPP courses is meant to offer an oasis to these learners. The courses aim to do so by addressing contextual demotivating factors (e.g. a lack of confidence,

---

[2] As stated on the Korea Institute for Curriculum and Evaluation website (KICE, 2023), the CSAT

is an academically challenging and balanced test designed to measure student achievement and academic aptitude according to the National Curriculum standards for college education. The CSAT is developed and managed by [KICE] and commissioned by the Ministry of Education. CSAT aims to assess high-order thinking skills in the six study areas – [Korean] Language Arts, Mathematics, English, Korean History, Inquiry and Foreign Language/Classical Chinese." (Introduction of CSAT).

Before taking the CSAT, students receive about 10 years of compulsory English education.

meaningful purpose, improvement and experiences of success, and self-determination) identified in Kim and Kim's (2016, p. 151) metastudy through an intentional remotivating strategy (EPP contents and pedagogy) in line with recommendations by Jung (2011), which seem widespread.

Based on the first two sections above, EPP courses could foster comprehensive peace and communicative peace by giving students opportunities to learn about peace, to learn to (make/build) peace, to learn peacefully, and to "make peace with English" to borrow Friedrich's (2007) expression. These are discussed in the findings.

## Specific Context of Implementation

The two EPP courses were piloted in a department of English language and literature at a national university in rural Korea in 2022–2023. In this small department, which follows a so-called "democratic policy," each course is opened only annually, and all are electives with no prerequisites. As per university regulations, most employ relative grading.

The three-credit (45 hours), fifteen-week thematic courses were named EPP1: English Writing for Inner Peace (spring) and EPP2: English Writing for Interpersonal Peace (fall), respectively. In both, students explored their understandings and ideas about peace as a process and outcome as they attempted to clarify topic and focus, to work on voice in relation to their purpose and audience, to organize, develop, and format their ideas, and to increase fluency, meaningfulness, and accuracy in English writing through production of different genres.

The courses had distinct foci. EPP1 emphasized creative writing and academic expression, and EPP2 interactive writing and academic response. To support authenticity, both courses conducted in English centered on mostly learner-generated contents (based on their stories, situations, or views, real or imagined) in response to open-ended prompts. EPP1 mostly elicited reflection and self-expression about the presence or absence of peace in students' lives (e.g. in places, items, people, aspects of life, and memories) as well as ways of assisting themselves and/or others towards this positive end. EPP2 prompts were more directed at interactive communicative peace outcomes in progressively more challenging situations (e.g. declining invitations, refusing requests, voicing complaints, stating opinions over controversial issues, expressing disagreement, and translating self-criticism). Both courses adopted a "learn as you use" language syllabus (Hall, 2011, p. 195).

To achieve these, after a first phase of introductory and organizational lessons, learning was carefully scaffolded into cumulative writing cycles, which involved active participation and collaboration such that the classroom became "a meeting place for both silent meditation and verbal witness, of interplay between interiority and community" (O'Reilley, 1993, p. 32). EPP1 consisted of individual writing, starting with poetry. While independent, this creative writing served as a warm-up to the following academic expression tasks. Interaction took place during brainstorming and dialogic feedback tasks guided by the compassionate THICK procedure for feedback which is truthful, helpful, I-centered, clear, and kind (Wright, 2023). Each cycle ended with individual language awareness tasks focused on editing and revising. EPP2 involved individual prewriting planning followed by interactive writing tasks and dialogic feedback. Then, individual language awareness tasks focused on academic response to prompts about contrasts between genres, registers, and language choices made.

Assessment comprised mostly formative feedback (self, peer, and teacher) in response to in-class writing tasks (scored as completed for participation points). Summative assessment included delayed grading in EPP1 for final multimodal projects (an animated poem and a mounted paragraph), where students re-revised two favorite pieces for a virtual exhibit on Padlet (see Fig. 7.1), and "best of n attempts" grading of language awareness tasks in EPP2. In line with the course aims and students' needs, there were no exams. Instead, in the final class, students filled in a short reflection paper (also scored on completion).

To provide a peaceful learning environment for students, several pedagogical features were incorporated into EPP courses. Students completed most of their writing in-class in provided sketchbooks, which they could also freely illustrate. The decision to mostly teach unplugged (Meddings & Thornbury, 2009) was deliberately made to encourage

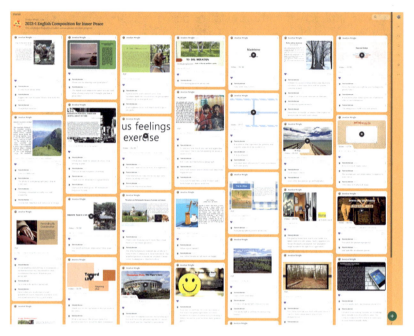

Fig. 7.1 Virtual exhibit

interaction, support meaningful emergent language, and reduce technological distraction. Although the genre was usually teacher-determined, the general writing prompts offered ample leeway to GRASP other aspects. (The acronym stands for designated Genre, elected wRiter voice, chosen Audience, selected Subject/topic, and intended Purpose for writing.)[3] In addition to having students write motivational messages to themselves (EPP1) or classmates (EPP2) at the beginning of the semester, hold awards nominations for themselves midway and at the end (EPP1), and write self-appreciation cards to themselves upon finishing (EPP2), the teacher offered constant encouragement and used cute Post-its to give THICK feedback. As well, she incorporated breathing, visualization, or stretching activities into lessons at key points, and always played soft

---

[3] Initially, the teacher had focused on GASP. However, it became apparent that students struggled with their voices in EPP2 as they adopted a plurality of stances sometimes informal/formal, familiar/unfamiliar, playful/serious, imagined/real while writing various types of texts.

instrumental music or recordings of nature sounds in the background. Altogether, the above design aimed in various ways to contribute to peace.

So far, 22 students (7 and 15) completed the spring course, and 25 the fall with approximately 65% being English majors and 35% coming from other disciplines. Students were mostly Koreans of mixed genders, in their sophomore to senior years. While the majority were in their early to mid-twenties, a few mature (transfer) students also participated. Given the host department offers few practical courses, all tend to be mixed-level. Based on beginning-of-the-semester surveys (Q1), student proficiency levels ranged from A1-C1 according to the Common European Framework of Reference for Languages (Council of Europe, 2023), with most between A2-B1. Given the size, nature of the courses, and the student diversity, the teacher adopted the role of *accompagnateur*, one who is present and supportive along a journey (Weigel, 2013).

# Findings

This section presents mostly qualitative learner data revealing insights into what worked and a couple of obstacles related to the four main goals (learning about peace, learning to (make/build) peace, learning peacefully, and learning to make peace with English), where relevant based on classroom observation, consensual data from production tasks in sketchbooks (SK) and reflection papers (RP), and elicitation data from four anonymous course questionnaires conducted electronically on the first day (Q1), around midterm (Q2), at the end of the semester (Q3), and before revealing grades (Q4). Given the nature of the data, most opinions and experiences expressed below reflect authentic developmental learner writing that was spontaneously produced rather than processed or polished. To preserve and respect student voice, quotes were not edited.

## Learning About Peace

There is a lot to learn about a concept such as peace! Students indicated that they learned ample through EPP courses. First, they learned about 'peaces' (Galtung, 1996), a core goal of the courses: "I found that there are many types of peace from inner, social and ecological peace. Through writing about peace, I could reflect many kinds of peace" (EPP1S16RP). Another asserts learning about the semantic range of the concept and the scope of application: "I leaned 'peace''s various meaning. I could know 'peace' can be applied many topics related with writting" (EPP1S12RP). Indeed, students learned about peace by looking at it through a choice of personally relevant topics spanning the full range covered in peace education (from the psychological, social, economic, political, cultural, spiritual, global, and ecological). Examples of self-nominated awards titles appear in Table 7.1.

Table 7.1 Awards nominations[4]

| Categories | Prizes | Titles | Sources |
|---|---|---|---|
| Poems | Best form | *Two Different Tears* | (EPP1S12SK) |
|  | Most creative/ original | *Broken Correction Tape* | (EPP1S12SK) |
|  | Best imagery (vocabulary) | *Snow Country* | (EPP1S1SK) |
|  | ... |  |  |
| Paragraphs | Best form | *My Enemy = Math* | (EPP1S6SK) |
|  | Best content | *My Life Lamp* | (EPP1S25SK) |
|  | Best style | *Who Protects Me* | (EPP1S18SK) |
|  | Best organization | *Peace Found in Cub Scouts* | (EPP1S12SK) |
|  | Best development | *Why do Women Quit Their Job?* | (EPP1S18SK) |
|  | Most accurate | *The Teacher with Whole Love* | (EPP1S25SK) |
| All | Best title | *Briquette is to Share Love* | (EPP1S11SK) |
|  | ... |  |  |

---

[4] Students customized categories, adding others such as Best rhyme, Best effort, Most relevant, Funniest, etc.

Based on observation, students generally chose to foreground peace rather than violence. This did not, however, prevent them from exploring and negotiating diverse topics like loneliness, self-hate, friendships with foreigners, "toxic" relationships, conflict at part-time jobs, ageism, visa issues, military service, the death of an adopted three-legged street dog, and more!

By the end of the course, a student recognized that peace is omnipresent: "I thought the word 'peace' is very close to certain people (soldiers, police) But I noticed peace is everywhere" (EPP1S20RP). Meanwhile, a different one commented on the proximity or availability of peace: "Peace is not so far. Depending on the process. I can feel peace at any time" (EPP1S8RP).

An acknowledgement that peace begins within was metaphorically expressed through this quote:

> Learning peace means having a heavy root against the wind. wind continuously blows though tree doesn't want. But if it's deeply rooted, it never lose. so I found out peace is created from myself, not an outside. And I learned the importance of reflecting myself with this reason. (EPP1S6RP)

More plainly but inclusively, a student remarked: "Peace starts with each individual. Peace begins in your (our) mind" (EPP1S21RP). This idea aligns well with the teachings of globally renowned peace activists (e.g. Mahatma Gandhi, Mother Teresa, Martin Luther King, Jr., Thich Nhat Hanh, etc.) encountered in EPP1. At least one student realized that peace requires personal effort: "I was able to think about when good peace would come to me. I could see that maybe I had to find it myself" (EPP1S14RP).

Most notably in EPP2, where the focus was on interpersonal relationships, students acknowledged learning about the contribution of writing: "Writing for peacebuilding purposes is important because it is the key point of building good relationships" (EPP2S8RP). This student highlighted awareness of the need for intentionality: "At the beginning of the semester, I didn't know mean of the writing for peacebuilding purposes. *Just, I knew ways to write for English* [emphasis added]. Now, I know that writing for peacebuilding purposes are important when relationships make positive" (EPP2S20RP). Meanwhile, another identified increased audience awareness:

> My feels about interactive writing are changed ... Begining of this semester, I felt interactive writing was easy and friendly. Because I thought interactive writings are only about chatting or text message. Now I know interactive writings can include any writing which has audience. I feel careful about interactive writing because interactive writing have audience. (EPP2S6RP)

The contribution of writing to peace was not obvious to all from the start, though, as this comment shows: "I learned that peace can be achieved not only by helping others, but also by writing and conveying something to others" (EPP1S24RP).

Peace encapsulates various virtues. Students prominently connected respect with peace when discussing their learning as in: "At first, I thought say in good words is the all of peacebuilding writing. Because I thought that get along with people is only purpose that I knew. ... now I believe that I can make our relationship better when we respect them" (EPP2S24RP). However, sometimes, it was self-respect they learned: "My first time of semester, I thought this class help me about 'How to respect myself' And now, 'that was right'" (EPP1S10RP). Positiveness, a virtue especially at the heart of Gomes de Matos' (1996) work, also commonly appeared in comments: "At the beginning of the semester, i know good conversation and respect is peacebuilding purposes. And now for peacebuilding, positive perspective is very important" (EPP2S27RP). Other peace virtues (e.g. empathy, flexibility) appear elsewhere.

Students also noted awareness of communication strategies contributing to peace: "At first, I didn't know about writing for peacebuilding purposes exactly. For now, I know it is a writing to enhance interpersonal peace, and develop negotiation and mediation skills" (EPP2S17RP).

One student revealed that peace can be shared and what this meant to them: "I think peace is very important in our life. Giving and receiving peace each other. I realize a lot of things that give me peace"

(EPP1S5RP). This theme inspired their writing, which evolved through the writing process from ideas to poem to paragraph to exhibit.

The above quotes presented several takeaways. Only one student claimed they did not learn much about the theme. However, their statement, "Most of the subject of writing sessions was 'Peace'. Honestly, I haven't learned anything specifically novel abot Peace. But I find having the chance to think about peace itself was close to the term" (EPP1S1RP), connects well to the next point.

## Learning to (Make/Build) Peace

Galtung (1996) distinguishes between making and building peace, with the first focused on resolving conflicts by changing attitudes and assumptions and the second on overcoming their root causes. Self-reports on the first survey (Q1) indicated that students fully expected to develop inner or interpersonal peace through EPP courses, and according to the end-of-semester survey (Q3), about 95% of students in both courses felt they achieved this objective. Their comments demonstrate ways they did so in the present and for the future.

First, reflection led to peace for some: "I realized what I needed for peace and I thought a lot about myself" (EPP1S23RP). For this student, it was a chance to reflect on the present; for another, it was an opportunity to revisit past memories. Specific ways reflection led to development mentioned were open-mindedness and adaptability: "I think about how to better peacebuilding. So I knew 'relationship"s way. I think deeply about various topic every weeks. I can understand many people's thinking. so my mind is flexible" (EPP2S25RP).

The writing process helped students make peace within. On prewriting, one student remarked, "I can know how to brainstorming before writting. This process can my mind clean and making good organization" (EPP1S16RP). For another student, self-expression was liberating: "I learn a lot about peace through my brainstorming through wrote a poem, paragraph too. I feel my burden is lifted when I write what's in my head" (EPP1S7RP). Writing also led to peace through self-exploration: "I got to know more about myself while writing poems and paragraphs. I feel peace while I write" (EPP1S5RP). The rewriting process was important for this student by helping them to grow: "The crucial point is, I am more confident with writing than before! I did so well to eroll in this class for I could have a chance to try and revise myself constantly" (EPP1S1RP). More specifically, other students noted the healing effect of creative writing in EPP1: "I could write different kind of poems and that makes me more creative and reflect my life. So it healed a lot" (EPP1Q3). In addition to regularly writing, students learned to peace through frequent compassionate feedback tasks: "Giving feedback in THICK repeatedly made me a better feedback giver. Thank you!" (EPP1S12RP). The cyclical learning enabled students to peacefully perform a potentially sensitive task.

Through their comments, students demonstrated understanding of Gomes de Matos' (2014) "peacebuilding, peacesupporting, peacesustaining function" (p. 419) of language. One who initially believed EPP courses would center on "a polite way to communication" realized later that it was more about how "to communicate harmoniously ... and according to the situation" (EPP2S18RP). Students also noted specific functions they practiced: "I didn't know about writing for peacebuilding purposes. But now, I know peaceful writing like how to refuse peacefully, how to apologize kindly, how to appreciate etc." (EPP2S23RP). Connecting with virtues, one student showed that such learning served to give voice to and empower them:

> At the beginning) I thought only optimistic ways are suitable for peacebuilding writing. To be peaceful, I thought there should not complaints, only should compromise. Now) I learned that I can reject someone's requests in peace and I can complain without offense. Respect and empathy are important. (EPP2S4RP)

This case clearly shows gains in freedom and self-determination (O'Reilley, 1993).

Taking on their voice, one student acknowledged the importance of quality of communication:

Actually, I didn't think about interactive writing. I just wrote what I want. However, ... I knew my bad habit through this class. My bad habit is that I write like bosses. It's not a good writing skill. I realized I have not to write bossy. When people read bossy sentence, they don't feel good. (EPP2S26RP)

On change due to language awareness about the value of self-adjusting tone, they also wrote: "I used to speak (write) sharply. But I realized sharp words are not good for the relationship. Now I am intered in the peacebuilding purposes. If you want to make peaceful world, you have to write well. It's really important" (EPP2S26RP). In EPP2, students intentionally practiced conveying different tones. According to one student: "I learn a lot about writing for peacebuilding purpose ... At the beginning of the semester, All I know about peacebuilding purposes writing were express love and respect. But Now, I know how to write harmoniously, kindly, graciously, indirectly and carefully" (EPP2S6RP). The above quotes demonstrate ways they learned to peace through language.

According to students, learning specific strategies also helped them develop. FENS (Roberts, 2020) is a conflict transformation technique, based on Marshall Rosenberg's (e.g. 2015) model of nonviolent communication, that emphasizes communicating about facts, emotions, needs, and solutions introduced in EPP2. One student noted personal benefits of the process: "When I am upset, organizing something [using FENS] helps me to calm myself down. Also, it helps me not to forget what I actually need and clearly see some situations" (EPP2S8SK). Taking perspective, others focused on benefits for readers, namely reader satisfaction and ease of response (EPP2S2SK) and better understanding and empathy (EPP2S15SK).

Several comments highlight learning of aspects of FENS, especially emotions and needs, which they spent more class time on, as in "I think that learning many feelings is the most important positive thing. It is important in relationship" (EPP2S20RP) and "I think this class is very important for students because I can explain what I need" (EPP2S7RP).

Beyond language and strategies, students developed sociolinguistic/ sociocultural context awareness through doing interactive writing: "I thought that peacebuilding could be made by good purposes wording.

But it's not true. Sometimes, good word can't resolve our problem. We need to focus on context and forms of writing for send peacebuilding messages" (EPP2S5RP).

Related to this, on extralinguistic knowledge, a student declared, "At first, all I knew about construction of peaceful writing was …. Sincerely, at the end of the writing! … However, now I know the structure of peaceful formal writing and I am actually a person who knows how to apply it to overseas direct purchase site sellers!" (EPP2S7RP).

Through reflection, the writing process, specific strategies, and tasks, students learned to (make/build) peace by writing better for more peaceful outcomes both with others and within.

## Learning Peacefully

Several pedagogical aspects helped students learn peacefully in EPP courses. The teacher's personality was one. As these comments from surveys show, students often described her in ways that fit her intended role of *accompagnateur*, as positive and caring: "I was happy because she always smiles and cared for students" (EPP1Q3) and "It was impressive that the professor cared about each and every student" (EPP1Q4). They repeatedly mentioned the impact of her passion and earnestness on individuals: "I am grateful that the professor gave her lectures with enthusiasm and responded sincerely when I asked questions" (EPP1Q4). They also noted a group effect: "Because it is a class where you can feel the passion of the professor, you can work hard together and feel comfortable through the connection with other students" (EPP1Q3). Kindness and attention, key elements of empathy, were two additional points they highlighted: "I felt that she was always kind to the students and paid a lot of attention to class preparation and progress. She prepares sketchbooks herself, carefully checks each and every part of each student's handwritten sketchbook …, and gives detailed feedback with post-it notes" (EPP2Q4). One comment, "Your lecture really soothed my heart. and helped me to love myself ♥♥" (EPP1S6RP), aligns with O'Reilley's (1993) statement that "good teaching *is* … therapy: good teaching involves reweaving the spirit" (p. 47).

Students touched upon aspects of teaching that contributed to peace by supporting learning including choice of topics: "It was good to be able to write creatively with self-directed topics" (EPP1Q3). Another was the teacher's explanation style: "You explained well in an easy to understand way" (EPP2Q4). Personalized tutoring was also mentioned: "I am grateful that the professor taught me in detail what I did not understand" (EPP1Q3). Several students signaled appreciation not only about the friendly feedback they received but its delivery, a sign the teacher practiced what she preached (i.e., not only that she taught THICK feedback to students but also gave it) as partly affirmed by this note: "Writing in English is different from Korean like grammar and vocabulary. I felt a lot of difficulties. I was encouraged through this class, because the professor's feedback was helpful" (EPP2S18RP).

Students indicated the quality of the group dynamic which contributed to a comfortable learning environment. For instance, some directly remarked on the kindness of their classmates and on how they supported each other: "The professor explained the contents of the class in detail, and the team members who worked together kindly conveyed the details. Thank you for your active help in resolving difficult and challenging issues" (EPP1Q4). Students reported pleasure sharing their work: "I feel great ... writing my poems and paragraphs. And I enjoy sharing my poems and paragraphs to my friends" (EPP1S2RP). This one underscored their joy of connecting and learning from each other: "During this class, it was good to express my opinion through English conversation with various people and to get feedback from people and fix it" (EPP2S1RP). Even students self-identifying as shy were positively impacted by collaboration: "Studying my friends together have gotten easier. Talking to my friends was easier than before because I was shy to talk with them" (EPP1S2RP). In addition to the classroom dynamic, students found the atmosphere contributed to peaceful learning as in this point: "listening some birds singing was peaceful" (EPP1S2RP).

Regarding assessment, two students specifically expressed satisfaction with not having tests. One explicitly stated their preference for tasks saying "the burden was small" (EPP2Q4) as a result. The lower-stakes evaluation scheme was certainly appreciated if rarely mentioned; there were no complaints about it.

Students learned peacefully, even claimed to have healed, in EPP courses thanks to their teacher's compassionate personality and pedagogy, and the classroom dynamic and atmosphere it cultivated. However, a program-level obstacle that seemed challenging for the teacher alone to transcend (since it was connected with department admissions, the democratic course registration policy, and, therefore inevitably, mixed-level classes) was raised by one student:

> It seemed that there were more students than expected who lacked English skills to write. Since the middle and high school English education curriculum in Korea does not focus on writing, it would be much more effective if there was a basic writing class, and it would be much more effective if you take that class first and then take this class. (EPP2Q4)

The collaborative learning strategy employed in class aimed to minimize this problem, but naturally, some students were better able or more willing to help others with difficulty. Possibly, certain adjustments to lesson pacing may further help compensate for this issue in following semesters.

## Learning to Make Peace with English

Evidence of remotivation and renewed positive attitudes towards English (language learning) indicate that students made peace with the language. The following are offered in support of this observation.

First, according to Kim and Kim (2016), novelty of experience can remotivate students. A couple indeed mentioned their motivation for taking EPP courses. One recalled what prompted them to register, "When I first signed up for the course, the lecture plan interesting and the name of the lecture caught my attention ... So I heard it because I thought it would be a good basis for me to put my resume in an overseas company later. That is what I think now, too!" (EPP2S7RP). Several students declared that EPP activities were new as in "Writting poem in English, this class, was the first time to me" (EPP1S16RP) and "it was a very fresh because I could think about interactive writing and interpersonal peace" (EPP2S23RP).

Unfamiliarity was also highlighted as in the following: "I felt confused about interactive writing at the beginning of the class because interactive writing is not importantly considered in korean curriculum, Interactive writing is still hard, but I feel more familiar compared to the beginning of the semester through practicing" (EPP2S8RP). As above and further below, numerous students noted feeling negative emotions (fear, nervousness, even awkwardness) writing in English or described the language as difficult at the beginning of the semester. Fortunately, with greater familiarity and practice, many expressed shifts to positive emotions.

Evidence students made peace with English in the EPP courses appears in multiple comments related to increased confidence such as: "At the begining of the semester, I didn't feel confident. Because, I always got bad scores when I writed for English at highschool. Now, I feel happy" (EPP2S20RP) and "At first, I felt stucked because I've never done completing paragraph by myself. But after I listened to this class, I feel more confident at writing" (EPP1S6RP). As another conclusively declared: "The most important thing, I learned 'English is not afraid thing!" (EPP2S9RP).

There may be various explanations for increased student confidence. One could be teacher engineering early encouragement. In week one of EPP courses, when the teacher asked students to write themselves motivational messages, they expressed their positive determination in various ways as: "You've got to take the chance" (EPP1S1SK) and "You can't go to heaven, if you run away everytime" (EPP1S25SK). Some visualized a better future: "I can better than yesterday" (EPP1S11SK). In EPP2, messages to partners usually aimed to uplift and expressed solidarity as in "Don't give up. Enjoy together" (EPP2S15SK).

Another reason could relate to early expectations of success maintained over the semester. According to the surveys, students started each EPP course with high (100%) expectations of progress in three areas (developing useful writing skills, learning new genres/styles of writing, and improving how they analyze writing) and, without exception, held these very positive attitudes throughout the course. (Final ratings decreased only for feedback skills and only for a couple students in EPP1).

Students reported actual opportunities to experience growth as in "At the beginning, I enjoyed writing especially poems, because it was creative as well as simple. For now, I feel that my writing skill is improved and i little proud of myself because I wrote a lot of paragraphs!" (EPP1S12RP) and "At the beginning of the semester, I was afraid to writing English paper. But now, I am satisfied my enveador and I feel confident. Because I know that my writing is better than first" (EPP2S15RP).

Various comments denoted changes in attitudes towards mistakes as the following indicate: "My confident about writing is changed after this semester. I always worried and scared about writing at the beginning of the semester. Because my faults in writings looks ridiculous. But Now, I feel confidence about writing because I realize faults can be revise" (EPP2S6RP) and "I never confident when I write in English. It was really hard to me. I worried grammar mistakes, confused the words. But I realized I don't have to worry about my mistakes. So I write the sentence with brave mind. I feel confident little than before. These day, I still have many mistakes but I fall in love in english writing" (EPP2S26RP).

Indeed, students appear to have been transformed through understanding the process: "When I started writing at the beginning of the semester, I was so scared about I'm wrong, That's why I was timid before. But, I understand what we doing! I'm learning and practicing. So I have to try everything that I can do. As the thought comes to my mind, I become brave! So I'm fearless about writing nowadays" (EPP2S24RP). Alternatively, prioritizing the process might have played a role as stated here: "As the process is more important than the result, the fact that I participated in the class itself was a valuable opportunity" (EPP1Q4).

Confidence could also be a result of students' challenging and persevering attitudes as these comments suggest: "I was a little lacking, but I was fortunate to be able to take classes together without giving up until the end" (EPP1Q4), and "I felt nervous and worried when I began of the semester. Because I don't have base knowledge of english grammer and word. Nevertheless I decided to challenging. As a result, I can feel a worthwhile" (EPP2S9RP). Overcoming difficulties was a key factor.

Positively reconceptualizing English could be a contributing factor as in this reflection: "I was scared before the semester. Because 'English' is a task to be accomplished. But now, I am interesting better using english" (EPP1S25RP). As learning English became more meaningful, this student gained courage.

In addition to confidence, students often expressed greater pride: "At the begining of the semester my writing need a lot of improvement. so thank you so much that you always give us "Language Awareness" exercise it help me a lot. ♥ Now I Feel more confidence to write something new, and I proud to my self that I can make a paragraph" (EPP1S7RP) and "At the beginning of the semester, I felt nervous. Because I didn't have a confidence about English writing. Now, I feel proud, Because I steadily attended this class and learned many writing skills" (EPP2S20RP).

Sometimes, students stated feeling greater comfort or ease as in: "It was difficult when I first started writing. But I feel comfortable writing now" (EPP1S22RP) and "At the beginning of the semester, I thought 'I can't! It's too difficult! I don't know how to write!' I had no confident in writing. But now, I'm very proud of me when I write my think, opinion easily" (EPP2S23RP). Greater ease from developing strategies was connected with empowerment: "Using english only makes me hard at beginning of the semester, but, now it is not. because using just easy words also can communicating with proffesor" (EPP2S21RP).

Acknowledging personal responsibility also helped them progress: "Language learning is all about how much time I commit myself to it. I feel more comfortable with basic level of writing. This has gotten easier. And now I'm ready to take one step further!" (EPP1S1RP). Effort overcame negative emotions: "Challenging is important. Just doing study is better than the worry time at all" (EPP2S6RP).

Finally, after taking EPP courses, students not only felt more positive in the present, but curious to learn more: "I want to know 'peace parable!'" (EPP1S25RP). Some envisage a bright future, one that includes new/additional English learning and skills: "Having Chance to be engaged in writing gave me more insights toward learning English. It was far beyond my preceded expectation. Now I want to take a step onto acquiring sophisticated conversational skills. I am delighted about having myself built a solid ground which will sustain my quntom leap toward another ground. throgh this class" (EPP1S1RP).

While students generally made peace with English and displayed attitudinal changes on self-reports, one contested area remained. At the midterm, a couple students communicated disappointment and showed a desire to further develop their language: "All material help me to improve my English writing skills, Just want to improve my grammar" (EPP1Q2), and "I want to more writing expressions! My writing skills are very boring" (EPP2Q2). Although EPP1 students completed language awareness tasks and improved their THICK feedback-giving ability (especially kindness), many could not easily give themselves or others helpful feedback on language accuracy. In EPP2, this kind of peer feedback was challenging for students, too. Even if students were quite pleased with the personalized feedback they received from their teacher, many had trouble editing work even with a correction guide. Similar comments did not appear on the final surveys. Nevertheless, as a result of this issue and observations of difficulty with form, the teacher modified language awareness tasks in EPP1 to have students systematically experiment with and compare freely available online editing tools. This proved helpful to a certain extent.

Summary of what worked:

- Generally, students developed their language proficiency and communication skills while learning about peace, learning to (make/build) peace, learning peacefully, and learning to make peace with English.
- Specifically, students developed their abilities to write and analyze writing in various genres and styles using strategies such as GRASP and FENS as well as to give THICK feedback.

Summary of challenges:

- Some students registered in EPP courses without having basic writing skills.
- Some students desired and needed more language-focused support than could be provided in class.

## Lessons Learned

Friedrich (2019) notes PL is sometimes met with cynicism and skepticism. When the teacher sought input for course titles from members of a PL group, most were supportive. A "critical friend," however, expressed the view that although the theme was important and EPP courses would be meaningful and original, the focus may be too specific. Moreover, it was pointed out that students' main goal might (only) be language proficiency. While perhaps valid for compulsory general English courses, feedback here has revealed that students were generally interested in and learned about peace, learned to (make/build) peace, learned peacefully, and learned to make peace with English as they improved aspects of their writing (and speaking) relative to their different starting levels.

Unequal comment distribution may indicate that students derived different benefits from the EPP courses. Certainly, one course cannot contribute fully to comprehensive peace and communicative peace. Together, the two courses offered greater access still, systematically developing more courses would enable going beyond the inner and interpersonal levels. Friedrich (2007) for one advocates for establishing a cross-curricular framework. Collectively, linguistics, language education, literature, and cultural studies departments could certainly contribute a lot to PLE.

While this innovation may be small scale for now, it need not be insignificant. Support comes in Galtung's (2008) wise words that "even if innovations are implemented only in one school or class, they can be valuable on a wider scale because of the demonstration effect" (p. 52). It seems that the first 47 EPP students have been mostly positively affected by their courses. If this report inspires other researchers, policy makers, educators, and activists, the impact may be felt more broadly.

# References

Birch, B. M. (Ed.). (2022). *Creating classrooms of peace in English language teaching*. Routledge.
Council of Europe. (2023). *The CEFR levels*. Retrieved August 30, 2023, from https://www.coe.int/en/web/common-european-framework-reference-languages/level-descriptions
Fisk, L. J. (1998). Underpinning a peace studies future. *Peace Research, 30*(4), 43–55.
Freire, P. (1970). *Pedagogy of the oppressed*. Penguin Books.
Freire, P. (1997). *Pedagogy of the heart*. Continuum.
Friedrich, P. (2007). *Language, negotiation, and peace: The use of English in conflict resolution*. Continuum.
Friedrich, P. (2019). *Applied linguistics in the real world*. Routledge.
Galtung, J. (1996). *Peace by peaceful means: Peace and conflict, development and civilization*. Sage.
Galtung, J. (2008). Form and content of peace education. In M. Bajaj (Ed.), *Encyclopedia of peace education* (pp. 49–58). IAP.
Gomes de Matos, F. (1987). Applied linguistics and the functions of peace in language education. *The Greek Journal of Applied Linguistics, 3*, 92–94.
Gomes de Matos, F. (1996). *Pedagogia da positividade: Comunicação construtiva em Português*. Universitária da UFPE.
Gomes de Matos, F. (2005). On communicative peace: Origins, goals, and applications. *Journal of Peace Education, 2*(2), 210–211.
Gomes de Matos, F. (2014). Peace linguistics for language teachers. *DELTA, 30*(2), 415–424.
Hall, G. (2011). *Exploring English language teaching: Language in action*. Routledge.
Jenkins, T. (2019). Comprehensive peace education. In. M. A. Peters (Ed.), *Encyclopedia of teacher education*. Springer.
Jung, S. K. (2011). Demotivating and remotivating factors in learning English: A case of low level college students. *English Teaching, 66*(2), 47–72.
KICE. (2023). *College scholastic ability test*. Retrieved August 30, 2023, from https://www.kice.re.kr/sub/info.do?m=0205&s=english

Kim, D. K. (2019). Issues of equity in Korean higher education: Academic deans' stances on the three-no's policy. In R. Chowdhury & L. K. Yazdanpanah (Eds.), *Identity, equity and social justice in Asia Pacific education* (pp. 167–183). Monash University Publishing.

Kim, T.-Y., & Kim, Y. (2016). EFL learning demotivation in the Korean context: Similarities and differences across school levels. *English Language & Literature Teaching, 22*(1), 135–156.

Kwon, S. K., Lee, M., & Shin, D. (2017). Educational assessment in the Republic of Korea: Lights and shadows of high-stake exam-based education system. *Assessment in Education: Principles, Policy & Practice, 24*(1), 60–77.

KOSIS. (2023). *Vital statistics of Korea.* Fertility rate. Retrieved August 30, 2023, from https://kosis.kr/statHtml/statHtml.do?orgId=101&tblId=DT_1B8000F&language=en

McInnis, D. J., & Wells, B. J. (1994). Peace education and its role in the EFL classroom. *Soka University Peace Research Institute Journal, 16*, 57–74.

Meddings, L., & Thornbury, S. (2009). *Teaching unplugged: Dogme in English language teaching.* Delta Publishing.

OECD. (2023). *Fertility rates* (indicator). https://doi.org/10.1787/8272fb01-en

O'Reilley, M. R. (1993). *The peaceable classroom.* Heinemann.

Oxford, R. L., Olivero, M. M., Harrison, M., & Gregersen, T. (2021). *Peacebuilding in language education: Innovations in theory and practice.* Multilingual Matters.

Roberts, B. J. (2020). *Conflict resolution training for the classroom: What every ESL teacher needs to know.* University of Michigan Press.

Rosenberg, M. B. (2015). *Nonviolent communication: A language of life* (3rd ed.). PuddleDancer Press.

Weigel, J. (Ed.). (2013). *To repair the world: Paul Farmer speaks to the next generation.* University of California Press.

Wright, J. (2023). Compassionate feedback. In Asmawi, A. B., Jacobs, J. M., Q. Guo, & Renandya, W. A. (Eds.), *Stories of teacher authenticity* (pp. 49–53). PeacheyPublications Ltd.

Wright, J. (2021, July 6). ELT Concept #12 – Communicative peace and (applied) peace linguistics. *Willy's ELT Corner.* Retrieved August 30, 2023, from https://willyrenandya.com/elt-concept-12-applied-peace-linguistics/?fbclid=IwAR2_k9MpgHhoKh9ovnHD3Wrxabzap8MaxPcxhhCT8nFdZfvv-

# 8

# Exploring Localized Adaptations of Critical Literacy Practices in Korean EFL Contexts

Young-Mee Suh and Seonmin Huh

## Rationale for an Innovative Instructional Model of Critical Literacy in EFL contexts

This book chapter introduces the need for localized adaptations of critical literacy practices in EFL educational contexts and argues that localized adaptations should balance educator, curriculum and learner factors toward development of critical literacies. This idea grows out of studies of critical literacies models (Bobkina & Stefanova, 2016; Janks, 2010; Lewison et al., 2008; Luke & Freebody, 1999) and two authors' ten-year empirical research into the pedagogy, teaching and the learning processes

Y.-M. Suh
Department of English Education, Hanyang University, Seoul, South Korea
e-mail: ymsuh012@hanyang.ac.kr

S. Huh (✉)
Division of English, General Education Center, Chungbuk National University, Cheongju, South Korea
e-mail: huhseonmin@cbnu.ac.kr

© The Author(s), under exclusive license to Springer Nature Switzerland AG 2025
H. Reinders et al. (eds.), *Innovation in Language Learning and Teaching*, New Language Learning and Teaching Environments,
https://doi.org/10.1007/978-3-031-83561-2_8

of critical literacies in Korean EFL contexts. We suggest the implementation of critical literacies that balances language development with expansion of critical thinking, integrating both rational and affective connections within the content of the curriculum, thus balancing individual cognitive growth with social growth as a citizen of international communities. This suggestion will contribute to successful localized adaption of critical literacy practices, as it invites an integrative and holistic method of implementing critical literacies to help learners grow linguistically, affectively, cognitively, and socially.

The word literacy does not only mean literacy in the narrow sense, but the word literacy is widely used in the context of emphasizing the acquisition and strengthening of newly required knowledge and competencies. Due to the rapid changes in the media environment, computers and communication, and artificial intelligence technologies, literacy education is essential for modern socioeconomic life and the functioning of democracy. Moreover, critical literacy skills, which are based on critical thinking and problem solving, are essential. Critical thinking is the process of analyzing, evaluating, and categorizing things rationally and logically, without being overcome by emotion, bias, or deference to authority. It is the process of comparing and examining situations in light of objective evidence, making cause and effect relationships clear, and drawing conclusions based on the judgment gained. It is a skill that helps us think best in any situation and is often referred to as a "survival skill", because it allows us to make good judgments and rational decisions. In other countries, critical thinking is so important that there is a lot of training to develop it.

Many scholars have defined what critical literacy is and we adopted the idea of critical literacy as a set of skills and competencies vital for engaging with diverse forms of information and media (Buckingham, 2003; Hobbs, 2010; Kellner & Share, 2005). Within our definition, critical literacies involve critical thinking, media literacy, digital literacy, and information literacy, enabling individuals to analyze, evaluate, and navigate complex information environments. These literacies empower individuals to question sources, assess biases, and understand cultural contexts, fostering informed and active participation in society. More specifically, for instance, when reading, readers should be able to "challenge not only propositional knowledge but also ideological assumptions in written texts" (Wallace, 1992, p. 60). According to Behrman (2006) and Huang (2011), readers should be critically aware that texts contain lexical and grammatical elements that are consciously chosen by the author to organize the content. Readers should recognize that the author's beliefs and values about the world are embedded in the text and think critically about its social context and ideology. Furthermore, readers are expected to engage in concrete, transformative action to change the world (Crookes, 2013; Janks, 2010). As such, the expectation of critical reading is that English language learners are not passive, receptive readers, but readers who have the capacity to critically engage with texts.

Critical literacy has a history of being marginalized from mainstream EFL literacy education and has been struggling to find its place. EFL literacy education usually centers around teaching and learning vocabulary, decoding, and reading comprehension (Ibrahim, 2022; Weng, 2023). EFL students focus on reading comprehension and decoding as those were often what they are tested for. They are expected to read texts for language learning and to accept texts rather than challenge them. In other words, they are expected to read and understand in a passive manner, and literacy education as a social practice has not been taught much in Korea where English is learned as a foreign language. Nowadays, however, EFL scholars have raised questions concerning how EFL literacy can find a space for critical literacy, when EFL learners need a strong focus on decoding and comprehension. Some empirical research on EFL critical literacy has started to be published and reported positive growth of students as critically literate beings. Some research argued that critical literacy can boost EFL learners' conventional, functional literacy skills with strong implications for EFL literacy education. For instance, Crookes (2013) reports that a critical approach to teaching EFL is "possible and do-able in all parts of the world, in South America, South Africa, Europe and East Asia" (p. 146), and there also have been a few reports of the application of critical EFL pedagogy in different educational systems in Asia; to name a few, China (Sun, 2019), Hong Kong (Wong et al., 2006), Iran (Ghahremani-Ghajar & Mirhosseini,

2005; Izadinia & Abednia, 2010; Rahimi, 2015), Israel (Hayik, 2015a, 2015b), Japan (Konoeda & Watanabe, 2008), Korea (Cho & Johnson, 2020; Huh & Suh, 2015, 2018; Kim, 2004; Kim & Cho, 2017; Shin & Crookes, 2005; Suh & Huh, 2014, 2017), Singapore (Kramer-Dahl, 2001; Kwek et al., 2007), and Taiwan (Huang, 2019; Ko, 2013; Ko & Wang, 2013; Kuo, 2009).

There are several models of critical literacy such as those put forward by The New London Group (1996), Luke and Freebody (1999), Cope and Kalantzis (2000), Lewison et al. (2008), Janks (2010), and Bobkina and Stefanova (2016). Firstly, Janks (2010)'s synthesis model of critical literacy education embedded the ideas of 'Domination, Access, Diversity, and Design'. The four concepts in this model are interdependent and integrated in instructional practice. Domination is about the view of "language, other symbolic forms, and discourse broadly, as a powerful means of maintaining and reproducing relations of domination (p. 23)." In this model, providing access to dominant forms and "different ways of reading and writing the world in a range of modalities (p. 24)" are important in terms of Access and Diversity. Requiring students to (re)generate numerous new meanings is also important in this model.

Next, Lewison et al. (2008) suggested an instructional model of critical literacy as follows:

> We see critical literacy instruction as a transaction among the personal and cultural resources we use, the critical social practices we enact, and the critical stance that we and our students take on in classrooms and in the world. (p. 5)

Personal and cultural resources include personal experience, social issues books, popular culture and media, textbooks, oral texts, student interests, and community issues.

Critical social practices include four dimensions: (1) disrupting the commonplace, (2) interrogating multiple viewpoints, (3) focusing on sociopolitical issues, and (4) taking action and promoting social justice. Critical stance also includes four dimensions: (1) consciously engaging, (2) entertaining alternate ways of being, (3) taking responsibility to inquire, and (4) being reflexive. The four dimensions are interrelated.

In other words, the critical literacy curriculum starts with students' personal knowledge, interests and issues. But even though it starts with the personal, it is always embedded in the social.

The models of critical literacy mentioned above are designed for implementing critical literacy with L1 or L2 English speakers. As we have tried to implement critical literacy in Korea, we realize that we need to have an instructional model of critical literacy, balancing conventional and critical literacies in EFL contexts. There are existing instructional models of critical literacy including conventional literacy in critical literacy instruction. Luke and Freebody's (1999) four resources model has components of conventional literacy skills such as code-breaking. The model places an emphasis on the development of the four major learner roles: code-breaker, meaning maker, text user and text analyst. As a code-breaker, learners are asked to complete decoding practice including phonics, word recognition, morphology and etymology. Secondly, as a meaning maker, the learners are asked to activate schema and predict what they are going to learn. They are also allowed to use comprehension strategies and guess the meaning of the new words. Thirdly, as a text user, the learners are taught to understand genre and what they can enact with texts. They also find, use, and respond to texts. Finally, as a text analyst, the learners place emphasis on understanding author's purposes, and how texts position them.

In a similar vein, Bobkina and Stefanova (2016) adopted four curricular components by Cope and Kalantzis (2000) and applied the model of critical thinking skills to their instruction. The adopted four curricular components are: situated practice, overt instruction, critical framing, and transformed practice. In the situated practice stage, the focus is on students' lives and experiences, their thoughts, opinions and expectations. No conscious reflection or metalanguage is used at this level. The students recall relevant knowledge and they are usually asked to participate in reader-response activities. In overt instruction, students are taught to understand general messages of the text and the various elements contributing to meaning are analyzed in detail. Critical framing involves connecting language with its social context and students are usually invited to teacher-directed discussion. Transformed practice refers to reshaping texts. What the students usually do at this level is to create their own text. The New London Group (1996) and Cope and Kalantzis (2000) suggested teaching metalanguage for skills-based learning as well as critical framing.

The studies just mentioned above considered conventional literacy in critical literacy instruction, but, the methods of balancing conventional and critical literacies have not been explored and theorized much in existing models of critical literacy. We believe that we need a more customized instructional model of critical literacy for EFL students and teachers. Huh's, 2016 research, titled *Instructional model of critical literacy in an EFL context: Balancing conventional and critical literacy*, was one of the efforts to introduce a model instructional approach to address both conventional and critical literacies in EFL reading class. She suggested three levels of engagement between the teacher and university students. Most of the interactions between a teacher and students in this model require starting from Level 1 where students discuss new vocabulary, read the texts, translate, and brainstorm what they already know about the topic. Then, these EFL learners personalize and socialize with the reading passages as a focus, through group discussion (Level 2). They summarize and synthesize what they read mainly to understand the authors' main idea or views and juxtapose that with their personal viewpoints. Level 3 involves critical engagement where students answer guided critical questions, identify underlying beliefs, and bring in alternative or missing perspectives. The emphasis is that the co-exitance of these three levels together can make EFL literacy education holistic. Level 1 is a prerequisite, especially with texts that challenge students in code-breaking. Level 3 needs a teacher's strong explicit guidance to engage students in reflection of ideological underpinnings and to help students understand what has been silenced and missing. While each level seems linearly progressive, depending on the level of difficulties of the texts and of familiarity with the topics, the lessons and students can freely jump around the levels. Each level helps the other levels be strengthened and balances conventional and critical literacies, boosting students' holistic growth as English literacy users. This model provides a groundwork for our thoughts on the EFL-specific instructional process of critical literacies. Based on this model, we conducted several empirical studies making efforts to implement critical literacy in Korea. This innovative process started from a preliminary study (Suh & Huh, 2014), and from this study, we believe action component and balancing criticality and affects should also be incorporated. We now turn to empirical studies that address this elaboration.

# Our Innovative Journey into Critical Literacy Instruction in Korea

## Finding a Room for Critical Literacy in the Dominance of Conventional Literacy

In Suh and Huh (2014), titled *Possibilities and challenges of a critical approach to reading instruction with Korean university students*, we introduced critical reading strategies to Korean EFL learners at universities in Seoul and Busan and reported the results of the instruction. The class was designed in two stages: Firstly, the students were invited to read texts in English by teaching one another in groups (reciprocal teaching). In the class, the students were encouraged to read English texts in a collaborative manner by asking about difficult parts to understand and helping one another achieve better comprehension. Secondly, they were encouraged to share their thoughts on the reading with critical perspectives. More specifically, they discussed what they thought of the issues in the text with the critical questions provided by the teacher. In the class, the teacher's role was mainly to provide comprehension questions followed by critical questions with the purpose of checking students' comprehension of the texts that they read and guiding them to express their thoughts about the issues in the texts with critical perspectives. At the beginning of the semester, the teachers initiated reading practices, but students took charge of reading practices at the end of the semester. The students selected their reading materials and presented how they read the text that they chose in terms of text comprehension and critical mode. The class revealed possibilities to implement a critical reading approach in EFL contexts. Most students reported that they were able to read English texts, beyond reading them line by line and translating them into their mother tongue of Korean. Collaborative reading in groups, teaching each other, was helpful and enabled them to increase their reading power. In addition, they enjoyed having opportunities to read texts in English with multiple perspectives, presenting different opinions from those of the authors. At the same time, the students reported some challenges that they had during the class. Foremost, they felt a burden to position themselves as readers with resistant perspectives. This is probably because Korean students tend to put much authority on the text. The students also felt uncomfortable sharing their opinions when they did not comprehend the texts well. Interestingly, they asked for more detailed guidance from the teachers on what to do in the reading class. Even though there is a line of thought that it is desirable not to provide specific guidelines to the students about ways to read text critically, the EFL students in our class want more specific guidance from the teacher.

What worked most effectively in this project in implementing critical literacy instruction was providing the students with time for vocabulary and comprehension checks in addition to time to summarize what they read. Teacher-initiated or student-collaborative reading in terms of text comprehension helped students get a sense of the social issues they came across, furthering their reading in a critical lens. What did not work well in this project was related to students' attitudes in discussing alternative perspectives. They often reported that it was tiresome to read with alternative perspectives and they tended to limit their discussion to the critical questions provided by the teacher. We learned from this study that a more balanced curriculum in terms of code-breaking and critiquing is needed in Korean educational settings. We also learned that making connections with students' personal experiences helped them open their minds and engage in the issues they dealt with. This led to Huh (2016)'s localized instructional model of critical literacy in EFL contexts—decoding and comprehension, personalizing and socializing with the reading, and critiquing and reflecting on the reading texts.

Suh and Huh (2017), titled *Korean university readers' growth through an integrated approach of conventional and critical literacy*, implemented a critical reading strategy of instruction based on Huh (2016)'s integrated model of conventional and critical literacy in an EFL context and Suh and Huh (2014)'s preliminary critical reading instruction. We designed a reading course based on the integrated model of three levels of engagement and implemented the model in each other's classes. We followed the same procedure when we taught our students in the course: decoding and comprehension, personalizing the reading contents, and critiquing and reflecting on the reading texts. In the classes, each teacher helped the students comprehend the texts that they read, analyze the texts critically, and engage in discussions around alternative perspectives of the reading. The analysis of the students' discussions and the teacher's observation notes revealed that the students became more strategic readers: for example, they were able to analyze the organization of the text and word choices, monitor their reading difficulties, and track the purposes, cultural biases, and beliefs in the texts. The students also emotionally engaged in what they read: they used emotionally charged words in their responses, connecting themselves to the texts through personal experiences and subjective feelings. Additionally, they emotionally connected with the target cultural groups for critical reflection on the social issues. Another theme that emerged was that they developed a critical stance about the writer's assumptions in the reading: they suggested alternative angles to interpret the social issues in the reading and took editors' positions to suggest what was missing from the texts. In addition, for presentations, they presented what they had discussed about the issues in the texts from a critical perspective and suggested better ways to present the issues to the class. This student-initiated reading practice assisted the students' abilities to take active stances on the issues.

This project was meaningful for us since it was revealed that it is useful for both teachers and students to follow the instructional model. As mentioned above, spending time on comprehension helped the students use not only cognitive strategies to figure out contents and organization but also metacognitive strategies to monitor themselves as readers. We also learned that it is possible to initiate critical reading by students and we need to follow the model in a flexible mode if we want students to practice as critical literate beings. More specifically, in one class, students were asked to select their own reading text regarding the issues that they dealt with in the class and present what they discussed in terms of missing perspectives and more democratic ways to present issues. This student-initiated reading practice was not implemented in the other class because students were satisfied with the readings in the class and were not willing to do further readings by themselves. More linguistically challenged students prefer to spend more time decoding and comprehending teacher's provided reading materials.

In addition, we realized that we need to be more careful choosing topics when designing critical literacy instruction. We dealt with several topics, including the Korean educational system, Asian sports, Western liberal education, and the American student loan system. The two former readings were familiar to the students whereas the other two were not. With the latter topics, we learned that it is important to spend more time to activate students' background knowledge and make connections with their personal experiences. For the next step, we would like to try a critical intercultural class with Korean elementary students. We believe it is important to raise critical intercultural citizenship in children, who often spend their time learning English in private institutes where they learn English by memorizing words, disseminating sentences, and being assessed by the teachers. We were also stimulated by critical literacy scholars (Crookes, 2013; Janks, 2010) who support action-provoking critical literacy, and we would like to see how students will react if we design and implement literacy classes focusing on action components in critical literacy education.

## Balancing Conventional Literacy and Critical Literacy to Contribute to Intercultural Citizenship

Our article (Huh & Suh, 2018), titled *Preparing elementary readers to be critical intercultural citizens through literacy education*, is our effort to connect critical literacy with intercultural citizenship education. In this project, we introduced a two-year critical citizenship literacy curriculum and suggested three pedagogical approaches for critical intercultural citizenship education. Dudley et al., (1999, p. 436) define critical citizenship literacy as "the capabilities that enable individuals to be active citizens who can negotiate the terms and practices of citizenship." In essence, it refers to the skills that empower individuals to engage as social agents, effectively navigating and influencing the principles and actions related to citizenship. This project challenges the commonplace celebratory intercultural education and nationalistic or civic responsibility-focused citizenship education to be more critical and socially agentic.

Furthering the commonplace intercultural education and civic education, this article provides concrete teaching pedagogies that can expand students' mindsets as intercultural citizens through critical literacy practices. Those teaching pedagogies are: dialoguing pedagogy, pedagogy of speaking for marginalized perspectives, and embracing pedagogy. Dialoguing pedagogy is the ways teacher encourage students to personalize the stories first, then have them think of experiences through dialoguing with each other and with book characters. Dialoguing pedagogy challenges students' personal thoughts and experiences. The pedagogy required for speaking for marginalized perspectives encourages actively searching for perspectives missing or marginalized from reading passages. Students identified the dominant cultural beliefs and rewrote new scripts with alternative beliefs included. This pedagogy visualized the dominant cultural beliefs and had students to challenge them, an important ability of intercultural citizens. Embracing pedagogy attempted to assist students to connect to physically and emotionally distant issues as though they were closer to their own, thus activating intercultural citizenship and relate to others, deepen their understanding and feelings of responsibility as intercultural citizens. Teachers encouraged students to activate their local knowledge and knowledge of the history of Korea within other contexts, write imaginative stories, and enact them as a way to elicit their intercultural understanding of other cultures. In this research we dealt with students' personal issues, the issues of familiar cultural stereotypes, distant social issues, and learned that each cultural issue needed discrete pedagogical facilitation. Depending on the familiarity of the cultural issues focused on, we need different teaching approaches of dialoguing pedagogy, pedagogy of speaking for marginalized perspectives, and embracing pedagogy.

Suh (2019), titled *A case study of critical reading in action with Korean university students in an EFL context*, elicited an action component in the critical literacy model developed in previous studies. The reading course was designed under the premise that it is important to actually participate in and take action for social change in critical pedagogy and the applicability of participatory critical pedagogy outside the classroom. The lessons progressed in three stages: (1) teacher modeling and student practice, (2) student-directed reading, and (3) student-initiated action. The reading class was managed in a flexible mode. In the first stage, the teacher introduced and modeled how to read texts critically. Then the students practiced critical reading with reading materials, which focused on the topics of gender roles and race selected by the teacher. In the second stage, students were allowed to select their own readings on similar issues. They discussed the readings in groups and were encouraged to ask and answer critical questions of one another to develop critical thinking as readers. In the final stage, students presented what they questioned about the readings and what they did as some form of educational action outside the classroom. The action project outcomes of the gender role readings included editing the article, a small campaign, a survey, and making a game to help women in financial crisis. Action project outcomes of the readings on race were a survey on race discrimination and reverse racism, making and distributing stickers, making a video and uploading it to YouTube, e-mailing the writer, donating to a funding group fighting race discrimination in the USA, sending SNS messages to friends, designing lesson plans about race discrimination, editing the article, and leaving YouTube comments. The class was a successful case of eliciting action components in a critical instructional model, as critical dialogue activities led students to come up with action-provoking questions about the readings and it brought about a variety of action outcomes. The students' responses to the class also revealed that they felt that they became more active readers with citizenships of the communities they belonged to by actually participating and taking action.

Conceptualizing critical literacies as developing active citizenship, we learned that action come in different forms and to different degrees. To elaborate, we learned that action does not always have to be connected to social activism, but raising students' critical consciousness about other cultural groups' histories and social injustice issues. In Huh and Suh (2018), we introduced how teacher pedagogy needs to be adjusted when addressing personally meaningful and familiar cultural topics to elicit students' positioning as intercultural citizens. Different teacher pedagogies worked to activate students' positioning as intercultural citizens using personally familiar topics including family life, school life, and gender representation as well as distant social issues of racism and apartheid in South Africa.

It was not possible to elicit some type of social action from elementary school students in the time allocated. This was because students tried to make sense of the materials in English and needed more time to digest and make sense of different life experiences and histories that are very different from their personal experiences. Especially with distant social issues, we feel that embracing pedagogy can be elaborated and developed more through empirical cases of this pedagogy to the level of social action. In the meantime, having elementary school students engage in understanding their own cultural knowledge, articulating boundaries, and being challenged to expand their comfort boundaries to reach out to other cultural groups' stories was one type of exercise in intercultural citizenship.

Different from Huh and Suh (2018), Suh (2019) showed diverse actions university students enacted. We observed that such diverse actions, resulted not only from critiquing the articles that they read with resistant perspectives, but also from empathizing and sympathizing with the ones who suffer. For instance, students felt sorry for their mothers or married women when they read an article about cooking and doing house chores mostly by women for family gatherings. Female students especially felt uncomfortable and irritated while reading about wage differences between men and women and felt pity for Afro-American girls who had difficulties in finding the right cosmetic colors for their skin. The students also felt injustice through discrimination against Asian students who wanted to be admitted to American colleges and felt very sorry for Islamic peoples and Afro-Americans who experienced discrimination in Seoul, Korea. They were willing to think hard about how they could democratize their society and fight these issues. With those observations, we agreed that it is necessary for us to invite students' feelings in the classroom. In addition, academic suggestions from Janks (2010) and

Leander and Ehret (2019) urging not only rationality but also affects in critical literacy education pushed us to design our next projects linking emotion to criticality.

## Critical Affective Pedagogy, Emotional Reading in Critical Reading

Two articles, *Critical affective pedagogy as a tool for holistic critical literacy practices* (Huh & Suh, 2020) and *Facing affects in an elementary level critical English literacy class: Utilizing affective turns in a critical literacy classroom* (Huh & Suh, 2021), discussed the important role of affects in critical literacy practices. Affects, especially negative affects, have been perceived as detrimental for language learning. Critical literacy education has emphasized rational approaches to engage in criticality and has not considered affective approaches to be useful. The two studies introduced here suggest another way to holistically engage in critical literacy practices and claim that critical literacy practices should be balanced between rationality and affects.

In the first research paper, *Critical affective pedagogy as a tool for holistic critical literacy practices,* critical affective literacy was taught. Native Americans and slaves in American history were the target topics. The example of a literacy activity is writing imaginative scripts between the characters from the books students have read and having students articulate their affective responses about the book characters' experiences. Students were invited to re-write the scripts to be critically and affectively more inclusive in diverse perspectives. Another literacy activity included asking critical questions to challenge the stories' main characters after engaging with their affects. Affects become strong resources for students to imagine other people's life experiences and a way students could further their critical reflections on the social issues. Critical affective pedagogy therefore helps us not to depend on rational criticality but to bring in affects, thus balancing both rationality and affectivity in critical literacy practices.

The second article, *Facing affects in an elementary level critical English literacy class: Utilizing affective turns in a critical literacy classroom*, elaborated on the notion of 'literacies in motion' (Leander & Ehret, 2019) to consider affective turns in literacy education. Affective turns are conceptualized as focusing on contradictory, unsettled, and holistic experiences and is connected to 'literacies in motion,' enacting literacies to vigilantly seek meanings. The nature of maneuverability is crucial to trouble our comfortable affects and meanings, that is, "undo" settled emotions and meanings (Massumi, 2002, p. 3). This act of 'undo' helped student see what could otherwise be, thus critically reflect on power dynamics and try to envision a better world. One student's literacies in motion have been captured to understand how complex affects interacted with his emerging meanings, mixing his affects with others in the present and imaginative worlds of book characters. Capturing those holistic intermingling of affects showed us his possible maneuvering across different cultural borders to fully understand other cultural groups' experiences. In this sense, 'literacies in motion' helps with maneuverability, capturing the invisible literacy engagement and helps us think of literacies as always moving and sometimes unclear, contradictory, and uninterpretable. At the same time, encouraging these active 'literacies in motion,' students can be always open for different meanings and would less likely think of their own meanings and meanings at the moment to be settled without questioning them. Critical affective pedagogy invites different literacy practices and helps us capture non-represented affective domains for critical literacy.

Suh (2023), titled *A case study of critical emotional literacy instruction in an EFL English reading class*, was a study to extend the boundary of knowledge in terms of balancing rationality and affects in critical literacy education at the tertiary level. The assumption of critical emotional literacy instruction is based on innovative thoughts on literacy education: Students not only need to cultivate critical thinking but also to develop emotional competence to reflect on their own feelings and to empathize with the feelings of others. Put differently, students should not only identify facts in the text but also have an emotional and critical attitude toward the text. The reading topics utilized in this research were about gender discrimination in the workplace and gender roles at home, and only newspaper articles were selected for reading texts. The activity that the students did in class was to discuss the texts with critical and emotional stances. Critical stances included: thinking about the purpose of writing, analyzing the characteristics of a text, understanding the author's point of view, identifying the author's bias on an issue in the text, and thinking of a more democratic way to deal with the issue. Emotional stances students used were as follows: making an emotional connection to what they read, examining the reasons for their feelings, understanding how others feel, analyzing how emotions are created and circulated, and thinking about ways to realize social justice regarding the issue. The main role of the teacher was to help the discussion take place in a flexible and cyclical manner, so that the discussion from a critical point of view could proceed to sharing emotions in class and vice versa. At the beginning of the course, students had difficulty understanding the emotions of others. Students had little experience recognizing the involvement of emotions in reading texts. They were used to reading texts without emotional involvement, so recognizing their own feelings about the texts and understanding the feelings of others was unfamiliar and difficult. Through reading multiple texts and trying to share their feelings about the texts, however, they were even able to come up with solutions to the issues revealed in the texts. To be more concrete, the beginning of emotional connection to the read article began when it was linked to personal experience on the issues. In the readings, students perceived "the suffered" as female rather than male. They often felt conflicting emotions (for example, denial vs. acceptance) of the issue in the reading and used negative emotional expressions (especially, negative emotional adjectives) frequently in sharing their emotions toward the reading. The expression of emotions associated with personal experiences appeared to be created and circulated as other emotions. The circulation of individual emotions formed empathy at a higher level through sharing the circulation of emotions felt from other students, and furthermore, they came to think about the source of the problem and its solution. The emotional engagement with issues in readings contributed to the students becoming more active in discussing missing perspectives and helped them become more balanced in thinking about the issues that they had read. In this way, it is possible to help students have more balanced perspectives on what they read, which further helps them transform into active readers and suggest ways to realize social justice for the issues that the articles discussed.

We learned that we can open a potential to activate students' affects to engage in critical literacies. In these projects, students were asked to focus on their affects about different social justice issues. In the process, we learned that encouraging positive affects in English classes can open students' capacity to face uncomfortable, unpleasant issues, and letting students feel okay to reflect, unpack, and observe their negative affects can help them use those negative affects to critically interpret social issues. Because affective dimension helped students trouble their commonplace thoughts and ideas and always seek alternative meanings in their literacy engagement, it can be an effective way to broaden students' critical literacy practices.

It is not without struggle to address students' negative affects. Elementary school students were emotionally vulnerable and sometimes felt overwhelmed with facing negative affects productively. Teachers did not want to hurt their affects and needed to be careful when introducing critical affective pedagogy. With university students, it is also not easy for the teacher to assist the students in addressing their negative affects. The students did have difficulties revealing their conflicting and negative affects and building their affects together with the issues they deal with in the class. The teacher, therefore, had to use the guidance questions to circulate their negative affects. On the whole, connecting negative affects with critical literacy development is not always a smooth path.

# What We Have Learned from Our Journey

## EFL-Specific Pedagogical Requirements

Successful localized adaptation of critical literacy practices encourages an individualized EFL-specific pedagogical model of critical literacy and requires specific alteration from the existing critical literacy models that are mostly created by scholars researching first language education or ESL education settings. Considering the double goals of teaching language and critical literacy practices, EFL educators should approach critical literacy education differently. To elaborate, teachers should not fail to address language goals and goals for critical literacy at the same time. EFL students should have an opportunity to engage in decoding, comprehension, critical analysis and social action to be critically literate beings in English, a foreign language. The existing models of critical literacy have focused on developing students' capacities for criticality, raising critical awareness and social action with less emphasis on language development or with first language and literacy learning in mind (Bobkina & Stefanova, 2016; Janks, 2010; Lewison et al., 2008). Luke and Freebody's (1999) four resources model addressed code-breaking, language learning requirement. We argue the importance of code-breaking even further for EFL education and suggest balancing conventional literacy, that is skill-based instruction, with development of critical literacy. When two pedagogical approaches are well-balanced, students have opportunities to be exposed to holistic literacy education.

Related to this, teachers' roles should also be thought through because EFL students have traditionally experienced dominantly conventional literacy education and students can feel disoriented and lost with critical literacy components. For EFL critical literacy education, we suggest gradual and explicit guidance from teachers when introducing critical literacies. Students show stronger ownership and initiation as they experience greater exposure to the critical literacy and social action portions of the curriculum, after teachers have guided them explicitly and gradually. Our studies suggest a gradual increase of students' participation and initiation and we utilize familiar topics first and then gradually engaged students in reading, writing about and discussing distant social issues. Teachers intervened a lot for linguistically challenging materials in the process. For familiar topics and easier language, students were successful in initiating and were immediately ready to engage in critical literacy. Instead of emphasizing student-centered interaction and teacher's intervention as less desirable, well-localized EFL-specific models of critical literacy should perceive the role of teachers to be more about flexible and active, dancing across the continuum of dominant discussion leader and minimal intervener of student discussion. The dynamic nature of teachers' role is required, to achieve both linguistic and critical goals.

Overall, we suggest that learners' factor in being able to learn language as well as expanding their thoughts regarding target contents. Students should grow in both conventional and critical literacies. Lack of exposure to both approaches in a balanced manner could limit their holistic literacy practices. Instead of thinking of conventional and critical literacies as discrete processes, they should be integrated in EFL literacy learning and implemented together to help develop students' English literacy skills as well as their critical intercultural citizenship skills.

A careful choice of discussion topics and degree of language difficulty is required. The topics should range from the those that are personally meaningful and relevant to the topics that challenge students' comfort zones and expand their linguistic knowledge and cultural boundaries at the same time. To overcome linguistic difficulties, it is important to find appropriate materials that are manageable for EFL students, such that they can break the codes and comprehend the contents. When the materials were too challenging for students, students could not move onto critical literacy practices.

## Broadening the Notion of Social Action in Critical Literacy

Previous research (Byram et al., 2017; Crookes, 2013; Janks, 2010; Lewison et al., 2008; Pandya & Avila, 2014) put an emphasis on transformative actions in critical literacy education. In Janks (2010), several social actions such as a letter-writing campaign for children with special dietary needs, the seed garden project and an alphabet book produced by teachers and their students were introduced. Other specific social actions in students' local contexts in previous research include searching for information on the internet, recycling, drawing, audit trail of learning, surveying, writing a letter to the librarian, school posters, Facebook comments, awareness-raising leaflets, and collaborative advertisements for peace. Those actions previously mentioned were completed in Argentina, Australia, Canada, South Africa, and the USA, but there is little reporting on social actions in critical literacy education in the EFL context.

Based on previous first language and ESL critical literacy models which include action components in critical literacy, we thought that critical literacy education in the EFL context should also include social action components. The university students participated in the critical reading with action research that dealt with two topics in their class, gender and race. Student-initiated actions after raising critical awareness and/or emotionally engaging with the topics included editing the article, e-mailing, small campaign (such as distributing stickers), survey, making a game, donating, YouTube activity, and SNS activity. We think that our efforts to broaden the portion of social action in critical literacy education with university students was successful since the students did become involved in specific actions aimed at assisting people in need, as related to the issues that they had discussed in a class. Their actions were small but community-sensitive, and those actions showed possibilities of connecting critical mode to action mode in critical literacy practices in an EFL context. One important thing, however, is that teachers need to guide students gradually to access the action process, and taking action isn't solely tied to participating in social activism. It can involve raising awareness of historical and social injustice issues within different cultural groups as our project with elementary kids revealed. Transformed action can manifest in various forms and intensities.

## Seeking Possibilities for Balancing Affects and Criticality

Our research tries to expand the scope of students' growth in both the rational dimension of criticality and the affective dimension. We believe that students' engagement with both their rational criticality and affects, being ready to be vulnerable linguistically, cognitively, and affectively, would introduce more than one way to enact critical literacies. The importance of balancing criticality with affects has been unpacked and concrete teaching strategies, curriculum layouts and teachers-student interactions explicitly discussed. Previous research on critical literacy has had a strong emphasis on the notion of criticality as one type of rationality, which implies detaching students' affects from critical engagements and being objective about target social issues without personal and affective interpretations. However, our studies indicate that affects, both positive and negative ones, contribute to students' understanding of others with different cultural perspectives and at deeper levels. Students' inner observations of their own affects, imagining what other people would have felt in those social injustice situations and juxtaposing them with their own affects have also contributed to students' critical reflection and strong connections to distant social issues. Even with those issues that were close to their everyday life experiences, focusing on rational analysis as well as affective analysis contributed to students' disruption of their own personal and cultural boundaries. This serves as strong evidence of developing intercultural citizenship and embracing more than one way of being in the world. Within this framework of analysis, affects should be welcomed and invited to boost students' critical literacy practices and should be an important component of a critical literacy educational model.

We also discovered that the implementation of affects may sometimes be overwhelming and not work well. The reason for this is the students' discomfort and vulnerability when opening up their affects and sharing, which is something Korean university students were not used to doing in Korean settings. The therapeutic approach to affective literacy education was difficult to implement and the researcher had to adjust her approach to make it more manageable for Korean university learners. In this sense, we believe that critical affective literacy should also be locally meaningful, and with specific pedagogical adjustments. Simplifying the critical questions and focusing on having a conversation rather than disclosing extremely difficult or vulnerable affects were important in our local contexts.

On the whole, as Janks (2010) claims, it is hard to change our pedagogic habitus, and we had a hard time changing our familiar ways of teaching literacy to critical literacy education. It was new, bothersome, and challenging to position ourselves as teachers moving beyond conventional language teachers. At the same time, however, we wanted to change and embody critical practices into our own educational contexts. The projects we introduced in this chapter reveal our effort to become comfortable with the new pedagogic habitus, pursuing students' language development, criticality, affectivity, and social action at the same time.

## Where Do We Go from Here?

In this chapter, we reconsidered the existing models of critical literacy suggested by Western scholars and suggested a linguistically, affectively, cognitively holistic integrative approach to the teaching of critical literacy in EFL context. This suggestion arrived at from the necessity of having a specific critical literacy model in an EFL context, contextually adaptable in South Korea. We argue that an innovative critical literacy model in EFL contexts should have a conventional literacy instruction component but also be holistic in nature, connecting personal engagement and action with a critical stance. This argument expands the notions of the critical literacy model in previous research in the sense that it includes critical thinking, sympathizing, or empathizing with others' emotions, social-political action, awareness of action, and language development. We expect this idea to be adaptable, localized, personalized, and contextualized in different educational situations in EFL contexts. In South Korea, we explored the challenges and possibilities required to instruct critical literacy skills in classes (mostly reading) at the primary level and the tertiary level with young age learners and adult learners. For the last decade, in the Korean EFL context, we documented what we experienced and what we learned as language teachers and researchers while implementing critical literacy instruction in Korea.

We hope the reports in this chapter will provide insights to readers who are interested in critical literacy instruction in EFL contexts. As previously mentioned, we learned that teachers' roles are very important in successfully implementing critical literacy instruction in the EFL context. Teacher factors include providing critical questions and guidance as students often feel uncomfortable, resistant, and tiresome when they were asked to take critical stances. Teachers need to gradually guide students to move from disrupting the commonplace to taking action promoting social justice. It is desirable for teachers to model first in critical literacy instruction, and then this should be followed by a student-initiated and centered mode with their own critical questions. It is desirable to prepare an explicit, teacher-initiated critical literacy curriculum in an EFL context. Critical literacy teachers also need to prepare structured curriculums in terms of topics, texts, teaching materials, and designing processes. On the other hand, learner factors that play important roles in successfully implementing critical literacy in an EFL context are willingness to cross cultural borders and understand others' thoughts and emotions in different cultures to develop global intercultural citizenship, in addition to broadening the spectrum of the meaning of action in critical literacy. EFL students should be exposed to conventional literacy education as well as critical literacies through the lens of criticality and affects, desirably followed by a social-action project. On the whole, the learners in our classes showed positive possibilities to position themselves as learners balancing affect, logic, and language development in the localized adaptation we suggested.

Finally, we are hopeful that readers will be able to plan and implement better lessons based on the ideas and experiences shared in this chapter and support their students to develop critical literacy skills. While implementing critical literacy in conventional language classes in Korea, we came up with a number of discussion questions which will help broaden the scope of future studies. We would like to encourage readers to think about the following discussion questions and find their own answers, making links with what we have introduced in this chapter and developing a clearer understanding of critical literacy instruction in EFL contexts.

- What topics in your local contexts can you bring into your critical literacy curriculum?
- Do you like to include familiar local and culture-specific topics in your lessons? Are you willing to consider unfamiliar topics to challenge your students? How do you balance the continuum of familiarity and unfamiliarity of discussion topics?
- Do you have appropriate materials that balance both language development and critical literacy development simultaneously? How do

you use materials for the dual purposes of language development and critical literacies?
- How do you access the materials in your local contexts to develop your students conventional, critical and affective literacy skills? How do you use the materials to help students develop both conventional, critical and affective literacies?
- How do you organize your literacy curriculum? What teaching approaches do you implement? When your curricular goals include developing holistic literacy users, what curriculum components should be improved and what new teaching approaches should be considered further?
- What are your ideas of explicit, dominant teacher guidance for your students' holistic literacy skills? Do you think teacher domination to be positive or detrimental for your students' growth as literate beings? Why or why not?
- What appropriate teaching activities and strategies (reflecting, disrupting, inviting multiple perspectives) can be used for your critical literacy curriculum?

Our research focused on critical literacies centering on reading and writing classes. The notion of critical literacies encompasses, however, broader concepts of media literacy, multimodal literacies and information literacies. We want to suggest future research to address the dynamic nature of critical literacies and participants' ways of making meaning from different modes of literacies and their maneuvers to develop critical literacies skills. Inclusion of broader concepts of literacies would require research methodologies and data analytic frames to be multimodal as well. Our studies dealt with cultural issues of family, school, gender difference, racism, educational and cultural discrimination. On the other hand, as society transforms, new social and political issues can and should be addressed. Locally meaningful topics should also be actively reflected in future research. We suggest future researchers actively look for local issues, diversify their critical literacies research topics, and consider new social and political issues that reflect social transformation. Furthermore, we were uncomfortable with being too revolutionary and included politically sensitive topics, such as South and North Koreas and dealing with ideological diversity in our class discussion. We believe our students as well as we, teachers and researchers, were pioneering EFL critical literacy research and it was not easy to include politically sensitive issues. In this sense, how to address locally sensitive political issues in critical literacy research should also be a part of researchers' journey in this field. Both researchers went through our emotional, affective struggles and had to deal with the identity conflicts of being EFL language teachers and critical literacies educators. We wrestled with the ideas of what it means to be an EFL language teacher with commitment of addressing critical literacies in our local context. Our stories could be documented through the lens of ethnography research methodology to inform other EFL critical literacies educators and researchers. This type of teacher identity research should add important insights in the future. Our research focused on elementary and university levels, as the dominant educational frame for adolescent groups in Korea centered around high-stake testing and these groups were not accessible for more innovative research projects. We need future research to investigate the possibilities of critical literacies education with adolescent groups and learn about the teaching and learning processes with broader age groups.

# References

Behrman, E. H. (2006). Teaching about language, power, and text: A review of classroom practices that support critical literacy. *Journal of Adolescent & Adult Literacy, 49*(6), 490–498.
Buckingham, D. (2003). *Media education: Literacy, learning, and contemporary culture*. Polity Press.
Bobkina, J., & Stefanova, S. (2016). Literature and critical literacy pedagogy in the EFL classroom: Towards a model of teaching critical thinking skills. *Studies in Second Language Learning and Teaching, 6*(4), 677–696.
Byram, M., Golubeva, I., Hui, H., & Wagner, M. (Ed.) (2017). *From principles to practice in education for intercultural citizenship*. Multilingual Matters.
Cho, H., & Johnson, P. (2020). Racism and sexism in superhero movies: Critical race media literacy in the Korean high school classroom. *International Journal of Multicultural Education, 21*(2), 66–86.

Cope, B., & Kalantzis, M. (2000). *Multiliteracies: Literacy learning and the design of social futures*. Routledge.
Crookes, G. V. (2013). *Critical ELT in action: Foundations, promises, praxis*. Routledge.
Dudley, J., Robinson, J., & Taylor, A. (1999). Educating for an inclusive democracy: Critical citizenship literacy. *Discourse: Studies in the cultural politics of education, 20*, 427–441.
Ghahremani-Ghajar, S., & Mirhosseini, S. A. (2005). English class or speaking about everything class? Dialogue journal writing as a critical EFL literacy practice in an Iranian high school. *Language, Culture and Curriculum, 18*(3), 286–299.
Hayik, R. (2015a). What does this story say about females? Challenging gender-biased texts in the English-language classroom. *Journal of Adolescent & Adult Literacy, 59*(4), 409–419.
Hayik, R. (2015b). Diverging from traditional paths: Reconstructing fairly tales in the EFL classroom. *Diaspora, Indigenous, and Minority Education, 9*(4), 221–236.
Hobbs, R. (2010). *Digital and media literacy: A plan of action*. The Aspen Institute.
Huang, S. (2011). Reading "Further and beyond the text": Student perspectives of critical literacy in EFL reading and writing. *Journal of Adolescent & Adult Literacy, 55*(2), 145–154.
Huang, S. (2019a). EFL learners' critical multimodal reflections on the politics of English. *TESOL Journal, 10*(3), 1–17.
Huh, S. (2016). Instructional model of critical literacy in an EFL context: Balancing conventional and critical literacy. *Critical Inquiry in Language Studies, 13*(3), 210–235.
Huh, S., & Suh, Y.-M. (2015). Becoming critical readers of graphic novels: Bringing graphic novels into Korean elementary literacy lessons. *English Teaching, 70*(1), 123–149.
Huh, S., & Suh, Y.-M. (2018). Preparing elementary readers to be critical intercultural citizens through literacy education. *Language Teaching Research, 22*(5), 532–551.
Huh, S., & Suh, Y.-M. (2020). Critical affective pedagogy as a tool for holistic critical literacy practices. *Journal of Language Sciences, 27*(4), 215–237.
Huh, S., & Suh, Y.-M. (2021). Facing affects in an elementary level critical English literacy class: Utilizing affective turns in a critical literacy classroom. *English Language Teaching, 33*(4), 45–61.

Ibrahim, N. K. (2022). *Critical literacy approach to English as a foreign language: From theory to practice*. Springer.
Izadinia, M., & Abednia, A. (2010). Dynamics of an EFL reading course with a critical literacy orientation. *Journal of Language and Literacy Education, 6*(2), 51–67.
Janks, H. (2010). *Literacy and power*. Routledge.
Kellner, D., & Share, J. (2005). Critical media literacy is not an option. *Learning Inquiry, 3*(2), 59–69.
Kim, S., & Cho, H. (2017). Reading outside the box: Exploring critical literacy with Korean preschool children. *Language and Education, 31*(2), 110–129.
Kim, Y. M. (2004). Critical reading practice for EFL readers. *Foreign Languages Education, 11*(2), 47–76.
Ko, M. (2013). A case study of an EFL teacher's critical literacy teaching in a reading class in Taiwan. *Language Teaching Research, 17*(1), 91–108.
Ko, M., & Wang, T. (2013). EFL learners' critical literacy practices: A case study of four college students in Taiwan. *The Asia-Pacific Education Researchers, 22*(3), 221–229.
Konoeda, K., & Watanabe, Y. (2008). Task-based critical pedagogy in Japanese EFL classrooms. In M. Montero, P. C. Miller, & J. L. Watzke. (Eds.), *Readings in language studies* (vol. 1; pp. 45–61). International Society for Language Studies.
Kramer-Dahl, A. (2001). Importing critical literacy pedagogy: Does it have to fail? *Language and Education, 15*(1), 14–32.
Kuo, J. (2009). Critical literacy and a picture-book-based dialogue activity in Taiwan. *Asia Pacific Education Research, 10*(4), 483-494.
Kwek, D., Albright, J., & Kramer-Dahl, A. (2007). Building teachers' creative capacities in Singapore's English classrooms: A way of contesting pedagogical instrumentality. *Literacy, 41*(2), 71–79.
Leander, K. M., & Ehret, C. (Eds.). (2019). *Affect in literacy learning and teaching: Pedagogies, politics and coming to know*. Routledge.
Lewison, M., Leland, C., & Harste, J. C. (2008). *Creating critical classrooms: Reading and writing with an edge*. Routledge.
Luke, A., & Freebody, P. (1999). A map of possible practices: Further notes on the four resources model. *Practically Primary, 4*(2), 5–8.
Massumi, B. (2002). *Parables for the virtual: Movement, affect, sensation*. Duke University Press.
Pandya, J. Z., & Avila, J. (Eds.). (2014). *Moving critical literacies forward: A new look at praxis across contexts*. Routledge.

Rahimi, A. (2015). Why does critical literacy hit a snag in the Iranian EFL setting? *Colombian Applied Linguistics Journal, 17*(1), 53–63.

Shin, H., & Crookes, G. (2005). Exploring the possibilities for EFL critical pedagogy in Korea—a two-part case study. *Critical Inquiry in Language Studies, 2*(2), 113–138.

Suh, Y.-M. (2019). A case study of critical reading in action with Korean university students in an EFL context. *English Teaching, 74*(4), 225–248.

Suh, Y.-M. (2023). A case study of critical emotional literacy instruction in an EFL English reading class. *Studies in British and American Language and Literature, 148*, 165–192.

Suh, Y.-M., & Huh, S. (2014). Possibilities and challenges of a critical approach to reading instruction with Korean university students. *English Language Teaching, 26*(3), 39–62.

Suh, Y.-M., & Huh, S. (2017). Korean university readers' growth through an integrated approach of conventional and critical literacy. *English Teaching, 72*(4), 23–51.

Sun, L. (2019). Words & actions: An EFL teacher's critical literacy goals and their enactment in a reading class in China. *Multicultural Education, 26*(3–4), 10–16.

The New London Group. (1996). A pedagogy of multiliteracies: Designing social futures. *Harvard Educational Review, 66*(1), 60–92.

Wallace, C. (1992). Critical literacy awareness in the EFL classroom. In N. Fairclough. (Ed.), *Critical language awareness* (pp. 59–92). Longman.

Weng, T. (2023). Creating critical literacy praxis: Bridging the gap between theory and practice. *RELC Journal, 54*(1), 197–207.

Wong, P.-Y.C., Chan, C.-W., & Firkins, A. (2006). School-based critical literacy program in a Hong Kong secondary school. *Hong Kong Teachers' Centre Journal, 5*(1), 129–139.

# 9

# Content and Language Integrated Programs at a Korean Science and Engineering University

Eun Gyong Kim

## Area of Innovation

Korean colleges and universities, including tertiary science and engineering schools, started offering English-medium instruction (EMI) classes in the 1990s. The number of EMI-offering institutions soared in the mid-2000s, when the Korean government aggressively promoted EMI in higher education (Byun & Kim, 2011). While Korean universities' interest in EMI has begun to wane, EMI still has a strong presence in science and engineering schools. At Ulsan National Institute of Science and Technology, all the classes are conducted in English, and at Korea Advanced Institute of Science and Technology (KAIST), 75% of the undergraduate courses and 63% of the graduate courses are offered using EMI (Registrar's, 2022).

---

E. G. Kim (✉)
School of Digital Humanities and Computational Social Sciences, Korea Advanced Institute of Science and Technology, Daejeon, South Korea
e-mail: egkim@kaist.ac.kr

This chapter discusses innovative content-language integrated classes at KAIST. It is indicated as *innovative* in the sense that such classes have not been implemented at other science and engineering schools in Korea. KAIST is one of the most reputable institutions in Korea: it has been ranked highest among Korean institutions in world university ranking systems (QS, 2023). It was established by the Korean government in 1971. The size of the student population is 11,515: 3,880 undergraduates and 7,635 graduates (KAIST, 2023). It consists of 5 colleges of Natural Sciences, Life Science and Bioengineering, Engineering, Liberal Arts and Convergence Science and Business, 7 schools, 13 graduate schools, and 27 departments, including Mechanical Engineering, Electrical Engineering, Civil and Environmental Engineering, and Computing.

Schmidt-Unterberger (2018) classified EMI teaching in higher education into five different types: 1. Pre-sessional ESP/EAP, 2. Embedded ESP/EAP, 3. Adjunct ESP, 4. EMI, and 5. ICLHE. Pre-sessional ESP/EAP courses prepare students with discipline-specific language skills (ESP: English for specific purposes) or academic language and study skills (EAP: English for academic purposes) before they start their academic program. In Embedded ESP/EAP, content and language instructors collaborate to create a course that caters to the specific linguistic demands of a subject area and that is part of a regular curriculum or academic program. Adjunct ESP is offered in connection with a particular content course, and language teaching is specific towards the needs of that course. In EMI classes, instructors teach their subject content in English without an explicit objective of language teaching or developing students' English ability. ICLHE, or Integrating Content and Language in Higher Education, classes aim for both the students' acquisition of content and the development of language skills. Full content-language integration requires language instructors' active involvement in curriculum design and course delivery and may be difficult to achieve in higher education.

The two innovative classes with a content-language integrated approach at KAIST are referred to as Adjunct ESP for undergraduate students and Embedded ESP/EAP for graduate students. For an investigation of the two EMI-related language programs, data were collected through questionnaire surveys from students who had taken either the adjunct undergraduate ESP classes or those who had been enrolled in the graduate ESP scientific writing courses. Also, email or online interviews with the content and EFL (English as a foreign language) professors involved in the development and offering of the undergraduate and graduate courses, teaching assistants, and students were conducted. In addition, performance measurements such as graduate students' pretest and posttest scores were collected. Furthermore, course materials, such as syllabi, lesson materials, and test materials, were collected.

For data analysis, text analysis was used for the written responses of the questionnaire surveys and interview data, and descriptive statistics for the survey data and test scores. Content analysis was done on course materials.

# Adjunct ESP Classes for Undergraduate Students

## Impetus for the Innovation

KAIST was the first Korean institution to implement an all-out EMI policy at the undergraduate level: the school required the class of 2007 to take all their classes in English with only a few exceptions. It was a radical approach to EMI teaching as no other Korean institutions had taken such an extensive EMI policy. Presently, 83.6% of the undergraduate classes are conducted in English, while the percentage of EMI classes at 13 other major universities in Korea is on average 19.9% (Nam & Gwag, 2019).

In implementing such a sweeping, comprehensive EMI policy, students' lack of English proficiency for EMI has consistently been identified as the major issue at the university. The vast majority of the undergraduate students at KAIST are Koreans who are not fluent speakers of English and are also graduates of specialized science high schools, where excellence in mathematics and natural sciences, not language education, is of primary importance (Kim, 2017). Moreover, Korean students in general are rarely exposed to EMI teaching until high school. For these reasons, most KAIST undergraduates feel linguistically inadequate in EMI classes.

In order to help students with the lowest English ability to improve their academic English skills, the EFL office at the university started an extensive pre-sessional EAP program in 2014. The program is offered in multiple levels in four English language skills and has had successful outcomes. Students' course evaluations have shown high levels of satisfaction over the EFL courses with an average score of 4.58 out of 5.00 between 2020 and 2022 (Table 9.1). Moreover, it has shown that undergraduate students' performance in all EFL courses, measured by the differences between the pretest and posttest scores, improved by 17% on average during the same period (Table 9.2).

EFL professors, however, realized that many students were still having trouble in EMI classes essentially because of their lack of language skills needed for their subject content. In order to introduce integrated content and language learning, the EFL office reached out to several departments

Table 9.1 Students' evaluations of EFL courses (5.00)

| Year | 2020 | | 2021 | | 2022 | | Average |
|---|---|---|---|---|---|---|---|
| Semester | Spring | Fall | Spring | Fall | Spring | Fall | |
| Enrollment in EFL courses | 1296 | 1026 | 1217 | 1049 | 1253 | 1101 | 1157 |
| Number of EFL courses | 68 | 59 | 69 | 59 | 66 | 63 | 64 |
| Average | 4.58 | 4.57 | 4.60 | 4.50 | 4.68 | 4.57 | 4.58 |

Table 9.2 Differences (%) in pre- and post-test scores (by year) among undergraduate EFL courses

| Year | Int. speaking & listening | Int. reading & writing | Presentation & discussion | Advanced listening | Advanced writing | Advanced reading | Average |
|---|---|---|---|---|---|---|---|
| 2020 | 28.31 | 18.93 | 16.07 | 5.48 | 17.78 | 10.72 | 16.22 |
| 2021 | 27.66 | 26.11 | 31.43 | 10.41 | 15.79 | 6.23 | 19.61 |
| 2022 | 17.84 | 20.52 | 17.19 | 4.73 | 22.87 | 6.70 | 14.98 |
| Average | 24.60 | 21.85 | 21.56 | 6.87 | 18.81 | 7.88 | 16.94 |

to start collaboration with content professors. Unfortunately, no departments came forward with their willingness to collaborate. Semester-long commitment from content professors and their departments was difficult to attain. Instead, the EFL office decided to implement Adjunct ESP classes as part of an intensive English program called the Academic English camp for the newly admitted in 2018.

## What Has Been Done

Five 101 courses in biology, chemistry, computer programming, mathematics, and physics for first-year students were chosen for Adjunct ESP. The class was developed following Coyle's 4Cs Conceptual Framework (Coyle, 2007). 4Cs refer to content, communication, cognition, and culture. Content is related to subject matter; communication, language; cognition, learning and thinking; and culture, social awareness of self and otherness. In the Framework, interrelationship and integration among the 4Cs are underscored: acquiring subject knowledge (content) entails learning and thinking (cognition), and language (communication) facilitates understanding (cognition) of the subject matter, for example.

A typical Adjunct ESP class consists of pre-language class (30 min) and post-language class (120 min.), both conducted by an EFL professor, in relation to a content class (60 min). The pre-language class includes tasks to activate students' background knowledge, vocabulary previews, and the teaching of note-taking strategies. The post-language class involve tasks to reinforce what students have learned in the content class and to facilitate their understanding of it, such as summaries of the content class and group presentations on parts of the content class.

## How It Has Been Received

The results of questionnaire surveys show students' high degrees of satisfaction with both the language and content classes: on average 4.26/5.00 over the content classes and 4.27 with the pre- and post-language classes (Tables 9.3 and 9.4). The questionnaire survey was divided into two sections: one regarding content classes and the other regarding language classes. It included items such as if the content class was good overall, if its level of difficulty was appropriate, if the pre- and post-language classes were helpful, if EFL instructors' teaching methods and the quality of their classes were good overall, if the EFL classes were helpful for improving their understanding of the content class, if the levels of difficulty of the EFL classes were appropriate, and if the EFL classes were fun. On average, 147 students per year participated in the survey between 2018 and 2022: 104 in 2018, 144 in 2019, 156 in 2020, 171 in 2021, and 158 in 2022.

The questionnaire also asked for students' opinions about the most difficult part of the content classes and the most helpful part of the pre- and post-language classes. The highest percentage of students answered that the most difficult part of the content classes was vocabulary, except for with the subject of physics, followed by listening in English (Table 9.5).

In the interviews that asked about the specific aspects of the content and language classes they found helpful or unhelpful and improvement measures they would like to suggest, five content professors, five EFL professors, and 121 students, and nine teaching assistants participated.

Table 9.3  Students' evaluations of content classes (/5.00)

| Content area | 2018 | 2019 | 2020 | 2021 | 2022 | Total |
|---|---|---|---|---|---|---|
| Biology | 3.99 | 4.64 | 4.33 | 3.79 | 4.36 | 4.22 |
| Chemistry | 4.05 | 4.41 | 4.59 | 3.85 | 4.30 | 4.24 |
| Physics | 4.06 | 4.36 | 4.37 | 4.37 | 3.20 | 4.07 |
| Programming | 4.19 | 4.58 | 4.36 | 4.26 | 4.44 | 4.37 |
| Mathematics | 4.18 | 4.68 | 4.42 | 4.47 | 4.37 | 4.42 |
| Average | 4.09 | 4.53 | 4.41 | 4.15 | 4.13 | 4.26 |

Table 9.4  Students' evaluations of pre- and post-language classes (/5.00)

| Content area | 2018 | 2019 | 2020 | 2021 | 2022 | Total |
|---|---|---|---|---|---|---|
| Biology | 3.85 | 4.63 | 4.29 | 4.24 | 4.24 | 4.25 |
| Chemistry | 3.86 | 4.53 | 4.32 | 4.00 | 4.27 | 4.20 |
| Physics | 3.92 | 4.52 | 4.45 | 4.36 | 3.58 | 4.17 |
| Programming | 3.99 | 4.61 | 4.34 | 4.21 | 4.36 | 4.30 |
| Mathematics | 4.13 | 4.68 | 4.55 | 4.44 | 4.31 | 4.42 |
| Average | 3.95 | 4.59 | 4.39 | 4.25 | 4.15 | 4.27 |

Table 9.5 The most difficult part of the content lecture (multiple choices possible)

| Year 2022 | Biology | Chemistry | Mathematics | Physics | Programming | Average |
|---|---|---|---|---|---|---|
| Number of responses | 147 | 170 | 184 | 169 | 156 | 165 |
| Vocabulary | 74 (50.3%) | 89 (52.4%) | 101 (54.9%) | 89 (52.7%) | 67 (42.9%) | 50.6% |
| Listening in English | 65 (44.2%) | 59 (34.7%) | 72 (39.1%) | 93 (55.0%) | 56 (35.9%) | 41.8% |
| Concepts | 31 (21.1%) | 72 (42.4%) | 46 (25.0%) | 97 (57.4%) | 53 (34.0%) | 36.0% |

The student interviewees favored particularly student-centered activities and groupwork, or collaborative work, which were present in all language activities. They also appreciated the authenticity of the content classes, as they were exposed to EMI classes at KAIST for the first time.

The EFL professors, however, found difficulty in customizing their language classes for content classes and said that they had to put numerous hours in class preparation. As they were not experts in the content areas, and students were considered the best in science and mathematics among Korean high school graduates, their understanding of the content materials required great efforts from them. Approvingly, EFL professors' lack of expertise in the content areas were supplemented by the teaching assistants, who were higher-year undergraduate students. That is, in the ESP classes, they acted as effective facilitators, providing content knowledge when content professors are not available.

Although all the content professors said that they were satisfied with the adjunct ESPEnglish for Specific Purposes (ESP) classes, or the pre- and post-language classes, their collaboration did not go beyond the early stage of course development. Furthermore, most of them had a one-way teacher-centered lecture style, exhibiting the needs for instructional training and improvement.

## What Should Be Done to Make Improvement

Both content professors' and EFL professors' active involvement and collaboration are required for creating effective adjunct ESP classes. Unfortunately, it is often the case that such a task is not perceived as important or of immediate concern for either content and EFL professors. That is, both content and EFL professors are occupied with their primary obligations, such as research and teaching academic classes or regular EFL classes, respectively. However, developing language skills required for subject content is crucial for EFL students to have academic accomplishment. Therefore, to be able to enlist cooperation and commitment from both content and EFL professors, the administration's understanding of the importance of such classes and proper compensation for both professor groups are necessary. Also, as TAs play essential roles in conducting ESP classes, they too need to be appropriately acknowledged and compensated.

# Embedded ESP Courses for Graduate Students

## Impetus for the Innovation

For graduate students at a reputable research-focused institution like KAIST, publishing papers in international journals is a crucial part of their studies, or a graduation requirement. Nevertheless, most of the students are EFL speakers who need to develop both general English skills and discipline-specific writing skills for writing papers in English.

The EFL program at KAIST has offered scientific writing (SW) classes without distinction as to major, and most graduate students have taken them. The EFL program administers course surveys among students every semester, and EFL professors noticed that students had consistently complained about similar problems with regards to SW courses: course materials were too general, classroom activities and assignments were not related to their majors, and lessons were not specific enough to deal with the manuscript guidelines and styles of different majors. To address these issues, the program administrators and teaching staff decided to offer discipline-specific SW classes, or embedded ESP SW courses, in the fall of 2018.

## What Has Been Done

In the fall of 2018, embedded ESP courses started in just two major areas: computer science and mathematics. The head and teaching staff of the two departments positively responded when they were contacted by the EFL director and teaching staff. Since then, the number of departments and programs that collaborate with EFL professors for the development and offering of embedded ESP SW courses has consistently increased. Currently, in the fall semester of 2023, the number has reached 14 majors and programs, including materials science and engineering, human–computer interaction, mechanical engineering, biological sciences, bio and brain engineering, medical science, biomedical science and engineering, mathematical sciences, computer science, AI, chemistry, chemical and biomolecular engineering, business and technology management, and electrical engineering.

In interviews with six EFL instructors teaching embedded ESP SW classes, they shared what had been entailed in their course development and offering: collaboration with content professors, acquisition of content knowledge, material development, and utilization of teaching assistants and students. For course development, an EFL professor contacted a content professor in the major area of his or her interest, and they discussed the writing needs of his or her major area. Following the discussion, the EFL professor designed course objectives, goals, assignments, and projects.

Moreover, in order to develop their content knowledge, EFL professors read journal articles and textbooks in the major field. However, they still felt that the level of the content knowledge that they had acquired did not match the level of students' knowledge or expertise and that it was not sufficient to give proper feedback on students' written work. This feeling of inadequacy may be inevitable as these students are among the best Korean students with considerable knowledge and expertise in their major area. To deal with this problem effectively, EFL professors utilized students' expertise in class and actively adopted student-centered teaching methods such as peer-editing. Also, teaching assistants, with their advanced knowledge in their field, played an important role in class activities, providing discipline-specific feedback on students' writing.

## How It Has Been Received

Overall, the embedded ESP SW classes have been received well by students. The EFL program administers course surveys every semester, as discussed earlier, and the student survey of the embedded ESP SW courses asked how helpful the course was in improving students' research writing skills and if the course helped students to write a scientific research paper that is suitable for publication. With the survey results showing 5.19 out of 6.00 on average between 2020 and 2022, it can be said that students are relatively satisfied with the courses (Table 9.6).

Moreover, students enrolled in the embedded ESP SW courses were required to take the pretest and posttest. Students were to write a summary of their research paper or a review article on their research topic. The summary was graded in five areas: how well it described the context or background of their paper (background), how well it explained the purpose of their paper (scope), how well it explained the value of their paper (value), their use of grammar and language (clarity) and the length of their summary (conciseness). Each area was graded as "poor (0)," "good (1)," or "excellent (2)," and a total score ranging from 0 to 10 was awarded.

Test results show on average 15.7% of improvement between the pretest and posttest scores in the last three years (Table 9.7). There was

Table 9.6 Survey results of ESL SW courses (out of 6.00[a])

|  | 2020 | 2021 | 2022 |
|---|---|---|---|
| Number of responses | 256 | 195 | 338 |
| Course average | 5.10 | 5.26 | 5.21 |

[a]Very helpful = 6.00, Helpful = 5.00, Somewhat helpful = 4.00, Somewhat unhelpful = 3.00, Unhelpful = 2.00, Very unhelpful = 1.00

a substantial drop in the average of Fall 2022, when the instructional delivery mode returned from online to in-person. The cause-and-effect relationship between the change in the instructional mode and the drop in the difference is not clearly proven. Nevertheless, it is recommended that the strengths of online instruction should be more integrated into in-person instruction as students have displayed preference for online instruction over in-person instruction in scientific writing classes (Table 9.8).

Furthermore, email or zoom interviews were conducted among the content and EFL professors who had been involved in embedded ESP SW courses. They were asked why they became involved in the course development and offering of an embedded ESP SW course, if they were satisfied with the course, what they would like to improve about it, if any, and if they were satisfied with collaboration with content or EFL professors. Almost all the professors, that is, all five content professors

Table 9.7 ESP Scientific Writing courses

| Term | Instructional delivery mode | Difference (%) between the pretest and posttest scores |
|---|---|---|
| Fall 2020 | Online | 12.36 |
| Spring 2021 | Online | 10.70 |
| Fall 2021 | Online | 21.62 |
| Spring 2022 | Online | 21.02 |
| Fall 2022 | In-person | 12.76 |
| Average | | 15.69 |

Table 9.8 Students' preference over online vs. in-person instruction in Scientific Writing

| Year | Term | Responses | Responses (%) In-person | No preference | Online |
|---|---|---|---|---|---|
| 2020 | Spring | 211 | 23.7 | 20.9 | **55.5** |
|  | Fall | 298 | 26.5 | 23.5 | **50.0** |
| 2021 | Spring | 252 | 23.8 | 20.2 | **56.0** |
|  | Fall | 254 | 16.1 | 22.0 | **61.8** |
| 2022 | Spring | 330 | 11.5 | 15.5 | **73.0** |
|  | Fall | 309 | **43.0** | 20.7 | 36.3 |

and all but one EFL professor, shared favorable views of embedded ESP SW classes.

However, the EFL professors pointed out the lack of collaboration with content professors as an important problem. In the initial stage of course development, content professors offered their input in course design, but their cooperation and assistance did not go beyond the initial stage. Hence, the utmost concerns that the EFL professors had about the development and offering of an embedded ESP SW course were insufficient collaboration with their counterpart content professors, followed by their own lack of content knowledge, and insufficient administrative support.

Furthermore, nine teaching assistants and 42 students participated in semi-structured email interviews. They were asked why they were involved in or took their ESP SW course, if they were satisfied with it, and how they would like to improve it. Some said that they were satisfied with their course's relevance to their field, but others found their course limited in its relevance to their field. It is often the case that there is a wide scope of subfields in the same major area, so it is difficult for one course to meet students' various writing demands. This problem could be resolved by opening more SW courses specific to different subfields, but it would require more investment from the university.

## What Should Be Done to Make Improvement

For EFL professors, who are language specialists, to be able to provide language instruction that cater to specific disciplines, several components are essential: steady, dependable collaboration with content professors, development of content knowledge, and utilization of competent, knowledgeable teaching assistants. Content professors at a research-focused institution tend to be occupied with their research obligations, as mentioned earlier. For them to be actively involved in the development of embedded ESP SW courses, they first need to see the importance of participating in such a task, and the administration needs to provide them with fitting incentives.

Also, to develop content knowledge, EFL professors need to put in much more effort than what they would normally put in for their regular language classes. For them to be able to be involved in the development and offering of an embedded ESP SW course, they need to see the importance of such a task, as with the case of content professors, need a strong sense of commitment, and require an appropriate incentive for their extra work. Teaching assistants may play a much more important role in embedded ESP SW courses than in other classes as EFL professors depend on their input in the course development and delivery much more substantially than in regular EFL classes. They sometimes act as a vicarious instructor, providing feedback on students' written work, and guiding EFL professors' preparation for their course especially when content professors are not available for assistance. Their efforts too need to be acknowledged with an appropriate incentive.

## Lessons Learned

Implementing a new instructional method that benefits students immensely, such as Adjunct ESP and embedded ESP SW, and maintaining the quality of such classes require the understanding, strong commitment, and immense investment, whether time or monetary, from all those involved. In particular, interdisciplinary collaboration is critical for the success of content-language integrated classes. Students' academic performance improves through discipline-specific language support; content professors become more articulate in explaining or lecturing about their content knowledge with the help of EFL professors who are language specialists; and EFL professors develop content knowledge and may strengthen their institutional status through collaboration with content professors (Chanock, 2013; Eriksson, 2018; Jaidev & Chan, 2018; Lasagabaster, 2018).

As discussed earlier, it is difficult to achieve an effective level of interdisciplinary collaboration between content and EFL professors. Content professors are pressured by their research and other responsibilities and are often under time constraints. EFL professors are burdened especially by the need to develop content knowledge and the need to put enormous effort into developing content knowledge and designing content-language integrated courses. Therefore, it is crucial that the development of such a course is initiated with the understanding of and support from departmental and central administration. Moreover, in addition to the benefits to students, individual content and EFL professors should see benefits for themselves for being involved in such a course, for example, enhancing their linguistic capability and professional expertise. There is a need for consistent publicity activities that can share successful outcomes of the existing content-language integrated classes.

This chapter has examined innovative content-language integrated classes at KAIST, and its findings have some pedagogical implications. EFL and content professors at Korean science and engineering universities, where most classes are offered in EMI, and at other Korean universities with an EMI policy will find the findings useful in improving EMI classes through introducing elements of CLIL (content language integrating learning) into classes.

## Discussion questions

1. What are the benefits of content-language integrated classes for EFL students attending a university with an EMI policy?
2. What are the measures that could be taken to increase content professors' involvement in the development of content-language integrated classes?
3. What types of assistance can be offered for an EFL professor that develops or intends to develop a content-language integrated course?

**Conflict of interest**   We have no known conflict of interest to disclose.

# References

Byun, K., & Kim, M. (2011). Shifting patterns of the government's policies for the internationalization of Korean higher education. *Journal of Studies in International Education, 15*(5), 467–486.

Chanock, K. (2013). Teaching subject literacies through blended learning: Reflections on a collaboration between academic learning staff and teachers in the disciplines. *Journal of Academic Language Learning, 7*(2), A106–A119. https://journal.aall.org.au/index.php/jall/article/view/256

Coyle, D. (2007). Content and language integrated learning: Towards a connected research agenda for CLIL pedagogies. *International Journal of Bilingual Education and Bilingualism, 10*(5), 543–562. https://doi.org/10.2167/beb459.0

Eriksson, A. (2018). Redesigning a Discipline-Specific Writing Assignment to Improve Writing on an EMI Programme of Engineering. *Journal of Academic Writing, 8*(2), 48–66.

Jaidev, R., & Chan, P. (2018). Embedding communication in the disciplines: A tale of two faculties. *Innovation in Language Learning and Teaching, 12*(3), 199–211. https://doi.org/10.1080/17501229.2016.1156685

KAIST. (2023). *Morea about KAIST*. Koread Advanced Institute of Science and Technology (KAIST). Retrieved September 3 from https://www.kaist.ac.kr/en/html/kaist/01.html#0114

Kim, Y. (2017, July 13). Suhak·gwahak pyeonsikan gwahakgo chulsindeul "yeongeo gangui duryeowoyo" 수학·과학 편식한 과학고 출신들 "영어 강의 두려워요" Graduates of science high schools, where mathematics and natural sciences are mainly taught, fearful of English-medium classes. *The Chosunilbo*. https://www.chosun.com/site/data/html_dir/2017/07/13/2017071300161.html

Lasagabaster, D. (2018). Fostering team teaching: Mapping out a research agenda for English-medium instruction at university level. *Language Teaching, 51*(3), 400–416. https://doi.org/10.1017/S0261444818000113

Nam, H., & Gwag, E. (2019, May 21). Yeongeo ansseuneun 'yeongeo gangui'…daehak pyeongga norigo magujabi gaeseol 영어 안 ㅆ는 '영어 강의'…대학평가 노리고 마구잡이 개설 (No English used in English-medium (EM) classes; universities open EM classes indiscriminately for better university ranking). *Segye Ilbo*. https://www.segye.com/newsView/20190520511336

QS. (2023). *QS Asia University Rankings 2023.* Quacquarelli Symonds (QS) Limited. Retrieved September 3 from https://www.topuniversities.com/university-rankings/asia-university-rankings/2023

Registrar's, A. (2022). *EMI statistics.* KAIST.

Schmidt-Unterberger, B. (2018). The English-medium paradigm: A conceptualisation of English-medium teaching in higher education. *International Journal of Bilingual Education and Bilingualism, 21*(5), 527–539. https://doi.org/10.1080/13670050.2018.1491949

# 10

## A Case Study of an AI-Assisted CLIL Approach: A College English Course for Global Citizenship and Global Competence in an EFL Setting

Eun-Jou Oh

## Area of Innovation

This study introduces a CLIL model designed to cultivate global citizenship and global competence in an EFL tertiary setting through the use of machine translation (MT hereafter) as a pedagogical translanguaging tool and presents a case study detailing the implementation of the model amidst the challenges of the Corona pandemic in 2021. The conceptualization and implementation of the proposed model were driven by three overarching factors. Firstly, it aimed to complement the effectiveness of English-only instructional practices in ELT within a tertiary context where English is taught as a foreign language by adopting pedagogical translanguaging. Secondly, it was motivated by the alignment of higher education's mission with the necessity to adapt to the dynamic demands of contemporary society, thereby equipping students

---

E.-J. Oh (✉)
Korean Bible University, Seoul, South Korea
e-mail: eunjouoh@bible.ac.kr

© The Author(s), under exclusive license to Springer Nature Switzerland AG 2025
H. Reinders et al. (eds.), *Innovation in Language Learning and Teaching*, New Language Learning and Teaching Environments,
https://doi.org/10.1007/978-3-031-83561-2_10

with the requisite skills to confront the multifaceted challenges of globalization. Lastly, AI tools emerged as a pivotal facilitator for innovation in effectively integrating these two motivating factors into practice.

## Pedagogical Translanguaging: A Departure from English-Only Instructional Strategies

The 1990s marked a pivotal period for English education in South Korea, coinciding with the global discourse on globalization driven by neoliberal ideologies (Tsui & Tollefson, 2007). This era witnessed a paradigm shift in educational priorities, notably highlighting the importance of enhancing national competitiveness through improved English proficiency across various Asian nations (Butler, 2011). This transition in South Korea can be attributed to significant global events such as the Asian Games and Olympics in the 1980s, which sparked a heightened interest in English language acquisition (Yim, 2017), situating the country within Kachru's *expanding circle* of English use (1985). Furthermore, South Korea's accession to the OECD in the 1990s further intensified discussions on globalization, prompting a transformative shift in English education from a grammar-focused to a communication-centric approach (Chang, 2019).

A prominent manifestation of this shift in higher education was the adoption of English-medium instruction (EMI). By the early 2000s, EMI gained considerable traction in South Korean universities, with approximately 30% of classes in Seoul and 10% nationwide being conducted in English by 2011 (Kim et al., 2017). Leading engineering institutions such as the Korea Advanced Institute of Science and Technology (KAIST) and Pohang University of Science and Technology (POSTECH) were early adopters of EMI, as highlighted by Kim et al. (2017), contributing to the perception of EMI being associated with elitism.

However, the swift implementation of EMI from the top-down has been criticized for overlooking the linguistic challenges faced by stakeholders simultaneously (Kim et al., 2017). In contrast to the idealized notion of an English-only classroom endorsed by policymakers, observations in EMI settings suggest that the use of multiple languages and various modes of communication is commonplace (Kim, 2022; Williams, 2023), highlighting translanguaging as a viable alternative to monolingual English instructional approaches. Moreover, research (Choi, 2013; Kim & Shin, 2014) indicates that strict adherence to English-only practices may prove ineffective, particularly among students with lower proficiency levels in EMI or CLIL contexts.

Originating from William's seminal work in 2002, translanguaging is fundamentally characterized as the process of receiving information in one language and utilizing it in another (as cited in Poza, 2017). It is presented as a theoretical framework that transcends conventional linguistic boundaries, encompassing cognitive and semiotic systems (Li, 2018). As evidenced by its proliferation across nearly 3,000 publications within the domain of ELT (Prilutskaya, 2021), the concept of translanguaging has garnered significant attention in contemporary multilingualism research. However, the exploration of translanguaging as an alternative to English-only instructional practices for EFL students with lower proficiency levels in CLIL settings is novel and requires innovative experimentation challenging conventional ELT paradigms.

## The Alignment of Higher Education's Mission with Contemporary Needs

The alignment of higher education's mission with contemporary needs in the globalized world is imperative for educational institutions to remain relevant and effective. Communication-centric approaches, exemplified by initiatives such as EMI in higher education, underscore institutions' commitment to meeting the evolving demands of a globalized society. In the realm of college English programs, a noticeable shift in educational paradigms has occurred over time. Initially focused on knowledge acquisition through traditional subjects like literature, history, and philosophy texts, these programs were rooted in the broader framework of general studies, aiming to provide students with a well-rounded education (Kwon, 2000), particularly before the onset of globalization.

However, a discernible transformation in priorities emerged in the 1990s and the 2000s, as evidenced by Kim and Im's (2013) comprehensive analysis of educational objectives on college English programs across 36 universities. Their findings highlighted a recurring emphasis on the cultivation of practical English proficiency, with speaking, reading, listening, and writing prioritized in descending order.

This transition unfolded within the context of neoliberal globalization, reflecting nuanced shifts in societal needs geared towards enhancing national competitiveness. Universities responded pragmatically by implementing English graduation certification systems, incorporating standardized tests such as TOEIC, TEPS, and TOEFL (Kim & Im, 2013). Adaptations to meet the escalating demand for English as a lingua franca (ELF) were considered essential imperatives in higher education during the transition from the 20th to the twenty-first centuries.

However, the perception of globalization has undergone a significant shift in recent years. Once venerated as a symbol of progress and modernization, globalization is now confronted with numerous challenges, including economic instability, exacerbated inequality, forced migration, and global health crises such as the COVID-19 pandemic (Kobrin, 2020; Roberts & Lamp, 2021). This paradigmatic shift has underscored the importance of global citizenship education (GCED) as a central agenda in higher education (Black et al., 2023; Borkovic et al., 2020; Horey et al., 2018).

In light of these challenges, there is a pressing need for higher education institutions to reorient their educational content and trajectory. College English programs, as compulsory components accessible to all university students, present an opportunity for innovative approaches to address the urgent demands of the contemporary era. By incorporating value-oriented characteristics and serving an extensive population, these programs can contribute significantly to the cultivation of global citizenship and global competence. Thus, they fulfill their role and responsibility as educational institutions in the twenty-first century.

## Impetus for the Innovation

The rapid evolution of information and communication technology (ICT) has brought about significant transformations upon the communicative milieu within our globally interconnected societies. Traditional paradigms of literacy, previously anchored in textual media, prove inadequate in navigating the multifaceted landscape of technologically mediated communication prevalent in contemporary society. Within this dynamic milieu, translation technology has emerged as a pivotal tool for individuals utilizing second languages. The pervasive integration of online MT into everyday activities underscores its indispensability within the present communication setting. The adoption of neural MT powered by deep learning since the mid-2010s has revolutionized due to its increased accuracy and convenience of interface after going through its inception in 1949 with basic approaches like the direct translation model, followed by the rise of rule-based systems until 1989, transitioning to corpus-based methods in the 1990s (Jiang et al., 2024). Research conducted by Vieira et al. (2023) delineates MT's predominant utilization for multilingual text comprehension, followed by recreational endeavors, internet exploration, language acquisition endeavors, social media participation, textual messaging, and real-time conversational exchanges.

Amidst the continuous evolution of MT and its integration into various societal contexts, its utilization in L2 education remains an area of ongoing development. While MT has undergone consistent quality enhancements, its application in L2 writing has garnered significant attention and spurred a considerable amount of research; refer to Jiang et al. (2024) for the systematic review on this research.

Despite the limited exploration of MT-mediated reading, Oh (2022) and Oh and Kim (2024) delved into the potential mechanism of MT in MT-assisted L2 reading, using Kintsch's CI model for L2 reading comprehension (Oh, 2014). This exploration facilitated the integration of learners' L1 reading competence and L2 proficiency into instruction and assessment, thereby fostering their developmental potential.

The primary challenge in CLIL implementation arises from the inherent complexity of its content (Coyle & Meyer, 2021). The college

English course model aimed at fostering global citizenship and competence often involves grappling with intricate global issues conveyed in sophisticated language. Within this context, MT emerges as a transformative tool, enabling ELLs to fully utilize their linguistic resources and mitigate the constraints of relatively low L2 proficiency. Embedded within the translanguaging framework, MT serves as an effective pedagogical tool, bridging cognitive and linguistic gaps in comprehending global citizenship concepts and issues. This resonates with one of the central objectives of translanguaging—to optimize learners' language utilization for meaningful comprehension and expression.

The rapid proliferation of AI-driven translation further underscores this transformative trajectory, as its integration across various societal domains continues to expand exponentially. Given that AI-powered translation tools inherently involve the use of learners' L1, their consistent presence within ELT necessitates conceptualization and theoretical frameworks to effectively incorporate L1 use into pedagogical practices. Integrating MT and other AI-assisted translation tools within the framework of pedagogical translanguaging represents a progressive step towards theorizing their role in ELT. In this context, the proposed model demonstrates considerable potential as a foundational framework, particularly within the realm of CLIL, catering to university-level students studying English as a foreign language.

## Specific Context of Implementation

The college English course model aimed at fostering global citizenship and global competence was developed in 2020, employing the backward design approach (McTighe & Wiggins, 1999), which is widely utilized in competency-based curriculum development. The model then has been progressively refined at Korean Bible University, where the author oversees and teaches college English courses. The case study presented here pertains to the initial implementation of this model, spanning two semesters in 2021.

The course development was supported by a grant from the National Research Foundation of Korea (NRF, 2020S1A5A8043039). The first phase of course development involved comprehending the concepts of GCED and global competence and their relevance to English Language Teaching (ELT). The author's foundational understanding of the subject was established through the development and implementation of a course entitled "Becoming a Global Citizen." This endeavor was supported by the 2020 Global Citizenship Education Course Development Support Program, which is administered by the Asia–Pacific Centre of Education for International Understanding (APCEIU) under the auspices of UNESCO. This course, offered as part of the university's general education curriculum, informed the author's design of the college English course contents.

Key materials for developing the college English model included GCED101 online course videos offered by APCEIU and the 2018 PISA global competence framework. These sources represent the dual focus of the model, catering to both instrumental and value-oriented needs. Following Dill's (2013) definition of a global citizen as someone possessing global consciousness and global competence, materials on global consciousness were sourced from UNESCO, emphasizing ethical goals such as tolerance, world peace, and moral responsibilities for global welfare. The PISA global competence framework addressed more instrumental aspects in that it was developed by the OECD to equip students with 21st-century skills essential for success in the global economy. Additionally, specific components of the framework such as cognitive processes and a questionnaire delineating subcomponents of global competence, were deemed to be practically useful for elucidating the concept of global competence.

## The College English Course Model for Global Citizenship and Global Competence

Under the framework of backward design (McTighe & Wiggins, 1999), the four desired results were formulated and articulated under the overarching concept of "understanding." A notable aspect of backward design is its categorization of the cognitive process of "understanding" into six distinct performance domains: explaining, interpreting, applying, perspective-taking, empathizing, and self-understanding. By aligning these domains with specific desired results, supported by acceptable evidence and learning experiences, learners are guided in systematically cultivating profound understanding throughout their educational journey. The four desired results encompassed within the domain of understanding include: (1) Understanding globalization and global citizenship, (2) Understanding global competence, (3) Understanding technology tools, and (4) Understanding English communication. Table 10.1 presents performance domains relevant to each desired result.

## Setting

The implementation took place at Korean Bible University in Seoul as a mandatory foundational course spanning two semesters in 2021. The university offers college English courses in two tracks: Track A, which emphasized listening and speaking and was taught by native speakers, and Track B, which focused on reading and writing and was taught by non-native speakers. Participants in this study opted for Track B.

The courses, titled College English I and II (CEI and CEII hereafter), were held twice a week, with each session lasting 75 minutes and totaling 3 credits, in an online format due to the pandemic situation. The classes were conducted in collaboration with a cooperating researcher who was responsible for managing writing-related activities, such as providing a mini-lesson on MT use, offering guidelines for MT-assisted writing for personal response essays, and evaluating the essays with feedback. Additionally, English presentations in CEII, implemented as out-of-class learning activities, were facilitated by a native English-speaking instructor, referred to as Sally, who has been teaching at KBU since 2013. Sally served as an audience member and discussant during these presentations.

In CEI, there were 33 students enrolled who scored between 350 and 550 points on the diagnostic test (mock TOEIC) administered upon admission., CEII, which served as a continuation of CEI in the second semester, had 26 students enrolled, all of whom had taken CEI for the research in the first semester. Seven students were waived for CEII and

Table 10.1 Desired results with performance domains

| Desired result | Performance domains | Descriptions |
|---|---|---|
| Understanding globalization and global citizenship | Explaining | • Explaining the closely interdependent globalized world through interconnectedness<br>• Describing who a global citizen is<br>• Explaining core themes of GCED |
| | Interpreting | • Discerning contradictions and paradoxes evident in various phenomena of the globalized world |
| | Self-understanding | • Recognizing oneself from the perspective of a global citizen |
| Understanding global competence | Explaining | • Explaining the components of global competence |
| | Applying | • Analyzing how global issues relate to the core themes of GCED<br>• Maintaining ongoing interest in and update relevant content regarding current issues<br>• Applying critical literacy skills |
| | Perspective-taking | • Analyzing diverse perspectives reflected in media coverage of global issues |
| | Empathizing | • Understanding and empathizing towards the diverse backgrounds in which various perspectives on global issues are formed |
| | Self-understanding | • Recognizing the competencies in oneself necessary for successful demonstration of global competence |
| Understanding technology tools | Applying | • Utilizing MT for reading media articles<br>• Utilizing MT to express one's opinions in writing and speaking |
| | Self-understanding | • Understanding suitable methods for utilizing MT for effective information acquisition and English learning in relation to one's own L2 proficiency |

(continued)

Table 10.1 (continued)

| Desired result | Performance domains | Descriptions |
|---|---|---|
| Understanding English communication | Explaining | • Explaining units of English language and types of sentences (simple, complex, compound, and compound-complex sentences) |
| | Applying | • Comprehending the precise meaning of authentic English texts<br>• Writing summaries of global issues and personal reflections<br>• Presenting global issues in English |
| | Self-understanding | • Understanding one's English proficiency through self-assessment of necessary skills for ongoing engagement in reading authentic global media articles |

did not need to take the course in the second semester because they either submitted a required TOEIC score according to university regulations or had completed an English course offered prior to the start of the semester. All students were freshmen in departments of Nursing, Social Welfare, Theology, Early Childhood Education, and Computer Software. The sample size for the analyses decreased to 27 for College English I and 19 for CEII respectively when the missing data were excluded.

## The Implementation of the Courses

Amidst the COVID-19 pandemic, instructional sessions were transitioned to online delivery, excluding the midterm and final examinations, which were conducted in person. The grading scheme for the courses consisted of attendance (10%), midterm exam (20%), final exam (20%), article analysis assignment (10%), article presentation (10%), personal response essays (PR, hereafter) (20%), and a mock TOEIC test (10%). The midterm and final exams covered vocabulary, sentence types, reading comprehension of GECD scripts, critical literacy (e.g., distinguishing between fact and opinion, analyzing informative or persuasive writing), and providing descriptions of key issues, perspectives, and GCED themes reflected in each seed article, along with writing comprehensive personal responses to the seed articles. Activities related to article analyses and presentations were evaluated based on completion, as templates provided specific guidelines to ensure successful task completion. PRs were graded by the cooperating researcher with feedback.

The main educational materials consisted of multimodal texts acquired from three sources: (1) GCED open online course videos provided by UNESCO, (2) OECD publications on PISA global competence (OECD, 2018), and (3) online English media articles.

To achieve the four desired results, the course was organized into four modules. Module 1 was dedicated to establishing the foundational knowledge necessary for proficient comprehension of English text and use of MT in both reading and writing tasks. Module 2 was primarily designed to foster global citizenship and featured materials and activities sourced from GCED101 videos provided by APCEIU. Module 3 incorporated resources from the PISA global competence framework. Module 4 involved students in analyzing authentic media articles from platforms such as CNN, NPR, CBS, BBC, and The New York Times (Table 10.2).

Module 1 content included lectures on chunking skills, which covered units of language, sentence types, and sentence error types, along with guidelines for employing MT for composing PRs.

The second module incorporated six GCED videos, with four presented in CEI and two in CEII, designed to explore concepts such as globalization, global citizenship, core themes of GCED, and the essence of GCED. During the viewing of the English GCED videos, students were required to complete dictation worksheets and comprehension guide questions. Subsequently, each student assumed the role of a leader in cooperative reading activities. The leader prepared by studying the comprehension lecture based on the video scripts provided by the instructor in advance and led translation activities within small groups during Zoom class sessions. Following the conclusion of each set of activities related to GCED videos, students composed PRs, comprising of a summary paragraph and a reflection paragraph.

**Table 10.2** Learning materials and modules of the College English I & II

| Materials | Contents | | Activities |
|---|---|---|---|
| | College English I | College English II | |
| MODULE1 [foundational knowledge]<br>• Lecture videos | • Chunking<br>• How to use MT for writing | • Types of common errors | • Dictation/comprehension guide<br>• Collaborative Reading<br>• PR writing |
| MODULE2 [GCED]<br>• GCED101 videos<br>• Comprehension lecture videos | • Video1. Interconnectedness and interdependence of the globalized world<br>• Video2. Challenges and contradictions of globalization<br>• Video3. Definition of global citizenship<br>• Video4. Five themes of GCED | • Video5. Emergence of GCED as global education agenda<br>• Video6. What is GCED? | |
| MODULE3 [global competence]<br>• OECD (2018) document | • PISA global competence framework (constructs of the survey)<br>• Critical literacy<br>• Article analysis assignment | • PISA global competence framework (typologies of cognitive processes)<br>• Review on critical literacy | |
| MODULE4 [article analysis]<br>• Sample seed media articles | • Covid-19 vaccine patent (CNN)<br>• Carbon emission of global rich (CBS) | • ROUND1: Climate Migration (CNN); Afghanistan: How many refugees are there and where will they go? (BBC)<br>• ROUND2: Climate change is about greed. It''s time for big oil to pay us (CNN); Key things the Facebook whistleblower told a Senate panel (CNN) | • Article analysis<br>• TAR<br>• Korean presentation (CEI)<br>• English presentation (CEII)<br>• PR writing |

*Note* TAR refers to Think-Aloud Reading. Sample TAR articles include Covid vaccines: How fast is progress around the world? (BBC) and Clegg: Facebook is mainly 'barbecues and bar mitzvahs.' (BBC)

The third module commenced with a lecture in CEI, elucidating the components of the PISA global competence framework and its educational significance. In CEII, cognitive skills specified in the PISA framework were explicitly explained. Critical literacy, encompassing lectures on discerning between facts and opinions, as well as informative versus persuasive writing, was exercised through article analyses in both courses. A structured template for article analysis, incorporating issue analysis, thematic analyses based on GCED themes, and perspective analysis, was provided in CEI and used in both courses.

In module 4, the instructor presented seed articles addressing global issues such as human rights, global health, and sustainability, from which students selected one for analysis. Students studied the comprehension lecture corresponding to each seed article, prepared by the instructor for article analysis. Subsequently, after individually reviewing the comprehension lecture, they shared their analyses within their respective home groups, where members selected the same seed article.

Furthermore, students were tasked with autonomously sourcing and perusing an additional article relevant to their selected seed article topic. Throughout this independent reading phase, students engaged in TAR with the assistance of MT, and subsequently submitted video recordings capturing the entire TAR process as a designated assignment; refer to Oh (2022) for the specifics of TAR. These individually reviewed media articles were then incorporated into the presentation ppt of the seed article, a collaborative endeavor undertaken by members within the same home group. Subsequently, each member, as experts of their respective seed article, delivered their presentation on their chosen seed article to peers who had reviewed different seed articles in a jigsaw format.

The presentation adhered to a structured format comprising issue analysis, thematic analysis, perspective analysis, summaries of individually reviewed TAR articles, and subsequent discussions. Collaboratively prepared presentation slides were crafted in English by members of the home group and presented in Korean during expert group sessions. Additionally, in CEII, an English presentation segment was introduced as part of extracurricular learning activities subsequent to the Korean presentation. Home group members alternated in delivering presentations in

Table 10.3 Schedule of College English I and II

| College English I | | | | College English II | | | |
|---|---|---|---|---|---|---|---|
| W1 | Diagnostic Test & OT | W9 | Module3 | W1 | OT & Module2 | W9 | Module4 |
| W2 | Module1 | W10 | Module3 | W2 | Module2 | W10 | Module4 |
| W3 | Module2 | W11 | Module4 | W3 | Module2 | W11 | Module4 |
| W4 | Module2 | W12 | MOCK TOEIC | W4 | Module1 | W12 | MOCK TOEIC |
| W5 | Modele2 | W13 | Module4 | W5 | Module3 | W13 | Module4 |
| W6 | Modeul2 | W14 | Module4 | W6 | Module3 | W14 | Module4 |
| W7 | Module2 | W15 | Final Exam | W7 | Module3 | W15 | Final exam |
| W8 | Midterm Exam | | | W8 | Midterm Exam | | |

English in the same expert groups, with Sally serving as additional audience. During English discussions on relevant topics, students utilized MT to enhance comprehension and articulate their opinions, effectively bridging any cognitive and linguistic barriers encountered in the discourse. Upon concluding the expert group presentation, students transitioned to composing personal response essays in both courses.

The skeleton of the implementation of the courses is provided in Table 10.3.

# Findings

The courses, following the proposed model, underwent evaluation based on students' perceptions regarding the four desired results, utilizing a combination of quantitative and qualitative data. Quantitative data comprised the following: two surveys gauging students' perceptions of the four desired results, the PISA global competence questionnaire and a self-efficacy questionnaire focusing on their proficiency in four language skills. All surveys and the PISA global competence questionnaire employed an 11-point Likert scale, ranging from 0 indicating "strongly disagree" to 10 indicating "strongly agree." The self-efficacy questionnaire used a 7-point Likert scale, ranging from 0 indicating "strongly disagree" to 7 indicating "strongly agree."

The initial students' perceptions survey, administered upon the completion of CEI, inquired whether students felt capable of performing specific performance domains of understanding related to each desired result. Similarly, upon the conclusion of CEII, students were asked to assess themselves broadly in terms of the four desired results of the course.

The PISA global competence questionnaire was administered at the beginning and conclusion of CEI, and upon the conclusion of CEII to assess global competence. Similarly, the self-efficacy survey was conducted at the commencement and conclusion of CEI. Notably, significant improvements were observed in all four skill areas, rendering the questionnaire unnecessary for administration in CEII.

## Quantitative Data Analyses

Overall, student" perception surveys consistently yielded high ratings across all four desired results. Table 10.4 illustrates the range of ratings on items pertaining to performance domains within each desired result following the completion of CEI and subsequently CEII. The improvement between the two courses affirm the model's effectiveness in facilitating student" achievement of each desired result.

The analyses conducted using independent samples $t$-tests on the students' responses to the PISA global competence questionnaires, both pre and post1 (CEI) and pre and post2 (CEII) revealed significant improvements in various areas. Following the completion of CEI, students demonstrated enhanced self-efficacy regarding global issues, increased awareness of global issues, improved perspective-taking abilities, heightened engagement with global issues, and a greater sense of global mindedness. These improvements were consistent with the course content, which focused on exploring global issues through the analysis of various media articles.

The only difference between CEI and II lies in the inclusion of English presentations featuring a native English-speaking audience member and

**Table 10.4** The results of students' perceptions surveys after CEI and CEII

| Desired result | CEI (n = 27) | | CEII (n = 19) | |
|---|---|---|---|---|
| | Items | Means | Items | Mean (SD) |
| Understanding globalization and global citizenship | Six items on three performance domains | From 7.963 to 8.481 | 1. I identify as a global citizen | 9.417 (1.577) |
| | | | 2. This course has played a crucial role in shaping my identity as a global citizen | 9.895 (0.459) |
| Understanding global competence | Six items on four performance domains | From 7.936 to 8.481 | 1. I have acquired the global competencies essential for navigating the challenges of the twenty-first century | 9.263 (1.628) |
| | | | 2. This course has significantly contributed to my acquisition of global competencies | 9.684 (0.749) |
| Understanding technology tools | Three items on two performance domains | From 8.185 to 8.407 | 1. This course has facilitated the development of my proficiency in utilizing MT for learning English | 9.579 (8.377) |
| | | | 1. The use of MT has aided in English language learning | 9.263 (1.628) |
| | | | 2. The use of MT has aided in fostering global citizenship identity and global competencies | 8.632 (2.290) |
| | | | 1. The use of L1 has aided in the learning of English | 9.368 (0.955) |

(continued)

Table 10.4 (continued)

| Desired result | CEI (n = 27) | | CEII (n = 19) | |
|---|---|---|---|---|
| | Items | Means | Items | Mean (SD) |
| | | | 2. The use of L1 has contributed to the development of global citizenship identity and global competencies | 9.211 (1.357) |
| | | | 3. Employing MT to engage in English discussions is an effective method for enhancing English proficiency | 9.316 (1.883) |
| | | | 4. Employing MT to engage in English discussions is an effective method for fostering global citizenship and global competencies | 8.895 (1.883) |
| Understanding English communication | Three items on three performance domains | From 7.667 to 8.000 | 1. This course has assisted me in acquiring the ability to accurately grasp meanings through sentence analysis | 8.947 (1.929) |
| | | | 2. The proficiency in sentence analysis has facilitated the accurate comprehension of meanings through the use of MT | 9.316 (1.336) |
| | | | 3. This course has facilitated the development of my proficiency in English reading skills | 9.053 (1.649) |

(continued)

Table 10.4 (continued)

| Desired result | CEI (n = 27) | | CEII (n = 19) | |
|---|---|---|---|---|
| | Items | Means | Items | Mean (SD) |
| | | | 4. This course has facilitated the development of my proficiency in English writing skills | 8.684 (2.120) |
| | | | 5. This course has helped me in assessing my own English proficiency | 9.263 (0.991) |
| | | | 6. This course has helped me in fostering my self-directed learning disposition in English language acquisition | 8.947 (1.929) |

discussant in CEII. This addition was deemed to have triggered significant improvements in awareness of intercultural communication, interest in learning about other cultures, and attitudes towards immigrants after the completion of CEII because no significant improvements were observed after CEI in this component of the questionnaire. Although adaptability showed an increase from 6.608 to 7.194, it did not reach a significant level in CEII, either. Similarly, while there was a slight increase in respect for people from other cultural backgrounds, this increase was not statistically significant, likely due to the relatively high initial rating of 8.863.

Significant enhancements in students' self-efficacy across all language skills areas were evident in CEI. Notably, despite the limited emphasis on English listening and speaking activities in CEI, the observed improvement underscores the efficacy of increased exposure to authentic English input via translanguaging learning experiences facilitated by MT, as supported by the descriptive analyses of survey items.

## Qualitative Data Analyses

Qualitative data were obtained through content analysis of personal response paragraphs written by students in CEI and descriptive responses provided in the surveys after the completion of CEII. Furthermore, a teacher's perspective was captured through an interview excerpt from Sally after CEII.

The content analysis of reflective paragraphs of PRs shows the extent of students' understanding of global citizenship and the attainment of the learning objectives as presented in Table 10.5.

Table 10.5 Key themes from College English I, PR writing content analysis

| PR | Key theme | Example sentence |
| --- | --- | --- |
| PR1 | • Had not known how much we are interconnected and interdependent even in the smallest, daily actions<br>• Will reconsider and be careful about the impact of my actions to others | • After reading the text, I could clearly imprint on my head that I am a member of the global community and felt how many people's lives are contained in my life |
| PR2 | • Shocked to know the degree of global inequality<br>• Interest in human rights of unprotected children and women | • I didn't know much about global wealth inequality. Now I understand what it is |
| PR3 | • Understanding of global citizenship as sense of belonging and responsibility<br>• Willingness to take actions and work with others | • I want to be a global citizen who is passionately committed to social justice, participates in communities at various levels, from local to global, and collaborates with others to make the world a more equal and sustainable place |
| PR4 | • Understanding of the five core areas of GCED<br>• Particular interest in one of the five areas | • With a lot of education about human rights, I have always thought about my own human rights, but never properly regarded human rights as a tool for respecting and protecting the human rights of others |

*Note* Extracted from Kim and Oh (2023)

The qualitative analysis of students' responses to the survey items in CEII unveiled their appreciation for the efficacy of each class activity within the model. Notably, students' responses revealed a virtuous cycle wherein engagement in activities like reading media articles, presenting them, and sharing opinions facilitated the acquisition of knowledge on contemporary global issues. This heightened understanding subsequently fostered the development of multiple perspectives, problem-solving skills, and a deeper interest in global affairs through discussions. For instance, Student10 articulated, "Through collaborative reading activities, I was able to clarify definitions and concepts about what it means to be a global citizen. Additionally, through English presentations and Korean seed article presentations, I was able to cultivate perspectives on how to approach issues as global citizens." Moreover, students were prompted to reflect on their own role as global citizens in reflective writing, thus perpetuating the cycle of learning and personal growth; S8 commented, "Furthermore, it was beneficial to not only engage in these activities but also to consolidate my thoughts and reflections by writing personal responses".

The value of exposure to diverse perspectives and the cultivation of problem-solving skills was also highlighted. For instance, S5 mentioned, "Analyzing articles enabled me to develop the ability to view global issues from various perspectives. Consequently, I also acquired the skill to propose solutions to these issues."

As for the use of MT for language learning and the development of global competence, the significant contribution of MT to students' overall learning experience and engagement was noted. MT facilitated comprehension and active involvement by overcoming language barriers and instilling confidence. For instance, S8 noted, "If I had to use only English, I might have wanted to give up midway because it would have been difficult. However, by using MT, I was able to proceed with the activities without any significant obstacles." Increased ease in dealing with authentic materials covered in the course, thanks to MT, indicates that MT effectively bridged the cognitive and linguistic gap embedded in these CLIL courses, making it an effective tool for pedagogical translanguaging.

In particular, S8 explained how s/he carefully adjusted her translanguaging for writing and speaking with the use of MT in mind. "It seems that writing PR in English had the greatest impact. While initially composing in Korean, I anticipated which words might be used and consciously adjusted the difficulty of words and the length of sentences to ensure that the English sentences did not become too complex. The same was true for drafting the English presentation script. I made efforts to avoid listing unfamiliar words without understanding and instead substituted them with words I knew, ensuring that the script conveyed accurate meaning. This process helped improve my writing skills. Lastly, during the Seed article presentation, I aimed to include keywords to ensure the PowerPoint slides were concise yet informative, which also contributed to improving my writing skills."

The role of L1 was deemed pivotal in clarifying their thinking to actively participate in the courses. S15 remarked, "Before speaking English, I believe it's essential to first organize my thoughts regarding my global citizenship identity and global competence. Then, expressing those thoughts in English becomes easier and more effective for English communication." Similarly, S18 stated, "No matter how good something may seem, if you cannot interpret or understand it, it becomes not something good but simply something unknown. That's why I believe reading and understanding are crucial. That's why I think Korean usage has been helpful." These comments highlight that clear thinking and understanding precedes all other activities for them to be effective, and the use of L1 fulfills this need.

Regarding self-understanding, interactions with Sally prompted realizations about the importance of pronunciation, as expressed by S6 and S15. Notably, S17 identified areas for improvement across different activities such an English presentation, PR writing and GCED sessions, motivating further efforts to address language shortcomings; "In terms of English presentations, although I had plenty to say and was passionate about presenting, my speaking skills were lacking. This motivated me to study conversational skills in the future. Regarding PR activities, despite my efforts to utilize translation tools appropriately and work hard independently, I found myself heavily reliant on translation tools. Feedback from professors also highlighted recurring mistakes, prompting me to strive harder to overcome my shortcomings. This experience reinforced my determination to continue making efforts. Lastly, during GCED sessions, I noticed my grammar weaknesses, particularly when explaining sentence structures. As a result, I dedicated extra effort to watching instructional videos to improve my understanding."

Overall, the integration of MT-assisted translanguaging activities and collaborative learning frameworks in the curriculum nurtured students' language proficiency, self-awareness, and autonomy, fostering a conducive environment for growth and development.

## Teacher's perspective

Sally was interviewed via Zoom one week after the second semester was over. When asked to reflect on her overall experience with the course, Sally expressed initial concerns about its difficulty level and the varying proficiency levels of students. However, she was pleasantly surprised by the students' performance, noting their consistent effort and engagement throughout the course. Unlike past experiences where some students showed disinterest or lack of effort, Sally observed that all groups demonstrated a genuine commitment to the assignments.

> So for the most part, there was even one very emotional response, where I could see that this person really cared about this topic. Yeah, it was related to the Coronavirus response. So people who think that the vaccines are dangerous, which is a very relevant topic. But even sometimes [from my past experiences], if a topic is relevant, it's [still] difficult to get students to be interested in it, interested enough to learn new English vocabulary to talk about it. [But this time, it was different.] So even in the middle of this project, I started to feel really excited about who I was gonna get next. And what were they gonna say?

She also described feeling emotionally invested in the students' success, becoming excited about each group's presentations and crafting thoughtful questions to encourage their learning.

And I think it also, that's also partially why I put so much effort into making the questions. Because after the first group did so well, and then the second group did so well, I really felt motivated. And I, if I, if I were having a conversation with someone, what would I ask them about this? What would I want them to ask me? What are the kinds of things I want to talk about? Or as a person, what kind of I deserve to have an opinion about something, and these students deserve to have their opinion heard, whatever it is. So I think my feelings changed quite dramatically from the start of the presentation to the end of the presentation. Usually, I find these kinds of projects emotionally draining, because I so much want them to succeed. I saw very much wanting [them] to do well and to believe in themselves. And a lot of times I just can't get them to that point. But this time it was very different. And I think they felt it. They found how well they were doing. They felt right it was going. And then the conversation ended up being very interesting and satisfying, satisfying to hear satisfied.

Sally's post-semester interview underscores the transformative impact of students' deep engagement with learning materials on a teacher's motivation to genuinely interact with them. Her reflections highlight the symbiotic nature of language learning, wherein student agency catalyzes teacher engagement and vice versa. As students take ownership of their learning through MT-enabled activities, teachers are empowered to adopt more student-centered approaches. This transformative virtuous cycle is facilitated by a combination of value-oriented contents of global citizenship and global competence and translanguaging pedagogy realized through MT. This conclusion finds validation in the comprehensive analysis of students' reflective feedback on their course experiences, as exemplified by the commentary provided by S15:

> Honestly speaking, not only this semester but also throughout the year, I invested a lot of time in English classes, and it was challenging. However, looking back, I realize that opportunities to deeply learn and study English and global competency are rare unless you're in a language or global studies program at university. The time spent was extremely valuable and worthwhile. Although it was tough, the sense of accomplishment and pride I felt afterwards was rewarding, and I can feel my English skills

improving to the point where I recognize it myself. I consider it a meaningful and rewarding class. In that sense, I am grateful to the professors who have helped me in English class, and I feel good about developing a habit of approaching studying English steadily without fear or resistance.

## Lessons Learned

Certainly, before the implementation of these courses, there existed apprehensions regarding how students would perceive and respond to them, notwithstanding the reasoned process underlying the theorization of the role of MT in my planning. This uncertainty stemmed from the recognition that global issues present considerable complexity, often exceeding students' familiarity with them even in their L1, coupled with the demanding language proficiency requisite for comprehension. Nevertheless, the empirical findings gleaned from this study demonstrate that students not only adeptly engaged with the program but also exhibited measurable enhancements in self-efficacy and autonomy, outcomes realized through their persistent endeavors.

However, several challenges emerged during the implementation of the model. Primarily, students reported a significant workload associated with course participation. Conducted online, the flexible class schedule allowed students to allocate sufficient time for completing various activities, such as collaborative reading, article analyses, presentations, and discussions via Zoom. Given the necessity for prior preparation for most class activities, effectively engaging students with the course materials emerged as a pivotal factor, aligning with the proposed model's emphasis on intrinsically motivating students through MT-enabled translanguaging. Online format also allowed flexibility in content delivery for the instructors, as well. Transitioning to in-person classes in 2022 necessitated content reduction to accommodate available class time and alleviate student workload.

Additionally, the role of language proficiency remained critical in model implementation. The students involved in this case study exhibited language proficiency levels ranging from CEFR A2 to B1. Implementing the model with students of lower proficiency posed greater challenges, as the language complexity of authentic media articles remained formidable even with MT assistance. To address this issue, the utilization of ChatGPT emerged as a potential solution, prompting the author's ongoing efforts to tailor the model for students with lower proficiency levels.

Furthermore, the characteristics of participating students proved to be another critical factor. Students in this study opted for a program focusing on reading and writing skills, taught by a non-native English-speaking instructor, over courses emphasizing listening and speaking skills, delivered by a native English speaker. When in-person classes were implemented in 2022 and 2023, where students were assigned to courses without the opportunity to select, student interest and engagement levels varied compared to those observed in this study. A balance between content learning and language acquisition, as well as how the model can accommodate students' diverse learning styles and preferences, remain as questions for further research to enhance the sophistication of the model.

Several other challenges emerged upon transitioning classes to an in-person context. Despite implementing measures to prevent overreliance on MT, such as think-aloud reading (Oh, 2022) and multiple submissions of writing drafts (Kim & Oh, 2023), some students displayed ambivalence towards the active use of MT for learning GCED and global issues in English classes. Providing a rationale for the use of MT and learning GCED and global competence in this specific context is crucial for fostering positive attitudes towards MT and effectively engaging students in the learning process. To clarify the class focus, the course title was changed to "Global Citizens and English" starting in 2024.

The workload on the part of teachers also warrants attention. In 2021, CEI and CEII were implemented with the support of a research grant, allowing three instructors to collaborate effectively: the author, serving as the principal investigator responsible for course implementation; another researcher assisting with writing tasks and a native English-speaking teacher assisting with English presentations. However, in the transition to in-person classes, without tailored guidance in the writing process and English presentations, the author noticed varying levels of student engagement. Additionally, staying updated on global issues to effectively incorporate them into the curriculum may pose another challenge for teachers.

One potential solution to address these challenges is by leveraging linked communities of practice (CoP), where teachers with diverse expertise can collaborate (Kleinschmit et al., 2023). The author also explored this CoP for global citizens approach with students who have completed CE classes in an extracurricular context (Oh et al., 2023). If this type of online CoPs could be established among students with diverse cultural backgrounds while taking CE courses, intercultural competence can also be nurtured more effectively.

Recognized as a "substantial development leap," MT is reshaping the landscape of English language learning by challenging the notion of English as solely belonging to native speakers; instead, it is transforming English into a shared resource, undermining the normative status historically maintained by Kachru's (1986) *inner circle* (Yamanaka & Toyoshima, 2023). With the emergence of ChatGPT and its versatile applications in language learning, the educational landscape is undergoing profound transformations. In this dynamic environment, instilling confidence in both students and educators to embrace innovative methodologies is essential. Personally, this entire experience has reinforced my confidence in advocating for transformative educational practices, including the integration of MT as a pedagogical translanguaging tool.

## References

Black, R., Thomas, M. K. E., & Bearman, M. (2023). Producing the global graduate: Academic labour and imagined futures in critical times. *Pedagogy, Culture & Society*, 1–18.https://doi.org/10.1080/14681366.2023.2210595

Borkovic, S., Nicolacopoulos, T., Horey, D., & Fortune, T. (2020). Students positioned as global citizens in Australian and New Zealand universities: A discourse analysis. *Higher Education Research & Development, 39*(6), 1106–1121.

Butler, Y. G. (2011). The implementation of communicative and task-based language teaching in the Asia-Pacific region. *Annual Review of Applied Linguistics, 31,* 36–57.

Chang, B. M. (2019). English language policies in Korea and globalization. *Asia-Pacific Journal of Multimedia Services Convergent with Art, Humanities, and Sociology, 9*(1), 699–707.

Choi, S. J. (2013). Issues and challenges in offering English-medium instruction: A close examination of the classroom experiences of professors. *Studies in English Language & Literature, 39*(2), 275–306.

Coyle, D., & Meyer, O. (2021). *Beyond CLIL: Pluriliteracies teaching for deeper learning.* Cambridge University Press.

Dill, J. S. (2013). *The longings and limits of global citizenship education: The moral pedagogy of schooling in a cosmopolitan age.* Routledge.

Horey, D., Fortune, T., Nicolacopoulos, T., Kashima, E., & Mathisen, B. (2018). Global citizenship and higher education: A scoping review of the empirical evidence. *Journal of Studies in International Education, 22*(5), 472–492.

Jiang, L., Yu, R., & Zhao, Y. (2024). Theoretical perspectives and factors influencing machine translation use in L2 writing: A scoping review. *Journal of Second Language Writing, 64,* 101099.

Kachru, B. (1985). Standards, codification and sociolinguistic realism: The English language in the outer circle. In R. Quirk & H. G. Widdowson (Eds.), *English in the world: Teaching and learning the language and literature* (pp. 11–30). Cambridge University Press.

Kim, E. G., & Shin, A. (2014). Seeking an effective program to improve communication skills of non-English-speaking graduate Engineering students: The case of a Korean Engineering school. *IEEE Transactions on Professional Communication, 57*(1), 41–55.

Kim, E. G., Kweon, S.-O., & Kim, J. (2017). Korean engineering students' perceptions of English-medium instruction (EMI) and L1 use in EMI classes. *Journal of Multilingual and Multicultural Development, 38,* 130–145.

Kim, J. S. (2022). Bifurcated language policy and practice: English only policies vs. De facto translingual practices in English-medium instruction classrooms at a Korean university. *Korean Journal of English Language and Linguistics, 22,* 619–636.

Kim, S. H., & Im, J. (2013). The current state of college English education in Korea. *Modern English Education, 14*(2), 263–290.

Kintsch, W. (1998). *Comprehension: A paradigm for cognition.* Cambridge University Press.

Kleinschmit, A. J., Rosenwald, A., Ryder, E. F., Donovan, S., Murdoch, B., Grandgenett, N. F., Pauley, M., Triplett, E., Tapprich, W., & Morgan, W. (2023). Accelerating STEM education reform: Linked communities of practice promote creation of open educational resources and sustainable professional development. *International Journal of STEM Education, 10*(1), 16.

Kobrin, S. J. (2020). How globalization became a thing that goes bump in the night. *Journal of International Business Policy, 3*(3), 280–286.

Kwon, O. (2000). Korea's English education policy changes in the 1990s innovations to gear the nation for the 21st century. *English Teaching., 55*(1), 47–91.

McTighe, J., & Wiggins, G. (1999). *The Understanding by design handbook.* Association for Supervision and Curriculum Development.

Oh, E. J. (2014). Exploring a theory-based model of L2 reading comprehension: CI model for L2 reading comprehension. *Korean Journal of Applied Linguistics, 30*(3), 151–177.

Oh, E. J. (2022). Exploratory study on the use of machine translation for reading in college English classes. *Multimedia-Assisted Language Learning, 25*(4), 66–92.

Oh, E. J., & Kim, E. Y. (2024). Theorizing the role of machine translation in L2 reading: Validating the theory and exploring the learning potential through MT use. *Korean Journal of English Language and Linguistics, 24,* 1028–1050.

Oh, E. J., Kim, E. Y., Myeong, M., Jeon, S. H., Kim, Y., Jang, Y. H., & Yoon, S. (2023). Modeling a community of practice for global competence: A collaborative autoethnography of college EFL learners. *Korean Journal of General Education, 17*(5), 69–92.

Poza, L. (2017). Translanguaging: Definitions, implications, and further needs in burgeoning inquiry. *Berkeley Review of Education, 6*(2), 101–128.

Prilutskaya, M. (2021). Examining pedagogical translanguaging: A systematic review of the literature. *Languages, 6*(4), 180.

Roberts, A., & Lamp, N. (2021). *Six faces of globalization: Who wins, who loses, and why it matters.* Harvard University Press.

Tsui, A., & Tollefson, J. (Eds.). (2007). *Language policy, culture, and identity in Asian contexts.* Lawrence Erlbaum.

Vieira, L. N., O'Sullivan, C., Zhang, X., & O'Hagan, M. (2023). Machine translation in society: Insights from UK users. *Language Resources and Evaluation, 57*(2), 893–914.

Williams, D. G. (2023). Trust and translanguaging in English-medium instruction. *ELT Journal, 77*(1), 23–32.

Yamanaka, T., & Toyoshima, C. (2023). The critical influence of machine translation on foreign language education: A prospective discourse on the rise of a novel instructional landscape. *Ubiquitous Learning: An International Journal, 16*(2), 101–115.

Yim, S. (2017). Globalization and language policy in South Korea. In A. B. M. Tsui & J. W. Tollefson (Eds.), *Language policy, culture, and identity in Asian contexts* (pp. 37–53). Lawrence Erlbaum Associates.

# 11

# ChatGPT and Google Bard in Critical-PBLL: Korean University Student Perspectives

## Mi Kyong Kim

## Innovation Areas and Drivers

The present study goes beyond traditional skill-focused English courses, such as reading and listening, and proposes an alternative learning approach: learner-centered Project-Based Learning (PBL). In South Korea, there has been ongoing research on the integration of this approach into general English education (M. Kim, 2006, 2015). When applied to language education, this method is referred to as Project-Based Language Learning (PBLL), as coined by Beckett and Miller (2006). In the context of incorporating PBL into general English courses, the term PBLL is used. Unlike traditional skill-focused English teaching that emphasizes reading and listening, PBLL shifts the focus to a student-driven inquiry-based teaching method, wherein learners construct knowledge about the English language and the subject of

---

M. K. Kim (✉)
Chodang University, Jeollannam-do, Republic of Korea
e-mail: cpefl2006@hanmail.net

© The Author(s), under exclusive license to Springer Nature Switzerland AG 2025
H. Reinders et al. (eds.), *Innovation in Language Learning and Teaching*, New Language Learning and Teaching Environments,
https://doi.org/10.1007/978-3-031-83561-2_11

inquiry through their own explorations. To foster creative and critical thinking skills within PBLL, research has been conducted in the realm of Critical Project-Based Language Learning (Critical-PBLL), drawing from critical pedagogy as outlined by Freire in 1993 (M. Kim, 2021). Furthermore, recent studies have begun to incorporate Artificial Intelligence (AI) technology-based learning tools to aid in the completion of Critical-PBLL tasks (M. Kim, 2023). In English education, AI technology-based learning tools encompass three main categories: (1) text-based tools (e.g., automated translation systems, grammar checking tools, text generation AIs), (2) voice-based tools (text-to-speech AIs, automated translation with voice output, AI chatbots), and (3) content information tools (text, visual content, sound, coding-based generative AIs). Notable AI tools that provide text-based generative information include ChatGPT and Google Bard. When utilizing these tools in education, the focus should be on exploring practical applications from an educational content and method perspective, rather than limiting their use due to ethical concerns such as plagiarism (D. Kang, 2023; Y. Hwang, 2023). As an alternative and experimental study, this study aims to develop a pedagogical framework that utilizes text-based generative AI in Critical-PBLL and to understand learners' perspectives on this framework.

## PBL, PBLL, and Critical-PBLL

PBL is a robust learner-centered teaching method that involves learners in active inquiry to construct relevant knowledge (Legutke & Thomas, 1991). In this process, instructors shift from being knowledge providers to facilitators and collaborators (Beckett & Slater, 2005, 2020). Conventional PBL usually involves three phases: Phase 1 involves problem identification, where learners autonomously select a problem; Phase 2 entails task performance, during which learners explore and propose solutions to the problem; and Phase 3 involves presentation and evaluation, where learners share their findings and reflections with peers (I. Kang, 2017). These stages can be further subdivided into six stages, as proposed by Moss and Duzer (1998). PBLL refers to the application of PBL in language education, such as English education, with selective language interventions based on learners' proficiency levels and needs. Stoller (1997) extended the six-stage PBL framework to a ten-stage PBLL framework by incorporating language intervention stages. For example, language interventions related to information comprehension and credibility assessment might be integrated during the information collection stage. PBLL adapts to learners' language needs and proficiency levels. Critical-PBLL is a variation of PBLL that includes reflective and critical thinking development by integrating critical education processes into problem identification and task performance stages (M. Kim, 2021). This approach combines language intervention and critical education. Critical-PBLL employs the five-stage problem-posing education framework suggested by Nixon-Ponder (1995), incorporating stages like describing the content of the discussion, defining the problem, personalizing the problem, discussing the problem, and discussing the alternatives of the problem. It aims to foster reflective and critical thinking.

Reflective and critical thinking can overlap (Ennis, 1996; Halpern, 2014), whereas reflective thinking, according to John Dewey (1910), includes assessing and reassessing through a critical lens. In education, efforts are made to identify reflective thinking, using conceptual frameworks such as Hatton and Smith (1995) and van Manen (1977), which consider reflective thinking as a linear process. However, reflective thinking intertwines with critical thinking in complex and abstract ways, often following a spiral pattern. A conceptual framework like Jay and Johnson (2002) allows integrated analysis by considering characteristics of reflective thinking, such as additional perspectives, personal values and experiences, and a broad understanding of issues. In the context of Critical-PBLL, reflective thinking plays a vital role in promoting critical thinking. Research on PBL in English education focuses on enhancing English skills and learner-driven knowledge construction (J. Jung, 2019; M. Shin, 2018, 2019), developing critical and reflective thinking abilities (M. Kim, 2019; Kim & Pollard, 2017), intensifying engagement in unfamiliar learner-centered environments (M. Kim, 2015), and exploring the relationship between English proficiency and task performance (Kim, 2021).

This study aims to present a Critical-PBLL framework for a general English course in South Korea, tailoring language interventions to learners' needs and proficiency levels. The study seeks to conduct learner-driven inquiry processes that foster reflective and critical thinking, analyze learners' English learning experiences, and examine the impact of these activities.

## AI Technology-Based Learning Tools in ELT

Within Critical-PBLL, the study aims to utilize learning tools to assist learners, including those with limited English proficiency, in jointly performing tasks such as final outcome generation and presentation. General English education includes students from various departments with different English levels. Particularly, skills like speaking and writing, which are crucial in the final outcome presentation, are considered challenging even for proficient English learners. This might be due to a relatively lower emphasis on these skills in domestic English education. To facilitate task performance, one of the language-transcending practices called translanguaging (Garcia et al., 2017) is proposed to be used through AI technology-based learning tools that offer various language options (Vogel et al., 2018).

In language education, such as English Language Teaching (ELT), AI technology-based learning tools can be actively utilized to construct knowledge (Groves & Mundt, 2021). These tools broadly provide English learning resources in the form of (1) text, (2) voice, and (3) content. Firstly, text-based resources, such as automated translation systems (e.g., Naver Papago, Google Translate), grammar-checking tools (e.g., Grammarly), and text-based AI generators (e.g., ChatGPT), have been researched for their potential in English education. For example, the use of automated translation systems (Lee, 2020; Tsai, 2019) and grammar-checking tools (H. Yang, 2018) in English writing activities is analyzed for their effectiveness and advantages. Secondly, voice-based resources have recently gained attention. With advancements in text-to-speech technology, there are text-to-speech AI tools (e.g., Natural Readers) and voice-transformed outputs from automated translation systems (e.g., Naver Papago). Additionally, AI chatbots (e.g., Google Assistant) offer voice-based interactions. These tools have been analyzed for their potential in final outcome presentation processes (M. Kim, 2023) and English-speaking activities (Yang et al., 2022) during PBLL. Thirdly, content-rich materials and information generated by emerging generative AI tools are being explored for their potential as learning tools. Generative AI refers to AI models that generate content based on prompts. Such content can be in the form of text, visual content, sound, or even coding. Text generation AI tools like ChatGPT and Google Bard fall into this category. ChatGPT, a combination of Chat and Generative Pre-trained Transformer, was released on November 30, 2021. Google Bard was released on March 21, 2023. Recent research has explored the potential of using text-based ChatGPT as a language education tool. For example, ChatGPT has been proposed for use in Korean writing education activities, involving the development of usage guidelines, activity design, and analysis of participant experiences (Oh, 2023). The potential of ChatGPT in content-based language education methods, such as PBLL, has been investigated due to its context-aware wide-ranging information provision and multi-language capabilities (Shin et al., 2023; Sudajit-apa, 2023). Moreover, research is being conducted on prompt literacy. As ChatGPT generates responses based on the input prompt, understanding the prompt's role is crucial (S. Chang, 2023). Studies are being conducted to define and develop prompt literacy for effective usage of ChatGPT (Y. Hwang, 2023). In recent research on AI technology-based language education, there is a focus on the usage of automated translation systems rather than newly developed text-based AI generators. Research investigates the development of metalinguistic awareness, such as modifying and using automated translation outputs, to reduce learning anxiety (Lee, 2021; Roehr, 2007). Additionally, studies explore the technical limitations (Lee & Briggs, 2021), learning effectiveness (Clifford et al., 2013), and dependency (Stapleton & Kin, 2019) on automated translation systems.

Text-based AI generators hold significant potential for a Critical-PBLL general English course. Firstly, from a linguistic perspective, it provides actual results written in proper English, allowing learners to practice English logic, vocabulary, grammar, and writing. Secondly, it offers the flexibility of using both Korean and English prompts and outputs, enabling inclusive communication through practices like code-switching and translanguaging. Thirdly, its content provision suits content-centered language education methods like Critical-PBLL, where learners construct knowledge through inquiry and problem-solving processes. Based on these considerations, this study aims to develop and apply a Critical-PBLL general English course framework using text-based generative AI tools like ChatGPT and Google Bard, while assessing the potential and implications through learner experiences.

## A Framework for Integrating ChatGPT and Google Bard into a Critical PBLL General English Course

A framework for Critical-PBLL using ChatGPT and Google Bard was designed and implemented into a general English course. The Critical-PBLL approach combined (1) the problem-based learning process that stimulates reflective and critical thinking necessary for knowledge exploration and construction (Nixon-Ponder, 1995) with (2) language intervention (Stoller, 1997), and (3) integrated presentations and reflection. Students were encouraged to use various AI-based learning tools in a learner-centric manner during task execution. Firstly, the two AI generators, providing results in both content and language aspects, were utilized. Secondly, text-to-speech AI (Natural Readers) and an automatic translation tool (Google Translate and Naver Papago) were used to convert text to speech. The text-to-speech AI was predominantly used during the final stage of Critical-PBLL for oral presentations, while the text-based AI generators were employed throughout the entire process. The Critical-PBLL general English course was designed based on a modified version of the 12-step Critical-PBLL instructional framework (M. Kim, 2023). The tasks undertaken by learners through this framework included (1) Korean and English group journals and (2) group oral presentations. The Critical-PBLL framework in a general English course was operated with an educational curriculum as outlined below.

Step 1 (Understanding Source Material): In this step, language intervention (I) and the use of ChatGPT and Google Bard were employed. Firstly, the English learning process involved selecting an English-language article related to significant social issues relevant to the learners.

In the context of this study conducted in the first half of 2023, the issue of "South Korea's birthrate sinks to fresh record low as population crisis deepens" was chosen, which was widely discussed domestically and internationally. The article selected for analysis was "South Korea's birthrate sinks to fresh record low as population crisis deepens" published by The Guardian on February 22, 2023 (McCurry, 2023). Language intervention was conducted in five areas: (1) English logic, (2) coherence, (3) sentence structure, (4) vocabulary, and (5) reading comprehension. Additionally, the text language results from the two AIs were used to enhance vocabulary and comprehension.

Steps 2–9 (Writing English Group Journals): A total of seven steps were involved in crafting English group journals. Step 2 involved problem selection, where each group identified a paragraph, sentence, or word from the English article that sparked their curiosity. The content aspect of the AI generator results was used to explore the chosen problems and their related issues. In Step 3, the identified passage, sentence, or word was translated into Korean. The language aspect of these two AI results was employed for this task. In Step 4, personalization of the problem was achieved by connecting the chosen issue to the learners' own experiences and surroundings. The language aspect of ChatGPT and Google Bard results (Korean to English) was utilized. Step 5 involved discussing the problem from multiple perspectives, considering its social, cultural, economic, and historical contexts. Both the content and language aspects of the two AI results were used for this step. In Step 6, alternative solutions to the problem were devised. Both the content and language aspects of the two AI results were utilized. In Step 7, the initial draft of the group journal was completed. Tasks completed in Steps 2–6 were compiled by group leaders to create the draft journal. The logical structure was refined while reviewing the journal as a whole. For example, if an alternative solution was presented during the problem discussion, it was moved to a separate section. Both the content and language aspects of the two AI results were used. In Step 8, language intervention (II) was conducted. Faculty feedback primarily focused on English logic (coherence). In Step 9, the revised version of the English group journal was completed by integrating the modified content from the previous steps. Both the content and language aspects of the AI generator results were used.

Steps 10–11 (Group Presentation): Step 10 involved language intervention (III). Groups prepared English oral presentations, writing their speeches collaboratively. The professor explained the structure of the presentations (introduction, main points, conclusion) and provided models for the introduction and conclusion. Learners worked together to write their group presentations, and the final version was shared by the group leader through SNS messaging. This included English transition phrases. Learners also practiced their presentations outside of class, focusing on pronunciation, stress, and intonation. Text-to-speech AI tools (Natural Readers and TTS features of automatic translators) were utilized for practice. In Step 11, groups orally presented their findings in English and engaged in question-and-answer sessions. Question and answer sessions were conducted in Korean to expand the range of expressions. The content of the question and answer sessions was based on Part 2 of the final group journal, written in English.

Step 12 (Writing Final Draft of Group Journals): This step involved preparing the final version of the group journal, including the question and answer sessions. Both the content and language aspects of ChatGPT and Google Bard results were used for writing the final group journal. The final journals were submitted through the university's Learning Management System.

## Implementation in Context

In the first semester of 2023, a six-week (weeks 9 to 14) course based on text-based generative AI was conducted within the framework of Critical-PBLL for a general English course. The participants consisted of 20 students who agreed to take part in the study, all of whom were enrolled in the course titled "Basic English Utilizing AI" at a Korean university. A total of 20 students were divided into four groups of five, each group encompassing various academic years and majors. Participants engaged in various forms of research activities, including questionnaires, reflective notes, group journals, Social Network Services (SNS) messaging, and interviews. Prior to the study, a pre-questionnaire was conducted to assess participants' English proficiency, previous experience with AI-based learning tools, and familiarity with learner-centered approaches. Results showed a diverse range of English proficiency levels among participants, ranging from 1st grade to 6th grade in the national college entrance exam and TOEIC scores ranging from the 250 s to a perfect 990. Given the relatively higher English proficiency of students in the aviation field, the group leader was selected from an aviation major. The participants had no prior experience in diverse genres of English writing or spoken presentations. Furthermore, none of the participants had previous experience with AI-based learning tools. With the exception of a participant who had experience with learner-centered flipped learning, the rest were more accustomed to traditional instructor-led lecture-style classes. All participant names were pseudonyms.

This study aimed to analyze the learning experiences of participating students through the implementation of a Critical-PBLL general English course utilizing ChatGPT and Google Bard for six weeks (Weeks 9–14). Qualitative data was collected and analyzed for this purpose. Firstly, a total of 16 open-ended anonymous questionnaires were collected (Questionnaire, S1-S16). The questionnaire comprised three open-ended questions designed to gain comprehensive insights into participants' perceptions of the course framework. The questions focused on identifying advantages, disadvantages, and overall impressions. Secondly, 16 reflective notes were collected. Reflective notes were divided into seven sections to understand the learning experiences throughout the entire Critical-PBLL process. These sections included aspects related to English learning, AI utilization, knowledge construction, critical perspectives, group activities, the use of group SNS messaging, and overall impressions. Thirdly, four sets of group journals were collected. The course was divided into four groups, each submitting a group journal. Group journals were utilized as part of the learning model to promote knowledge construction through learner-driven exploration from a critical perspective. The journals were divided into two parts. Part 1 consisted of five questions following the five-step problem-posing approach of critical education (Nixon-Ponder, 1995). Part 2 involved question-and-answer sessions aimed at understanding the comprehensive perspectives presented in the oral presentations. Fourthly, four sets of SNS messaging were collected. In line with the Critical-PBLL group task and communication purposes, each group with a designated group leader who opened a group chat for communication. The messages were analyzed to understand communication patterns. Finally, interviews were conducted with 13 participants (Interview, S1-S13). These interviews were conducted via telephone during the summer vacation period in July 2023, considering students' remote residences and their academic/personal schedules. The interviews were semi-structured and lasted approximately 30 minutes per participant. The entire interview process involved recording, transcribing, and analyzing recorded conversations and researcher notes. The interview questions were structured around the sections in the reflective notes, with a focus on the advantages, disadvantages, and critical perspectives of using the two AIs, as well as experiences related to group journals and activities. The 13 participants had diverse backgrounds and English proficiency levels, with only two having previous experience in studying abroad. Participants had no prior experience with learner-centered classes or AI-based English learning tools, nor had they engaged in preparatory learning for formal English writing or spoken presentations.

The collected and analyzed qualitative data in this study underwent thematic analysis (Braun & Clarke, 2006), a qualitative data analysis method. To comprehensively and deeply analyze the vast amount of collected data, a method was employed that involved identifying themes within the data, structuring these themes to derive meaning, and categorizing related concepts. The researcher iteratively read through the data, noting keywords related to participants' experiences in using ChatGPT and Google Bard in the Critical-PBLL learning context. From these keywords, overarching concepts were identified, followed by the categorization of related concepts. Through integration, key categories were derived. Qualitative data analysis software, QSR-NVivo, was used to code the analysis data, allowing for the categorization of keyword and theme frequencies, as well as hierarchies of higher-level and lower-level concepts, ultimately leading to the extraction of key categories (Bazeley & Jackson, 2013). To ensure the qualitative research validity (Creswell & Creswell, 2018) of data collection and analysis, multiple strategies were employed, including triangulation, participant agreement, and peer debriefing. (1) Triangulation was achieved by using five types of extensive analysis data (questionnaires, reflective notes, final group journals, SNS messaging, and interviews). (2) Participant agreement was obtained during the first week of the Critical-PBLL course (Week 9). Participants were informed of the purpose of using and sharing submitted data for research purposes only and obtained their consent. (3) Peer debriefing was conducted by seeking perspectives from two fellow professors, who are members of the PBL research community within the campus, to gain insights on conducting the Critical-PBLL general English course and analyzing its results. The categorization structure derived from the qualitative analysis approach began with distinguishing between positive and negative learning experiences. This categorization was integrated into key categories through iterative and cyclical coding.

## Results and Discussion

Learners' experiences are classified into the following categories: knowledge construction, reflective thinking, playful learning, teacher as facilitator, excessive AI use and reduced discussion, and challenges in understanding prompts and tasks.

### Knowledge Construction

Research related to knowledge construction through project-based learning on inquiry topics and English proficiency has been consistently conducted in English education (M. Kim, 2019; M. Shin, 2019). Furthermore, within content-based English teaching methods like PBL in English education, there have been suggestions regarding the potential of text-based generative AI tools (such as ChatGPT and Google Bard) as learning tools (Shin et al., 2023; Sudajit-apa, 2023, July). In the context of this Critical-PBLL study that utilizes text-based AI generators, knowledge construction activities emerged as the most frequent segments, accounting for the highest frequency. Knowledge construction was divided into two aspects: inquiry topics and English language.

Firstly, knowledge construction on inquiry topics was analyzed in terms of the roles of the two AI generators, and usage patterns. One is that the roles of the two AIs were seen as positively contributing to various aspects, particularly their ability to rapidly extract a vast amount of information for knowledge construction. More specifically, they were perceived to aid in generating various perspectives related to inquiry topics and alternatives (problem-solving skills) and enhancing topic comprehension. The other is that usage patterns were categorized into overall usage patterns and task-specific usage patterns. Overall usage patterns encompassed (1) ways of utilizing ChatGPT and Google Bard. (2) The process of promoting prompt literacy was another usage pattern. Task-specific usage patterns were classified into (1) usage from the problem selection phase throughout the Critical-PBLL process. (2) Furthermore, it extended into the use within academic subjects and daily life. Secondly, knowledge construction on English language skills was analyzed in terms of the roles of ChatGPT and Google Bard, and usage patterns. One is that the roles of the AIs appear to contribute to the rapid extraction of diverse and extensive information, aiding knowledge construction. Specifically, it was seen that they assisted in deriving various perspectives related to research topics and alternatives (problem-solving abilities), aiding in understanding the topics. The other is that the usage patterns were divided into overall usage patterns and task-specific usage patterns. Overall usage patterns include (1) methods of utilizing the two AIs. (2) The process of developing prompt literacy was mentioned. Specific usage patterns for tasks were revealed, including (1) using the two AIs from problem selection to ongoing use in the Critical-PBLL process. (2) Furthermore, it was evident that it was used in major subjects and daily life.

In the context of learning English as a foreign language, as in Korea, the potential for English language learning through the outcomes of ChatGPT and Google Bard is significant. Firstly, text-based generative AI provides formal English. In other words, it encompasses structured English with aspects such as English logic (e.g., coherence based on principles like General to Specific, the use of signpost language, a logical structure comprising introduction, body, and conclusion), vocabulary (e.g., usage of modals and one-word verbs with collocations instead of phrasal verbs), and sentence structures (e.g., subject-verb agreement and diverse sentence types). Secondly, these outcomes represent authentic English used in English-speaking regions, rather than being crafted solely for language-learning purposes. Thirdly, employing real and formal English outcomes for learning allows learners to be conscious of lacking English logic, vocabulary, and sentence structures while progressing in their studies. Fourthly, this learning approach is distinct from English proficiency levels and offers easily accessible, personalized lessons based on actual English usage, catering to learner-driven individualization according to their English proficiency.

## Reflection

PBL, driven by learner inquiry, is under research for its potential to enhance reflective thinking skills (M. Kim, 2019; Kim & Pollard, 2017). In this study focused on Critical-PBLL using text-based generative AI, activities centered around reflective thinking were the second-highest frequency segment and were seen as positive learning activities. Critical perspectives were analyzed based on group journals submitted using an integrated reflective detection conceptual framework (Jay & Johnson, 2002). The results were as follows. Firstly, a broad contextual perspective was observed. The following shows that the investigation topic was discussed from four social perspectives. "We discussed this issue from a social perspective. There are four [social] perspectives on this topic" (Group journal, Team 2 collaboration task). Secondly, expressions of personal values, experiences, and beliefs were evident. The following shows that an opposing viewpoint based on personal beliefs (overgeneralization) was presented in response to the perspective that low birth rates result from women prioritizing personal freedom over marriage. "It is claimed that women prioritizing personal freedom over marriage is a major cause of low birth rates. However, **I believe** this statement is an overgeneralization" (emphasis added) (SNS messaging, Hyun Woo). Thirdly, additional perspectives were presented. During the question-and-answer session, as part of the conclusion of an English oral presentation, a student presented additional perspectives (balance in childcare policy and imbalance in policy benefits) on the investigation topic (solutions to low birth rate policies). "Childcare policies are implemented by the country or society to support and protect childcare. These policies aim to help parents provide quality childcare, promote the development and well-being of children, and alleviate economic burdens. However, these childcare policies can often lead to issues of imbalanced distribution of benefits or equilibrium" (Group Journal, Han Ul). Most of the segments related to reflective thinking were derived from group journals and SNS messaging. Activities utilizing SNS messaging seemed to enhance reflective thinking as they performed tasks based on Nixon-Ponder's (1995) problem-posing stage, which utilized question items in group journals. This suggests that activities using SNS messaging have contributed to enhancing reflective thinking skills.

## Playful Learning

The following segment with a high frequency also revealed a positive learning experience akin to playful activities (Tardy, 2021). A student referred to this as "playful studying" (Interview, S12). The results were as follows. Firstly, participants expressed that the Critical-PBLL approach using ChatGPT and Google Bard was refreshing and not burdensome. A student stated, "I found it fascinating to study in a new way" (Questionnaire, S16). Another student mentioned, "It was nice to break away from the traditional methods of learning English and find something fresh and interesting. I also learned new ways of studying English" (Questionnaire, S15). Furthermore, a student highlighted, "I could learn something different from what I have learned in school so far, and above all, I felt comfortable without pressure" (Interview, S11). Secondly, specific content-based English learning through Critical PBLL appeared to evoke interest. A student mentioned that activities like analyzing a single English article to identify issues were interesting (Reflection Note, Hyon Woo). Another student expressed, "Dealing with social issues through English newspapers made it engaging, and I felt proud to learn related knowledge [problems, societal perspectives, and alternatives] that I didn't know before" (Reflection Note, I-Han). Furthermore, another student shared, "I could discover new [exploration] issues and gain unexpected opinions. It was innovative as a new way of learning English" (Reflection Note, Yong He). In essence, learning English through Critical-PBLL involved studying content (research topics) and English simultaneously, based on English news articles dealing with social issues, identifying problems, exploring from various angles using the two AI generators, finding alternatives, and presenting results through English journals and oral presentations. Thirdly, the task-based, project-oriented learning process of Critical-PBLL has been compared to playful English learning. A participant expressed that the process of studying while performing tasks felt like a game or play, thus enhancing the efficiency of learning (Interview, I-Han).

The process of Critical PBLL utilizing ChatGPT and Google Bard revealed a form of playful learning where knowledge construction and task completion took place within a space akin to playful activities (Cook, 1997). This study was conducted in an elective English course. Due to the characteristics of elective courses being different from major courses, the researchers designed the majority of assignments to be completed during class time to reduce assignment-related burdens. Consequently, (1) time limits were imposed, (2) immediate "quests" (missions) were expected during group tasks, (3) instant rewards (group task completion or feedback) were provided during task performance, and (4) competition was inherent in group tasks. These game elements applied in the learning context, making the learning process engaging, are referred to as gamification (Figueroa, 2015; H. Lee & D. Shin, 2022). In this study, this form of gamification seemed to have promoted English learning as a playful element.

## Excessive AI Use and Reduced Discussion

In English education, the issue of learners becoming overly reliant on automatic translation tools has been studied (Stapleton & Kin, 2019). Similar concerns have also emerged in the use of text-based generative AI (Jackson, August 2023). This study centered around Critical-PBLL in a general English course, utilizing ChatGPT and Google Bard revealed a similar concern. The next high-frequency segment highlighted a negative learning experience, indicating that the excessive use of the AIs led to a reduction in the discussion process. In other words, the exploration and discussion stages were compressed, and this seemed to be correlated with the excessive use of the two AIs. Based on the convenience of instant information provided by the AIs and their usefulness in task performance, another student commented, "It feels like I can just use AI search based on what the teacher provided" (Interview, S1). This excessive use of generative AIs during task performance seems to have led to a reduction in group discussion processes. In other words, tasks were completed in a divided manner rather than collaborative, as sufficient information could be acquired without much discussion. A student revealed the need for discussion by saying, "Instead of discussing a certain topic, we just divided it into two parts. One person took one part, and another person took the other part. They just summarized their assigned parts later. Because of this, I think we need some time for exchanging opinions with team members" (Interview, S5). The excessive use of the two AIs during task performance and the resulting reduction in group discussions indicate a need for strategies to balance these aspects. For instance, starting with group discussions and then incorporating Google search engine use followed by the AI generators could explicitly encourage the exploration and discussion process, thereby promoting a more balanced learning experience.

## Challenges in Understanding Prompts and Tasks

The next high-frequency segment that emerged highlighted a negative learning experience related to the challenges faced during the initial stages of Critical-PBLL tasks. A student expressed, "At first, it was difficult because it was my first time encountering such tasks. It was a bit challenging to adapt at first, but after getting used to it, it became smoother" (Interview, S11). The challenges in the initial task performance seemed to be linked to (1) low prompt literacy and (2) unfamiliar tasks based on critical thinking.

Firstly, a student with low prompt literacy mentioned, "Using search terms [prompt literacy] was quite difficult. When I tried, I often got strange answers. You need to search accurately to get accurate results" (Interview, S8). (1) Improved prompt literacy was attributed to a better understanding of the research topic. Therefore, a higher understanding of the research topic appeared to enhance prompt literacy. (2) To foster this, separate guidelines and practices were suggested. Literacy can be categorized into four types: traditional literacy, digital literacy, AI literacy, and prompt literacy, which is an extension of AI literacy (Y. Hwang, 2023). Traditional literacy refers to reading and writing skills for text-based information, digital literacy includes skills for processing and utilizing video-based information alongside scientific advancement, AI literacy refers to understanding and utilizing AI technology, and prompt literacy is the ability to understand input values and utilize them in conjunction with generated AI outcomes. In the context of text-based generative AI usage, such as in this study, it appears essential to recognize and learn prompt literacy guidelines during the initial tasks. Secondly, unfamiliarity with tasks based on critical thinking, which forms the foundation of Critical-PBLL, seemed evident. A student mentioned, "I knew it was a social issue, but handling it directly was a bit tricky" (Reflection Note, S2). Specifically, challenges were noted during the early stages, such as problem identification and definition. A student commented, "Deciding what to designate as a problem was difficult" (Reflection Note, S2), and in an interview, the same student added, "I thought my head would explode" (Interview, S11), highlighting the difficulty in the problem identification step.

The challenges faced during the initial stages of critical thinking-based tasks seem to underline the importance of the teacher's facilitative role in task performance. A student noted, "Initially, I struggled with what to type, but the professor provided various insights that were helpful. Later on, I didn't face difficulties" (Interview, S13), highlighting the role of the teacher as a facilitator in task performance. Within Critical-PBLL, which emphasizes critical and reflective thinking, a new role for the teacher emerges. While traditional education often involves transmitting knowledge like a bank deposit (Freire, 1993), in Critical-PBLL, the teacher acts as a "coach and facilitator" (Stoller, 1997, p. 5), encouraging critical thinking-based tasks.

## Conclusion

In this chapter, I developed a Critical-PBLL framework in a general English course at a Korean university that promotes critical thinking through learner-driven exploration and reflection while constructing knowledge about English and exploratory topics. Additionally, to support Critical-PBLL tasks, text-based generative AI tools like ChatGPT and Google Bard are employed. Then, I explored the student learning perspectives on the course. Drawing from the empirical findings of the study, I conclude with the following three pedagogical implementations for Critical Project-Based Language Learning (Critical-PBLL) utilizing text-based generative AI tools. First, it is crucial to collaboratively develop prompt literacy guidelines with learners. The use of generative AI tools, such as ChatGPT and Google Bard, is indispensable and has demonstrated significant educational value. However, existing guidelines predominantly emphasize information verification and ethical considerations. Thus, guidelines addressing prompt literacy, a vital aspect of employing text-based generative AI, should be developed collaboratively within the context of English language instruction. Second, the English outputs generated by these generative AIs can be actively integrated into language learning. These outputs, which reflect authentic English as used in English-speaking environments, can serve as valuable language intervention tools, particularly in contexts such as Korea, where English is taught as a foreign language. Lastly, it is imperative to establish specific guidelines for the proper utilization of AI generators with learners. For example, a structured sequence could be implemented during brainstorming sessions, beginning with group discussions, followed by a Google search, and culminating with the incorporation of generative AIs. Such an approach would help regulate the excessive use of AI tools and facilitate more focused and productive discussion processes.

# References

Bazeley, P., & Jackson, K. (2013). *Qualitative data analysis with NVivo* (2nd ed.). Sage.
Beckett, G., & Miller, P. (Eds.). (2006). *Project-based second and foreign language education: Past, present, and future*. Information Age Publishing.
Beckett, G., & Slater, T. (2005). The project framework: A tool for language, content, and skills integration. *ELT Journal, 59*(2), 108–116.
Beckett, G., & Slater, T. (Eds.). (2020). *Global perspectives on project-based language learning, teaching, and assessment: Key approaches, technology tools, and frameworks*. Routledge.
Braun, V., & Clarke, V. (2006). Using thematic analysis in psychology. *Qualitative Research in Psychology, 3*(2), 77–101.
Buruk, O. (2023). *Academic writing with GPT-3.5: Reflections on practices, efficacy, and transparency*. Retrieved 10 August 2023, from the World Wide Web: https://doi.org/10.48550/arXiv.2304.11079
Chang, S. (2023). ChatGPT has changed the future of writing education: Focusing on the response of writing education in the era of artificial intelligence. *Writing Research, 56*, 7–34.
Clifford, J., Merschel, L., & Munné, J. (2013). Questionnaireing the landscape: What is the role of machine translation in language learning? *Research in Education and Learning Innovation Archives, 10*, 108–121.
Cook, G. (1997). Language play, language learning. *English Language Teaching Journal, 51*(3), 224–231.
Creswell, J., & Creswell, J. (2018). *Research design: Qualitative, quantitative, and mixed methods approaches* (5th ed.). Sage.
Dewey, J. (1910). *How we think: A restatement of the relation of reflective thinking to educative process*. Heath and Co.
Figueroa, J. (2015). Using gamification to enhance second language learning. *Digital Education Review, 27*, 32–54.
Ennis, R. (1996). *Critical thinking*. Prentice Hall.
Freire, P. (1993). *Pedagogy of the oppressed*. Penguin.
García, O., Johnson, S., & Seltzer, K. (2017). *The translanguaging classroom. Leveraging student bilingualism for learning*. Caslon.
Groves, M., & Mundt, K. (2021). A ghostwriter in the machine? Attitudes of academic staff towards machine translation use in internationalised Higher Education. *Journal of English for Academic Purposes, 50*(1), 1–11.

Halpern, D. (2014). *Thought and knowledge: An introduction to critical thinking* (5th ed.). Psychology Press.

Hatton, N., & Smith, D. (1995). Reflection in teacher education: Towards definition and implementation. *Teaching and Teacher Education, 11*(1), 33–49.

Hwang, Y. (2023). The emergence of generative AI and PROMPT literacy: Focusing on the use of ChatGPT and DALL-E for English education. *Journal of the Korea English Education Society, 22*(2), 263–288.

Jackson, L. (2023, August). *Revolutionizing academic writing: Exploring the transformative potential of ChatGPT chatbots for students and instructors.* Paper presented at the 2023 AsiaTEFL International Conference, Daejeon, Korea.

Jay, J., & Johnson, K. (2002). Capturing complexity. A typology of reflective practice for teacher education. *Teaching and Teacher Education, 18*(1), 73–85.

Jung, S. (2019). A case study of project-based learning in undergraduate general English class. *Journal of Education & Culture, 25*(5), 325–347.

Kang, D. (2023). The advent of ChatGPT and the response of Korean language education. *Korean Language and Literature, 82*(2), 469–496.

Kang, I. (2017). 4cha Sanop-hyongmyong sidae-ei PBLeui jaejomyong (In the era of the Fourth Industrial Revolution, a reexamination of PBL). *Seoul Education, 59*(4), Retrieved 10 August 2023 from the World Wide Web: https://webzine-serii.re.kr/

Kim, M. (2006). *The iron lady and the angry students: project-based learning using the internet critically in a Korean ELT university setting.* Unpublished doctoral dissertation, Monash University, Melbourne.

Kim, M. (2015). Students' and teacher's reflections on project-oriented learning: A critical pedagogy for Korean ELT. *English Teaching, 70*(3), 73–99.

Kim, M. (2019). Reflective practice in project-based culture learning: Content and quality of reflection. *English Language Teaching, 31*(4), 67–94.

Kim, M. (2021). Developing problem-posing education through project-based learning in an English writing course. *English 21, 34*(1), 109–136.

Kim, M. (2023). PBL using AI technology-based learning tools in a college English class. *Korean Journal of General Education, 17*(2), 169–183.

Kim, M., & Pollard, V. (2017). A modest critical pedagogy for English as a foreign language education. *Education as Change, 21*(1), 50–72.

Lee, H., & Shin, D. (2022). A class model with gamification and metaverse: Focused on long-term memory formation theory and virtual escape room game. *The Journal of Studies in Language, 38*(1), 33–52.

Lee, S. (2020). The impact of using machine translation on EFL students' writing. *Computer-Assisted Language Learning, 33*(3), 157–175.

Lee, S., & Briggs, N. (2021). Effects of using machine translation to mediate the revision process of Korean university students' academic writing. *ReCALL, 33*(1), 18–33.

Lee, Y. (2021). Still taboo? Using machine translation for low-level EFL writers. *ELT Journal, 75*(4), 432–441.

Legutke, M., & Thomas, H. (1991). *Process and experience in the language classroom.* Longman.

McCurry, J. (2023, February 22). South Korea's birthrate sinks to fresh record low as population crisis deepens. *The Guardian.* Retrieved 10 August 2023, from the World Wide Web: https://www.theguardian.com.

Moss, D., & Duzer, V. (1998). *Project-based learning for adult English language learners.* National Clearinghouse for ESL Literacy Education Washington DC. (*ERIC Digest* service no. ED427556).

Nixon-Ponder, S. (1995). *Using problem-posing dialogue in adult literacy education: Teacher to teacher* (p. 381677). Department of Education. ERIC.

Oh, S. (2023). A study on the case of using ChatGPT & learners' perceptions in college liberal arts writing. *Korean Journal of General Education, 17*(3), 11–23.

Roehr, K. (2007). Metalinguistic knowledge and language ability in university-level L2 learners. *Applied Linguistics, 29*(2), 173–199.

Shin, D., Jung, H., & Lee, Y. (2023). Exploring the potential of using ChatGPT as a content-based English learning and teaching tool. *Journal of the Korea English Education Society, 22*(1), 171–192.

Shin, M. (2018). Effects of project-based learning on students' motivation and self-efficacy. *English Teaching, 73*(1), 95–114.

Shin, M. (2019). Study of English teaching method by convergence of project-based learning and problem-based learning for English communication. *Journal of Korea Convergence Society, 10*(2), 82–88.

Stapleton, P., & Kin, B. (2019). Assessing the accuracy and teachers' impressions of Google translate: A study of primary L2 writers in Hong Kong. *English for Specific Purposes, 56*, 18–34.

Sudajit-apa, M. (2023, July). *The intersection of artificial intelligence and ESP: From linguistic analysis to implications for ESP pedagogy.* Paper presented at the Asia TEFL Webinar Series, Seoul, Korea.

Stoller, F. (1997). Project work: A means to promote language content. *Forum, 35*(4), 1–10.

Tardy, C. (2021). The potential power of play in second language academic writing. *Journal of Second Language Writing, 53*, 1–10.

Tsai, S. (2019). Using Google Translate in EFL drafts: A preliminary investigation. *Computer Assisted Language Learning, 32*(5–6), 510–526.

Van Manen, M. (1977). Linking ways of knowing with ways of being practical. *Curriculum Inquiry, 6*(3), 205–228.

Vogel, S., Ascenzi-Moreno, L., & García, O. (2018). An expanded view of translanguaging: Leveraging the dynamic interactions between a young multilingual writer and machine translation software. In J. Choi & S. Ollerhead (Eds.), *Plurilingualism in teaching and learning: Complexities across contexts* (pp. 89–106). Taylor & Francis.

Yang, H. (2018). Efficiency of online grammar checker in English writing performance and students' perceptions. *Korean Journal of English Language and Linguistics, 18*(3), 328–348.

Yang, H., Kim, H., Lee, J., & Shin, D. (2022). Implementation of an AI chatbot as an English conversation partner in EFL speaking classes. *ReCALL, 34*(3), 327–343.

# 12

# An Analysis of Flipped Learning Research Trends in Korean EFL Classrooms: Using Big Data Techniques

Hye-Kyung Kim and Sumi Han

## Flipped Learning

In education, innovation is essential to meet the changing needs of students. Traditional teacher-centered teaching techniques often place students in passive roles, who are merely informants (Freire, 1970; Jung et al., 2016). These teaching strategies can hinder students' critical thinking and creativity, and overlook individual students' differences in learning preferences and progress. In view of these shortcomings, modern education is introducing new strategies, and 'flip learning' is emerging as an important paradigm shift as one of those strategies (Bergmann & Sams, 2012).

---

H.-K. Kim
Tech University of Korea, Siheung, South Korea
e-mail: kimhk@tukorea.ac.kr

S. Han (✉)
Hallym University, Chuncheon, South Korea
e-mail: sumihan@hallym.ac.kr

Flipped learning differs from traditional teacher-centered approaches in several ways. Before class, students actively participate in content using technology-driven tools rather than passively absorbing it. This active approach is to embrace different learning styles and speeds while encouraging creativity and critical thinking. This innovative teaching method is especially important in English as a Foreign Language (EFL) classrooms. Since most Korean students are not surrounded by an English-speaking environment, new methods such as flipped learning can be beneficial to students who are placed in those environments. Using technology, students can independently access online materials or videos before class, and it is possible to prepare for deeper discussions and practice during class (Yoon, 2021). This new approach provides a more effective way to learn English (Kim & Han, 2021; Mok, 2014).

However, adopting new teaching methods in class often comes with challenges. In the case of flipped learning, it involves integrating with traditional teaching practices and finding the right materials, as well as addressing resistance from both teachers and students (Akçayır & Akçayır, 2018). Despite these challenges, flipped learning has become increasingly popular due to technological advances.

This study looks into the innovative use and results of flipped learning in the unique cultural and educational setting of Korean EFL classrooms. A main focus is the bibliometric and keyword analysis of flipped learning trends in these classrooms, using the strength of big data technology. This fresh approach is expected to highlight the effective use of flipped learning and the big changes it can bring about. As Korean EFL classrooms deal with their special challenges and chances, adding tech-based methods including flipped learning is a key move to improve educational quality.

# Impetus for the Innovation

## Driving Forces Behind Flipped Learning

Flipped learning is a fresh teaching idea that is changing the way we see education. Before class, students go over materials by themselves. Students can learn in their own way and at their own pace. Then, they go deeper into topics with group discussions and hands-on activities during class. Students work together, helping each other out and receiving guidance from their teacher. This way, classrooms change from teacher-centered to learner-centered (Bergmann & Sams, 2012; Kim, 2017; Strayer, 2012).

When technology started growing quickly in the early 2000s and more learning materials became available online, it became easier for students to study on their own. This change helped make flipped learning a popular choice in schools (Bishop & Verleger, 2013). Now, it is not just in some schools but all over the world. It is used in many areas, from regular school subjects to job training and even in learning new languages, helping students get ready for real-life situations (Abeysekera & Dawson, 2015).

Furthermore, the COVID-19 pandemic made us rethink how we teach and learn. Before it, flipped learning was just one of many teaching methods. However, with more classes moving online during the pandemic, it became a key way to teach (Bao, 2020; Kim et al., 2014). With less face-to-face time, students needed efficient ways to learn by themselves. In this context, flipped learning was the answer. It showed us how important it is for students to study on their own and be in charge of their learning.

## Positive Outcomes and Ripple Effects of Flipped Learning

One of the key benefits of flipped learning is its ability to create a more inclusive classroom environment. By engaging with lecture materials on their own time before class, students are better prepared to participate in deeper discussions and activities during class time. This prior preparation enables teachers to design class activities that cater to the diverse needs of their students, offering tailored instruction, support, and additional activities that align with each student's learning style (Abeysekera & Dawson, 2015; Mok, 2014). Another advantage is that flipped learning transforms the classroom into a hub of active learning, where students collaborate and engage in critical thinking. With foundational knowledge acquired before class, students are more equipped to tackle complex tasks requiring advanced thinking during class sessions. This approach to active learning not only enhances problem-solving skills but also prepares students for real-life challenges by promoting teamwork (Bishop & Verleger, 2013; Strayer, 2012). Moreover, the integration of technology in flipped learning to provide personalized learning paths and support active learning strategies represents a move towards a more learner-centered educational model.

Research on flipped learning with Korean EFL learners has found that this approach enhances students' English skills by increasing their motivation and engagement (Byun, 2019; Kang, 2015; Kim & Han, 2021; Lee & Wallace, 2018). Byun (2019) examined the use of TedED videos in a flipped English reading class and found that students who watched the videos before class improved their vocabulary and understanding of the topics. The variety of content on TedED also helped students with self-directed learning. Kang (2015) evaluated flipped classrooms in a college-level general English course and discovered that students showed significant improvement in vocabulary and grammar. The study also reported high student satisfaction and highlighted the important role of technology even though some students faced challenges in completing assignments. Kim and Han (2021) observed significant enhancements in English proficiency among first-year engineering majors over a year in college English courses. Lee and Wallace (2018) compared traditional and flipped learning in a college English course. They found that students in the flipped classroom had higher scores and were more engaged. Most students preferred this method, showing its benefits for teaching English. Furthermore, the integration of technology in Korean EFL education, especially during the COVID-19, has been explored, focusing on Learning Management Systems (LMS), mobile applications (e.g., KakaoTalk), and online platforms (e.g., Zoom, Google Meet). Educational technologies such as TedED and MOOCs have also been frequently employed as learning resources in various studies (e.g., Byun, 2019; Kang, 2015; Kim, 2015; Kim & Han, 2021).

In summary, flipped learning has brought important changes to education. By using technology to create personalized and active learning, it increases student engagement and success, while also preparing them for the challenges of today's world.

## Evolving Research Directions in Flipped Learning

Technological advancements have broadened the possibilities of using various educational technology tools and platforms, such as online videos, LMS, and lecture creation tools. These tools have paved the way for learners to engage in self-directed learning. Teachers, in turn, have harnessed these tools to deliver content more effectively (Bishop & Verleger, 2013).

Recent studies indicate that flipped learning not only improves students' self-directed learning capabilities but also enhances their collaborative, problem-solving, and critical thinking skills (Hung, 2015; Silverajah et al., 2022). Within a flipped learning environment, students gain exposure to diverse perspectives through discussions and collaborations, enriching their overall learning experience. Initially, flipped learning research was primarily concerned with learning outcomes and performance evaluation. However, as technology has evolved, the research scope has broadened, with a growing emphasis on enhancing various student learning abilities.

To explore English education research trends, methodologies such as meta-analysis and corpus-based analysis have been popular. Recently, bibliometric analysis has emerged as a preferred method due to its capability to identify key research themes and influential publications. For example, Dong et al. (2023) used this approach to examine the development of data-driven learning (DDL) over time. Bakelak and Rodríguez

(2022) analyzed English language teaching journals, focusing on contributions from Latin American authors. Kayadibi (2022) conducted a bibliometric analysis on 'bilingualism' from 1970 to 2021, highlighting the USA's leading role in bilingual education. Zhang (2020) looked at trends in second language acquisition between 1997 and 2018, using citation data to underscore key works and recent developments in the field.

Flipped learning has revolutionized language learning and teaching. The ability to restructure the traditional classroom and utilize technology to foster self-directed learning can potentially enhance student engagement, motivation, and overall language instruction effectiveness. Despite these advancements, the Korean EFL context faces unique challenges that flipped learning has yet to fully address. These include a heavy reliance on rote memorization, limited opportunities for authentic language use outside the classroom, and the varying levels of digital literacy among students and educators. Such limitations can hinder the full realization of flipped learning's potential in fostering a truly interactive and immersive English learning environment (Hung, 2015; Kang, 2015).

Since its introduction in Korea in the early 2010s, research in English education has expanded. However, there still remains a need to identify key trends and gaps in this research, particularly in addressing the aforementioned challenges. This study aims to address this by answering two primary research questions:

1. What does a bibliometric analysis reveal about publication trends in the field of English education using flipped learning in the Korean context?
2. What insights can a keyword analysis provide regarding primary themes in English education using flipped learning in the Korean context?

# Methodology of This Study

## Data Sources and Selection Criteria

This section delineates the methodology employed to investigate the research trends of flipped classroom techniques on English education in South Korea. The primary source for journal articles was the Research Information Sharing Service (RISS) of South Korea, an extensive repository of academic resources. Articles were selected based on predetermined criteria to maintain a consistent focus. The inclusion criteria for articles were as follows: (a) The study focused on research articles published in Korean academic journals, targeting Korean students and (b) articles published before 2023 were included. The search was conducted between February 11 and 13, 2023, using specific keywords to narrow down relevant studies. Article titles were searched using the following keywords, "flipped" and "English," along with their Korean equivalents ("플립드," "플립트," "거꾸로" + "영어"). As optional filters, the terms "teaching" and "learning" were also used. Throughout this search, a total of 216 articles were extracted.

## Data Crawling and Construction

Data crawling using Python was conducted to gather meta-information from the selected 216 articles. The meta-information for each article included (a) article title, (b) author, (c) author affiliation, (d) author keywords, (e) journal title, (f) publication year, and (g) abstract. Then, the meta-information of each article was examined thoroughly to exclude irrelevant studies: 40 articles were excluded as they were not relevant to the target research area and 6 articles were excluded as they were meta-analytic or synthesis studies. Plus, 12 studies were not included for analysis as the target subject was not Korean. Throughout this data cleaning, a total of 158 articles were included for further analysis. For each study, author name(s) and author affiliation(s) were translated into English, and any missing data such as author keywords were found in the journal articles and added to the dataset in English. The dataset was structured in a spreadsheet format as shown in Fig. 12.1.

## Data Analysis

Two types of big data techniques, a bibliometric analysis and a keyword analysis, were performed on the dataset to identify research trends or themes within the target domain. or both types of analysis, most frequent words or phrases are examined. Analyzing big data of educational, academic research offers a lens to examine vast amounts of information, providing educators and researchers with invaluable insights into learning patterns, student feedback, and the effectiveness of modern teaching methods such as flipped learning (Dietz-Uhler & Hurn, 2013).

First, the bibliometric analysis is used to examine the popularity and impact of certain articles, authors, and publications with data (de Bellis, 2009). Frequencies for each of the variables of the meta-information such as author and publication year were computed and examined. Second, the keyword analysis was conducted by examining author keywords and article titles, in turn, which are widely analyzed to identify main subjects and objects of focus in the articles. Author keywords are easy to grasp the key points of articles as they are given in the articles in four to five words or phrases following journal guidelines. In the pre-processing, synonyms and antonyms were classified into one keyword and (e.g., flipped class, flipped classroom, flipped learning; demotivation, motivation).

However, the number limit of keywords can exclude other key points of the articles. In this sense, analyzing article titles can offer additional insights that may not be captured by the author keywords. This can be particularly useful for identifying overarching themes, methodologies, or target groups that the keywords alone may not convey. Using Natural Language Processing (NLP) techniques with Python programming language, each title was only noun words or phrases were extracted and computed for their frequencies. To identify further focal points of research within the targeted domain, specific topics such as English skills, affective or conceptual themes, technology use, and words related to flipped-learning were identified.

# 12 An Analysis of Flipped Learning Research Trends ...

| No | Article Title | Author | Author Affiliation | Author Keywords | Journal Title | Year | Abstract |
|----|---|---|---|---|---|---|---|
| 1 | The Flipped Classroom Ap | Hyung-ji Chang | Sun Moon University | flipped classroom ; tourism English ; problem sc | English Teaching | 2020 | The purpose of this study was to |
| 2 | A Case Study of the Flippe | Erika Choe; M | Eulji University; Eulji University | flipped learning ; flipped classroom ; students' | Journal of Pan-Pacific Association of | 2016 | Research has proven the effective |
| 3 | A Flipped Learning English | Jung Lim Lee; | Dong-A University; Dong-A Univers | Flipped Learning ; EFL ; writing ; English profic | Studies in British and American Langu | 2020 | The present study aims to explore |
| 4 | The Perceptions of Elemer | Jung-Jin Kang | Gyeongin National University | flipped learning ; output ; English instruction | Primary English Education | 2015 | Flipped learning has recently been |
| 5 | The Effects of Flipped Lea | Yuhwa Lee; Ju | Keimyung University; Keimyung Ur | Flipped learning ; English grammar learning ; jus | Studies in British and American Langu | 2020 | The purpose of this study is to ex |
| 6 | Effects of Flipped Learning | Woo Young Ki | Hansei University | flipped learning ; teaching method ; vocabulary | Korean Journal of English Language a | 2018 | This study is designed to investiga |
| 7 | Flipped Learning in Korean | Youn-Kyoung | Daegu Catholic University | flipped learning ; Korean college English class ; | Studies in Modern Grammar | 2018 | The present study aimed at examin |
| 8 | Improving Korean Student | Jungyin Kim; S | Chonbuk National University; Gach | Flipped Learning ; game-based instruction ; Eng | English21 | 2019 | Flipped learning is a process-orien |
| 9 | Utilizing Flipped Learning | Juyoung Lim | Jungwon University | flipped learning ; EFL ; study on a movie ; a mc | STEM Journal | 2018 | The purpose of this study is to un |
| 10 | Contribution of Learning R | Kyong-Hyon P | Dankook University | flipped classroom ; learning readiness ; quiz ; gr | Foreign languages education | 2019 | The study is aimed at investigating |
| 11 | The Effects of a TTS-Base | Suk-Jin Do | Dongguk University | flipped learning ; TTS-based pre-reading activit | The Mirae Journal of English Languag | 2022 | This study investigated whether a |
| 12 | From Demotivated to Insp | Yoo Jean Lee; | Dankook University; Dankook Univ | flipped learning ; test-based English class ; dem | The Journal of Learner-Centered Curi | 2017 | This study investigates the effect |
| 13 | Learner Perspectives Tow: | Jihyun Byun | Hannam University | flipped learning ; TedED ; English reading ; bac | The Mirae Journal of English Languag | 2019 | The purpose of this paper is to ex |

**Fig. 12.1** Data structure

# Results

## Bibliometric Analysis

1. Publication trend over time

The number of publications per year was examined to identify trends in the field of flipped learning for English education. Figure 12.2 displays these annual publication counts. There has been a consistent interest in this topic from 2015 to 2022, with the years 2017, 2018, 2019, and 2020 seeing a higher number of publications than the others. Notably, 2018 saw the peak with 27 publications, indicating a zenith in research interest and activity in English education using flipped learning.

2. Journals of publication

Since 2015, research journal papers on the use of flipped learning for English education have been published across 58 different Korean journals. These journals can be classified into four areas: 33 journals

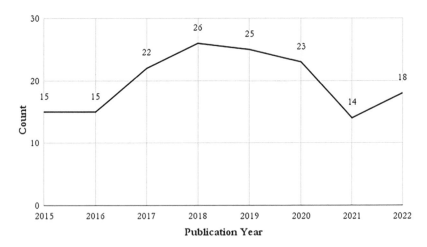

Fig. 12.2 Publication trend over time

in the fields of English Literature, Education, and Linguistics, constituting 56.90% of the total; 14 journals in education studies, making up 24.14%; eight journals in interdisciplinary studies, comprising 13.79%; and lastly, three journals in the humanities field, representing 5.17%.

Figure 12.3 displays the top 10 journals with the highest number of publications. Collectively, these journals account for 74 of the total 158 publications (46.84%), with each journal having five or more publications. The Journal of Learner-Centered Curriculum and Instruction (JLCCI) leads with 12 publications, followed by the STEM Journal and Multimedia-Assisted Language Learning (MALL), each with nine publications. The remaining 48 journals each have four or fewer publications. In summary, this figure acts as an informative roadmap for academics, educators, and stakeholders involved in English education and flipped learning, highlighting key journals and guiding those in search of comprehensive and authoritative research sources.

3. Authors of publication

The most prolific authors in the field of flipped learning for English education have been identified. A total of 136 unique authors were

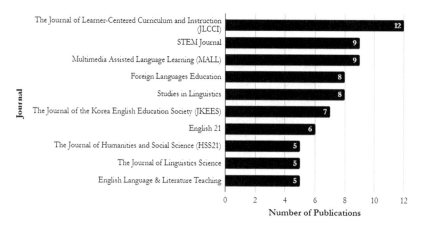

Fig. 12.3 Top 10 journals by publication count

identified in the dataset. As depicted in Fig. 12.4, the chart showcases the top 10 authors by their number of contributions. Leading the list is Kyong-Hyon Pyo from Dankook University with five publications, followed by Seung-eun Lee from Gwangju Women's University and Yuhwa Lee from Keimyung University, each with four publications. Their frequent appearances in the dataset underscore their expertise and active participation in this research area.

Regarding authorship, the majority of the 158 studies were published by either one or two authors. Specifically, 92 studies were single-authored (58.23%), 61 were co-authored by two authors (38.61%), three had three authors (1.90%), one had four authors (0.63%), and one featured seven authors (0.63%).

4. Affiliations of publication

A total of 99 unique affiliations were identified in the dataset as sources of publication, with the majority being universities (85 universities: 85.85%). Additionally, two high schools (2.02%), three middle schools (3.03%), and seven elementary schools (7.07%) were also identified. Furthermore, two notable educational institutions are KERIS

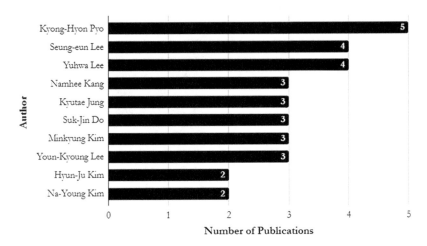

Fig. 12.4 Top 10 authors by publication count

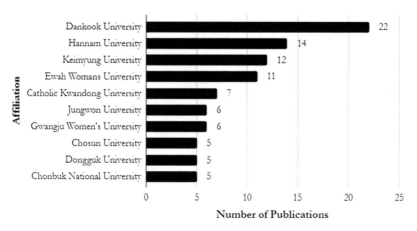

Fig. 12.5 Top 10 affiliations by publication count

(Korea Education and Research Information Service) and KICE (Korea Institute for Curriculum and Evaluation).

Figure 12.5 highlights the top 10 affiliations or institutions producing the most publications on flipped learning in English education. Four universities—Dankook University, Hannam University, Keimyung University, and Ewha Womans University—demonstrate the most active roles in producing and disseminating knowledge on this educational approach. Notably, Dankook University emerges as the leading center for research and innovation in this research domain.

## Keyword Analysis

1. Author keywords

Author keywords or keywords provided in the papers were analyzed to examine the trend of the research area. In Fig. 12.6, the top 10 author keywords are displayed, showing the core themes and areas of interest. A total of 765 keywords were identified in the dataset, and the 10 most frequent author keywords account for almost half of the total (48.37%). A total of 765 keywords were identified in the dataset and the

10 most frequent author keywords account for almost the half of the total (48.37%). Among them, 171 (22.35%) were related to keywords related to "flipped" including flipped learning (117 occurrences) and flipped (learning) class/classes/classroom/curriculum (54 occurrences). The other most frequent keywords are technology (online/mobile) (47 occurrences) and college English (27 occurrences). Self-directed (24 occurrences) and learner-centered (15 occurrences) directly indicate the learning nature of flipped learning. Among English skills, reading (18 occurrences) and writing (16 occurrences) were mostly examined. Motivation (17 occurrences) and satisfaction (15 occurrences) are key features of the affective domain.

2. Key research topics

Key research topics and themes were also examined through the article titles. Based on the analysis of author keywords, four key topics were selected: English skills, affective or conceptual words, technology use, and aspects of flipped learning. Initially, we searched for six English skill-related keywords: reading, listening, writing, speaking, grammar, and vocabulary. A total of 51 instances of these keywords were identified in 43 article titles: reading (16 occurrences), writing (13), vocabulary (7),

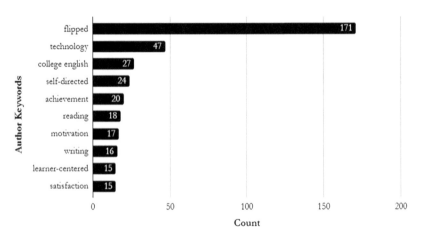

Fig. 12.6 Top 10 author keywords by count

grammar (7), speaking (6), and listening (2). Among these articles, eight examined the effects of flipped learning on more than one skill. Examples are "The effect of integrated English reading and writing classes using flipped learning on Korean university students' reading ability" and "The effects on learners' academic achievement, self-directed learning ability, and learning satisfaction in English reading and writing flipped learning course."

Second, affective or conceptual topics were identified in the article titles, with relevant words such as perception, attitude, (de)motivation being prevalent. Our count revealed perception (47 occurrences) as the most common, followed by satisfaction (25), attitude (19), (de)motivation (18), self-efficacy (6), and affective experiences or factors (5). Studies such as "Students' perception on the active flipped learning approach in the midst of the COVID-19 pandemic" and "EFL college students' affective experience in TOEIC grammar learning through flipped learning: A case of low-level learners." exemplify the focus on these affective aspects within the domain.

Third, we examined any special technology employed in the research from the title data, and when necessary, referred to the abstract and author keywords for additional information. In particular, some studies adopted existing in-house LMS tools such as Blackboard (e.g., Kang, 2015). A few studies utilized applications such as Social Network Service (SNS), KakaoTalk, and game applications for mobile-assisted language learning (e.g., Sung, 2015; Yoon, 2019). Due to the influence of the Covid-19, online platforms such as Zoom were increasingly used (e.g., Kang, 2021). Other technologies, such as TedED and MOOC, were also adopted as learning materials (e.g., Byun, 2019; Lim, 2018; Yoon, 2021).

Lastly, other topics related to flipped learning were also notable in the article titles: self-directed learning (20 occurrences), learning styles (4), and strategies (13). Example studies include "The effects of flipped learning on elementary school students' English achievement and self-directed learning readiness" and "The relationship between learning styles and learners' satisfaction in integrated English reading and writing classes using flipped learning."

# Discussion and Conclusion

## Key Findings

Key findings of the bibliometric and keyword analyses are as follows: In Korean EFL classrooms, flipped-based English education has been adopted as one of the most innovative teaching method. This approach is particularly innovative in Korean contexts as it revolutionizes traditional education by promoting active pre-class engagement through technology (Byun, 2019; Kang, 2021; Lim, 2019; Sung, 2015; Yoon, 2021). This method significantly enhances English language learning in environments where English is not the primary language spoken. From 2015 to 2022, there was steady and increasing research activity focused on flipped learning for English education in Korea. Especially in 2018, there was a noticeable spike in research, suggesting a key turning point, significant discovery, or the result of building upon work from previous years in the field.

Research on flipped learning with Korean EFL learners was not confined to a narrow set of journals but spanned a diverse range of 58 different Korean academic publications. A notable emphasis was observed in journals dedicated to English Literature, Education, and Linguistics. This distribution not only reflects a wide-ranging academic interest but also suggests that the implications of flipped learning are being explored from multiple disciplinary perspectives, enriching the overall discourse over the eight years. The prominence of articles in leading journals, especially "The Journal of Learner-Centered Curriculum and Instruction," cannot be understated. Such journals serve as authoritative platforms, driving research, setting standards, and influencing practices in this domain.

In terms of individual contributions, key figures have emerged as leading experts in this domain. Researchers such as Kyong-Hyon Pyo, Seung-eun Lee, and Yuhwa Lee have not only contributed significantly to the volume of Korean research but have also played a crucial role in shaping the discourse, setting research agendas, and influencing pedagogical practices. Their consistent contributions over the years demonstrate a deep commitment, expertise, and influence in targeting Korean English learners.

The role of academic institutions in fostering and supporting this research is evident. Korean universities, especially prominent ones such as Dankook University, have been pivotal hubs for research, discussion, and innovation in flipped learning. Their active involvement indicates robust academic backing, interest, and a commitment to exploring and refining educational methodologies for better outcomes.

Analyzing the prevalent terms and themes in the research provides further insights. The dominance of terms associated with the 'flipped' paradigm, as well as concepts such as self-directed and learner-centered learning in the author keywords, paints a clear picture of the central themes and focus areas underpinning the research in the Korean context. Moreover, the recurrent mention of terms such as perception, satisfaction, and attitude in the article titles suggests that researchers are not just focused on the mechanics of flipped learning but are also keenly interested in understanding its holistic impact. This encompasses both the cognitive outcomes, such as skill acquisition and knowledge retention, and the affective dimensions, such as student motivation, engagement, and overall learning experience.

Based on the results and findings of this study, a new pedagogy model for Korean English educators can be developed. This 'integrated flipped learning model' incorporates technology, skill development, and affective learning to enhance English language education. First, in technology integration, various tools are used to enrich the learning experience. LMS such as Blackboard facilitate content distribution, assessments, and feedback. Mobile apps, such as KakaoTalk, enhance student communication and engagement, while game-based methods help practice vocabulary and grammar. Platforms such as Zoom are crucial for virtual classrooms, especially during events such as the COVID-19 pandemic. Second, for skill development focus, the curriculum is designed to evenly cover essential English skills: reading, writing, speaking, listening, grammar, and vocabulary. This is achieved through a modular approach, focusing on each skill separately for effective learning and practice. Lastly, in affective learning consideration, personalization in learning addresses motivational, attitudinal, and self-efficacy aspects. Positive feedback and peer support are key, and the teaching methods aim to foster a supportive environment, encouraging a growth mindset and student engagement. This model should be flexible enough to adapt to the evolving educational landscape and technological advancements in various Korean EFL contexts.

## Limitations and Future Research Venues

Most research on flipped learning in the Korean English learning context has focused on college settings, raising questions about its effectiveness in other places like primary schools, high schools, or vocational training centers. This gap highlights the need to expand research to explore the best ways to implement flipped learning across different student groups and age levels.

In terms of language skills, Korean research has primarily focused on reading and writing. While these skills are crucial, listening and speaking are just as important, especially for real-world communication. These areas should receive more attention in flipped learning environments to create a more balanced approach to English education in Korea.

Another aspect that seems overlooked in current Korean research is the exploration of affective factors, such as self-efficacy, resilience, and emotional engagement. These factors are key to a student's learning experience and can significantly impact outcomes in a flipped classroom.

On the technology side, it is great that various tools have been adopted in flipped learning, but with technology constantly evolving, there is always more to discover. New platforms, apps, and digital resources regularly emerge, and understanding their impact on flipped learning could be very valuable. Future research could explore how these tools affect student engagement, support peer collaboration, or enhance content delivery.

## Concluding Remark

Reflecting on this study, we have deepened our understanding of flipped learning in South Korea and identified areas for further exploration.

Comparative analysis is crucial, highlighting the need to expand research by comparing flipped learning in South Korea with its use in other countries. These comparisons are essential for identifying specific challenges and opportunities, which will help create more globally relevant flipped learning strategies. Moving forward, the insights gained and the focus on comparisons will be key to building a more complete body of research in flipped learning. This approach will ensure its effectiveness in various educational settings worldwide, advancing the field of innovative language teaching and learning.

# References

Abeysekera, L., & Dawson, P. (2015). Motivation and cognitive load in the flipped classroom: Definition, rationale and a call for research. *Higher Education Research & Development, 34*(1), 1–14.

Akçayır, G., & Akçayır, M. (2018). The flipped classroom: A review of its advantages and challenges. *Computers & Education, 126*, 334–345.

Bao, W. (2020). COVID-19 and online teaching in higher education: A case study of Peking University. *Human Behavior and Emerging Technologies, 2*(2), 113–115.

Bergmann, J., & Sams, A. (2012). *Flip your classroom: Reach every student in every class every day*. International Society for Technology in Education.

Bishop, J. L., & Verleger, M. A. (2013). *The flipped classroom: A survey of the research*. ASEE National Conference Proceedings. Atlanta, GA.

Byun, J. (2019). Learner perspectives toward the TedED-based English reading class through flipped learning. *The Mirae Journal of English Language and Literature, 24*(2), 251–273.

de Bellis, N. (2009). *Bibliometrics and citation analysis: From the science citation index to cybermetrics*. Lanham, MD: Scarecrow Press.

Dietz-Uhler, B., & Hurn, J. E. (2013). Using learning analytics to predict (and improve) student success: A faculty perspective. *Journal of Interactive Online Learning, 12*(1), 17–26.

Dong, J., Zhao, Y., & Buckingham, L. (2023). Charting the landscape of data-driven learning using a bibliometric analysis. *ReCALL, 35*(3), 339–355.

Emock Bakelak, J. G., & Reyes Rodríguez, A. D. (2022). Bibliometric analysis in English language teaching and learning. *PODIUM, 41*, 119–140.

Freire, P. (1970). *Pedagogy of the oppressed* (M. B. Ramos, Trans.). Continuum.

Hung, H. T. (2015). Flipping the classroom for English language learners to foster active learning. *Computer Assisted Language Learning, 28*(1), 81–96.

Jung, S.K., Huh, S., Suh, Y, Lee, J.Y., Shin, H., Kim, H. K., & Ahn, S. (2016). *Critical pedagogy and English education.* Hankookmumhwasa.

Kang, N. (2015). The comparison between regular and flipped classrooms for EFL Korean adult learners. *Multimedia-Assisted Language Learning, 18*(3), 41–72.

Kang, Y. (2021). A study on problems of remote learning General English Class and improve plans in the age of COVID-19, Focusing on the core competence of D University. *Journal of Humanities & Social Science, 12,* 1013–1022.

Kayadibi, N. (2022). Bibliometric analysis of educational researches on bilingualism. *International Journal of Education and Literacy Studies, 10*(3), 80–90.

Kim, S. Y. (2017). Smart learning: Approaches and materials for language learning. *Multimedia-Assisted Language Learning, 20*(3), 62–83.

Kim, Y. S. (2015). The effect of the flipped class on the affective experience, learning achievement, and class satisfaction of college English language learners. *Foreign Languages Education, 22*(1), 227–254.

Kim, H. K., & Han, S. (2021). Effects of flipped learning in college English instruction on students' achievement, satisfaction, and perception. *Journal of Learner-Centered Curriculum and Instruction, 21*(3), 101–127.

Kim, M. K., Kim, S. M., Khera, O., & Getman, J. (2014). The experience of three flipped classrooms in an urban university: An exploration of design principles. *The Internet and Higher Education, 22,* 37–50.

Lee, G., & Wallace, A. (2018). Flipped learning in the English as a foreign language classroom: Outcomes and perceptions. *TESOL Quarterly, 52*(1), 62–84.

Lim, J. (2018). Utilizing flipped learning in the English language classroom: A study on a movie, *Love actually*-Based Curriculum. *STEM Journal, 19*(4), 91–108.

Mok, H. N. (2014). Teaching tip: The flipped classroom. *Journal of Information Systems Education, 25*(1), 7–11.

Silverajah, V. G., Wong, S. L., Govindaraj, A., Khambari, M. N. M., Rahmat, R. W. B. O., & Deni, A. R. M. (2022). A systematic review of self-regulated learning in flipped classrooms: Key findings, measurement methods, and potential directions. *IEEE Access, 10,* 20270–20294.

Sung, K. (2015). A case study on a flipped classroom in an EFL content course. *Multimedia-Assisted Language Learning, 18*(2), 159–187.

Strayer, J. F. (2012). How learning in an inverted classroom influences cooperation, innovation and task orientation. *Learning Environments Research, 15*(2), 171–193.

Yoon, H. (2021). The effects of MOOC based on flipped learning for college English class. *Korean Association for Learner-Centered Curriculum and Instruction, 21*(6), 17–29.

Zhang, X. (2020). A bibliometric analysis of second language acquisition between 1997 and 2018. *Studies in Second Language Acquisition, 42*(1), 199–222.

# 13

# ESP Research in Korea: Current Status and Implications for Korean ELT

Jihyeon Jeon🆔 and Eun-Young Kwon

## Introduction

The status of English as a global lingua franca has become more firmly established since the advent of the Internet. Historically, the pursuit of English proficiency in Korea was largely anchored in personal advancement or for nebulous future contingencies. Direct engagements with English, be it through travel to English-speaking countries or interactions with their residents visiting Korea, were relatively infrequent. Consequently, English instruction in Korea was predominantly oriented towards a holistic approach, or English for General Purposes (EGP), with exceptions made for imminent educational or vocational English assessments. The challenges associated with English Language Teaching

---

J. Jeon (✉)
Ewha Womans University, Seoul, Korea
e-mail: dearjeon@ewha.ac.kr

E.-Y. Kwon
AI Industry Research Center, Kwangwoon University, Seoul, Korea

© The Author(s), under exclusive license to Springer Nature Switzerland AG 2025
H. Reinders et al. (eds.), *Innovation in Language Learning and Teaching*, New Language Learning and Teaching Environments,
https://doi.org/10.1007/978-3-031-83561-2_13

(ELT) in Korea are not confined to just a few areas. In today's world, where individual choice plays a crucial role, advancements in information technology enable people to select movies, dramas, music, shopping, education, and more according to their preferences and interests. This shift has led to a decreased willingness among individuals to participate in activities that they have not personally chosen. Despite this trend, the options for personalization within Korea's ELT framework remain quite restricted. Both learners and educators often find themselves in a position where they must engage with material that does not align with their individual interests, strengths/weaknesses, or specific needs. However, with the rapid development of transportation and information and communication technologies, the use of English has changed in recent years. Koreans now find themselves increasingly immersed in English communications, not solely with native English interlocutors but also with non-native English speakers both offline or online (Jeon et al., 2011; Kim, 2018). The digital age further amplifies this trend, with the online communications facilitating myriad interactions in English. As there are more interactions in English, people began to be interested in diverse linguistic and cultural nuances, broadening their understanding of global perspectives.

As the number of online and offline communication for native and non-native speakers has increased, the number of cases where they communicate in English while doing a specific range of work to which they belong has increased (Amano et al., 2023; Frank, 2000; Guo, 2018; Jung, 2020; Tajino & Tajino, 2000). As the ultimate goal of Koreans learning in English was to communicate in English in their specialties, interest in English for Specific Purposes (ESP) education naturally arose. ESP proficiency requires an effective communication in specific domains, with the unique vocabulary, structures, and discourse styles inherent to each field. To convey messages effectively within such specialized contexts, a deep understanding of the specific discourse community and their accepted norms is essential. The type of English required to write a scientific paper (Kanoksilapatham, 2005) or facilitate interactions between hospital residents and patients or their peers (Eggly, 2002) are some examples of ESP.

The primary objective for Koreans in their pursuit of English proficiency is to ensure effective communication within communities where English is the predominant medium of discourse. In this context, the significance of ESP in enhancing the efficacy of English pedagogy cannot be overstated. Unlike EGP, ESP offers a narrower focus, enabling learners to concentrate on the immediately needed content, thereby optimizing the educational process. Furthermore, the approach of ESP education, which focuses on developing curricula, crafting materials, and implementing programs that are specifically designed according to the learners' needs, appears to be a viable answer to the issue of 'personalization' in Korean ELT. In this sense, a discussion on ESP education must be included in discussing innovative teaching in Korea. Unfortunately, however, the experience of ESP education is not shared or discussed visibly in Korea. Therefore, in this chapter, we would like to examine the current status of ESP in Korea, focusing on research articles to understand what we need for ESP education.

Internationally, the realm of English education has seen a surge in research pertaining to ESP, with the growing demand for specialized English communication across various sectors. This trajectory of interest can be traced back to the 1960s when scholars began distinguishing the nuances of English used in Science and Technology (EST) from that in other disciplines. By the 1970s, the demarcation between EGP and ESP became more pronounced. The pedagogical approach of Communicative Language Teaching (CLT) further invigorated specialized research in this domain (Howatt, 1984). The momentum in this field was notably accelerated with the inception of the journal *English for Specific Purposes* in 1986, followed by the introduction of *Journal of English for Academic Purposes* in 2002.

In South Korea, there has been a burgeoning interest in ESP. This is evident from the establishment of an ESP-focused Special Interest Group (SIG) by KATE in 2002, which has since been organizing annual ESP symposiums. The academic association called *ESP Korea* was established in 2016, and began to publish an academic journal *ESP studies* from 2019. Despite the growing enthusiasm surrounding ESP, however, we have to admit that, participation remains limited. When juxtaposed with the extensive and diverse ESP research being conducted internationally, the scope of domestic ESP research in Korea appears rather scarce. This paucity in volume poses challenges for a comprehensive meta-analysis of domestic ESP studies. Although the ESP field in Korea has few shared teaching experience and research is far from sufficient, accurately grasping the current situation is the foundation work that we need to do right away for innovative teaching.

For this study, the research articles published in *English Teaching*, one of the most established Korean academic journals for English education, will be analyzed in comparison with the articles published in *English for Specific Purposes* from the very first issue. Through Meta-analysis, the research articles will be categorized for systematic comparison. The main purpose of the articles will be categorized into English for Academic Purposes (EAP) or English for Occupational Purposes (EOP) before identifying specific content areas. The major genres-oral communication genre and written communication genre will be identified before looking at the sub-genres such as lectures, presentations, and conversations, research papers and e-mails, etc.

A systematic comparison of research articles in *English for Specific Purposes* with ESP articles published in *English Teaching* will provide a more detailed understanding of the present state of ESP research in Korea. This analysis aims to highlight the areas within Korea that have been the focus of more intensive research efforts as opposed to those that have been less explored, thereby identifying where further research in ESP is needed. Furthermore, leveraging these insights, this study proposes to develop a model of ESP pedagogy tailored for Korean EFL educators.

# Understanding ESP

## Concept of ESP

ESP is a subfield of Language for Specific Purposes (LSP) and can be defined as English communication within a specific domain (Swales, 1990).[1] ESP is tailored to the learner's needs, emphasizing the relevance between learning and actual communication. This distinguishes it from EGP. In South Korea, learning English to communicate in various situations, from elementary school to university English, falls under EGP. In contrast, learning a specific style of English used within a particular group is categorized as ESP. Effective communication within a specific group reflects the characteristics of that discourse community. For instance, a doctor communicating about medical activities in a hospital will be effective when adhering to the communication style of the medical discourse community. This style would differ from the doctor's communication in non-medical situations with the general public. The fundamental difference between EGP and ESP lies in the objectives and scope of English communication. Table 13.1 compares the essential differences between EGP and ESP.

From an objective perspective, while EGP aims for communication in general situations, ESP targets communication in specific situations. EGP encompasses a broad range of scenarios, whereas ESP focuses on predictable discourses within a particular domain. Thus, proficiency in EGP does not guarantee proficiency in ESP contexts and vice versa. For example, a Korean doctor proficient in EGP might struggle to communicate in medical situations in English. Similarly, a Korean scholar who can present research fluently in English might find it challenging to engage in casual conversations about food at a dinner party. From a motivational standpoint, while EGP learners might have vague and general motivations, ESP learners have very specific motivations, desiring professional communication within a particular group.

---

[1] Content-based instruction, a method frequently employed in the design of ESP courses, presents a distinct concept from that delineated by Hutchinson and Waters (1987).

Table 13.1 Differences between EGP and ESP

| | EGP | ESP |
|---|---|---|
| Objectives | Communication in general situations in English | Communication in specific situations in English |
| Range of learning | Wide-ranging | Restricted |
| Learning motivation | General motivation | Specific motivation |
| Instructional design | Many instances begin with a textbook or teacher-led approaches | Understanding the characteristics of the target discourse community and learner needs analysis are crucial |
| Instructor | English educators | Collaboration between English educators and domain experts is required |
| Learning materials | General learning activities and resources | Authentic tasks and resources |
| Assessment | Assessing the ability to communicate in general situations | Assessing the ability to communicate in specific target situations |

When designing instruction, EGP often starts with textbooks or teacher-led approaches. In contrast, ESP learners, having more specific motivations and higher expectations than EGP learners (Dudley Evans & St. John, 1998), require instruction based on understanding the characteristics of the target discourse community and a learner needs analysis. Teaching ESP can be challenging as it demands specialized communication in specific domains. For instance, teaching English paper writing in law requires domain knowledge, necessitating collaboration between English educators and domain experts. From an instructional and material perspective, ESP requires practical tasks and materials to ensure successful communication in the target discourse situation. To assess proficiency, while EGP evaluates communication in various situations, ESP assesses successful communication in specific target situations.

## Types of ESP

The ESP field is diverse, including EAP, EOP, English for Medical Purposes (EMP), English for Business Purposes (EBP), English for Legal Purposes (ELP), and English for Sociocultural Purposes (ESCP) (Belcher, 2009). The classification of these types warrants exploration.

ESP can be categorized differently based on perspective. From a purpose perspective, it can be broadly divided into EAP and EOP, based on whether the English communication is for academic or occupational purposes. For instance, students presenting, discussing, questioning, or writing papers in English, or scholars presenting research in their field, fall under EAP. English required for reports, presentations, correspondence, and documentation at work falls under EOP.

From a discourse community perspective, ESP can be further differentiated. A discourse community is a group with specific communication styles in particular situations, sharing common goals, communication genres, vocabulary, and recognized standards for content appropriateness and discourse expertise (Swales, 1990). Fields like EMP and ELP are classified based on discourse, but countless other domain-specific names, like Aviation or Tourism, can be generated. Bankers, doctors, nurses, lawyers, and tour guides belong to different discourse communities, each with distinct discourse features. In a globalizing and specialized society, to communicate professionally in English within one's field, one must be proficient in the specific discourse of that community. Hence, learning English for practical purposes should be approached from an ESP perspective. This increasing need for specialized English learning has led to ESP being termed as a means of international communication (Mackay & Mountford, 1978).

Both EMP and ELP can be categorized under EAP or EOP. For example, if a medical student reads books or discusses in English for studies, it is EAP. If a doctor communicates in English with patients or colleagues, it is EOP (Orr, 2002). Depending on when ESP education occurs, EAP and EOP can be further subdivided. Taking EBP as an example, the general business English acquired prior to delving into a business environment is termed English for General Business Purposes

(EGBP). Conversely, specialized English acquired during business operations is classified as English for Specific Business Purposes (ESBP). In the EAP context, English for General Academic Purposes (EGAP) refers to the broad content learned before specialized studies, whereas English for Specific Academic Purposes (ESAP) denotes the detailed content obtained while studying a specific domain.

## Analyzing ESP Research Articles

### Data Collection

To understand the trends in domestic ESP research, we examined studies published in the journal, *English Teaching*. The rationale for this choice is twofold: (1) *English Teaching*, established in 1965, is the oldest specialized academic journal related to English education in the country, and (2) it is suitable for comparative analysis to see how the state of related research has evolved over the decades. For data collection, this study initially extracted bibliographic data on 1,767 papers published in *English Teaching* from the Research Information Sharing Service (RISS). Subsequently, details such as the title, author name, publication year, volume and issue, author keywords, and abstracts of each paper were organized using Excel.

### Data Analysis

This chapter utilized Jeon's (2015) data analysis framework to assess domestic ESP research trends (see Table 13.3). The journal, *English for Specific Purposes* founded in 1986, is dedicated to ESP research and covers both EAP and EOP studies, making it an ideal source for understanding global ESP research shifts. Consequently, Jeon (2015) sought to identify frequently conducted research by examining the vocabulary in the titles of articles published in this journal over approximately 30 years, from 1986 to 2014.

## Analysis Process

Jeon (2015) determined that research titles are appropriate data for classifying research topics because they succinctly summarize the research and should adequately describe the content, allowing readers to distinguish a particular study from similar ones using the most representative terms (American Psychological Association, 2001). The software AntConc (version 3.4.3), commonly used for corpus studies, was utilized to discern the frequent vocabulary in the titles of articles from *English for Specific Purposes*[2] The titles from papers published between 1986 and 2014 were compiled into an Excel spreadsheet. These manuscripts were classified as: (1) original research articles, (2) discussion and research notes, (3) short communication, (4) research notes, (5) book reviews, (6) the author replies, and (7) other research. Entries like book reviews and the author replies, which are not research-focused, were omitted. Only categories like original research article, discussion and research notes, short communication, and research notes were retained, culminating in a compact corpus of 596 research titles. This was set up for a vocabulary frequency analysis, following the approach of Kwon (2015)[3] (Fig. 13.1).

Utilizing the AntConc tool facilitated a nuanced evaluation of term frequency based on word counts. Within the 1-gram analysis, it was observed that conventional English lexemes, particularly articles, consistently emerged as high-frequency words. This observation underscored the efficacy of the 2-gram and 3-gram analyses in discerning pivotal research-related keywords (Fig. 13.2).

To comprehend the contextual backdrop in which these salient keywords were embedded, the 4-gram and 5-gram analyses were deemed indispensable. A meticulous frequency assessment using AntConc revealed the frequent word clusters, as outlined in Table 13.2. By incrementally expanding the word count for analysis, a more profound

---

[2] The concept of employing vocabulary frequency in qualitative research was inspired by the discourse on the use of corpus analytical methods subsequent to Kwon's (2015) academic presentation.
[3] Adhering to the corpus research methodology outlined by Kwon (2015), the study aimed to discern the lexical frequency within research titles. Subsequent to converting PDF resources into text formats amenable to computational analysis, the exploration commenced using AntConc.

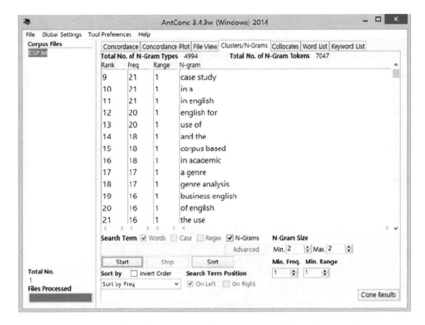

Fig. 13.1 Sample results of a 2-gram frequency analysis using AntConc

contextual understanding of the vocabulary was attained, taking into consideration both the thematic focus and the methodological framework.

## The Categories Found in *English for Specific Purposes*

Through the application of the AntConc software, we identified frequent vocabulary in the research titles of *English for Specific Purposes*. This analysis enabled the formation of the following primary categories[4]:

1. Types of ESP, distinguishing between EAP and EOP, along with their respective target discourse domains;

---

[4] Opting to utilize a constrained dataset, specifically research titles, facilitated a comprehensive overview of research themes spanning the entire publication history of a specialized journal, enabling the extraction of significant classifications.

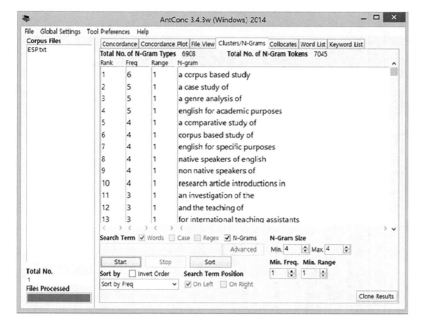

Fig. 13.2 Sample results of a 4-gram frequency analysis using AntConc

2. Discourse types, differentiating between oral and written communication, further subdivided by genres like research articles and presentations;
3. Central theme or subject of the research; and
4. Research methodologies, which include genre-focused, corpus-based, case report, needs assessment, and comparative studies.

Upon the extraction of these primary categories and the subsequent axial coding process, it became feasible to categorize the research papers into distinct sub-categories, as delineated in Table 13.3.[5]

Regarding the ESP types, a distinction emerged between EAP and EOP. Titles that were explicitly labeled "academic purpose" or those that clearly aimed at conveying or learning scholarly knowledge in a

---

[5] In this investigation, the application of corpus analysis as a foundational tool for qualitative inquiry revealed its efficiency, particularly when juxtaposed with conventional content analysis coding methods.

**Table 13.2** Frequent vocabulary compilation: An AntConc analysis of article titles from *English for Specific Purposes*

| Unit | Unit of AntConc analysis | | |
|---|---|---|---|
| | 2-gram[6] | 4-gram | 5-gram[7] |
| Criteria for frequent vocabulary | Frequent word clusters up to rank 75 that appear 7 or more times | Frequent word clusters up to rank 20 that appear at least 3 times | Frequent word clusters up to rank 35 that appear more than twice |
| Frequent vocabulary | – research articles<br>– corpus based<br>– case study<br>– genre analysis<br>– business English<br>– in scientific<br>– academic writing<br>– applied linguistics<br>– non native<br>– in medical<br>– comparison of<br>– needs of<br>– academic purposes<br>– perceptions of | – a corpus based study<br>– a case study of<br>– English for academic purposes<br>– a comparative study of<br>– native speakers of English<br>– nonnative speakers of English<br>– research article introductions in<br>– for international teaching assistants<br>– teaching of academic writing | – a corpus based study of<br>– non native speakers of English<br>– a genre base approach to teaching business English<br>– article introductions in applied linguistics<br>– by native and non native<br>– English as a lingua franca<br>– English for academic purposes<br>– in an EFL context the<br>– Italian and English sales promotion<br>– research article introductions in applied<br>– science journal paper writing in |

[6] From the 2-gram vocabulary frequency analysis, word groups that manifested a significant occurrence of 49 times were distinctly observed. Furthermore, to encompass a broad spectrum of research topics, this investigation identified keywords from lexemes that ranked up to the 75th rank, each with a minimum occurrence of seven times, ensuring a thorough lexical representation.

[7] The 5-gram vocabulary frequency analysis highlighted word groups with a frequency of three or more up to the third rank, and those appearing twice extended to the 35th rank. To provide a more encompassing view of keywords, selections were made from groups with a minimum frequency of two.

Table 13.3 Research categories in *English for Specific Purposes*

| Category | Subcategory |
|---|---|
| ESP type | 1. EAP<br>Target discourse area:<br>%1 law ② medical science ③ science/engineering ④ applied linguistics/TESOL ⑤ economics ⑥ business administration (finance, accounting, marketing, etc.) ⑦ others<br>2. EOP<br>Target discourse field:<br>① corporations ② other institutions |
| Discourse type | 1. Oral communication<br>Specific discourse genre:<br>%1 lectures ② presentations ③ Q&A sessions/conversations ④ others<br>2. Written communication<br>%1 Textbooks/materials ② research papers/theses ③ letters ④ e-mails ⑤ documents ⑥ others |
| Central theme (research content) | 1. Understanding the characteristics of the target discourse community<br>2. Course design/curriculum development<br>3. Teaching methods<br>4. Materials development<br>5. Assessment<br>6. others |
| Research method | 1. literature review/meta-analysis<br>2. genre analysis/corpus analysis<br>3. case reports/needs analysis<br>4. surveys/interviews/observations/experiments<br>5. mixed methods |

particular area were grouped under EAP. On the other hand, titles that contained terms like "professional" or "workplace" or those that were clearly intended for tasks in a specialized profession were classified as EOP[8]

For EAP research, the analysis identified several dominant content areas, which were grouped as:

(1) law, (2) medicine, (3) science/engineering, (4) applied linguistics/TESOL, (5) economics, (6) business-related fields, and (7) social

---

[8] The study did not differentiate between EOP and English for Vocational Purposes (EVP).

sciences. For EOP, the focus was on specific communication needs in particular fields or professions, allowing for distinctions between (1) corporations and (2) other institutions.[9]

Discourse types were primarily divided into oral communication and written communication. Based on frequently occurring genres, studies related to oral communication were further classified into (1) lectures, (2) presentations, (3) Q&A sessions or conversations, and (4) other genres, while written communication research was categorized into (1) textbooks/materials, (2) research papers/theses, (3) letters, (4) e-mails, (5) documents, and (6) others.

Content-wise, research themes encompassed (1) understanding the characteristics of the target discourse community, (2) course design/curriculum development, (3) teaching methods, (4) materials development, (5) assessment, and (6) others.

In terms of research methodologies, Gollin-Kies (2014) outlined distinctions between qualitative, quantitative, mixed-methods, and non-empirical research. In this particular study, given the sparse quantitative research within the ESP domain, the categorization based on recurrent terminologies was: (1) literature review, (2) genre analysis/corpus analysis, (3) case reports/needs analysis, (4) surveys/interviews/observations/experiments, and (5) mixed methods. When a study employed more than one method, such as integrating surveys within case studies or contrasting beginners with experts in genre analysis, a multiple coding was adopted.

## The ESP Type, Discourse Type/Genre, and Central Theme Found in *English Teaching*

Over the past 60 years, when examining research published in *English Teaching*, a wide range of topics within the field of English education have been deeply explored. However, research on ESP has been notably

---

[9] The discourse domains of EOP encompass a vast spectrum, including diverse businesses, medical institutions, hospitality sectors, and communication hubs. Due to the inherent complexity in categorizing such a broad range, a bifurcation was made between business entities and non-commercial institutions.

sparse.[10] When narrowing down to studies on English communication within specific discourse communities, only 26 papers related to ESP were found. As illustrated in Table 13.4, ESP-related papers began to emerge in the late 1990s. Most of these papers were published after 2000, with a significant increase in publications after 2010.

As indicated by the frequency of papers presented in Table 13.5, when categorizing the ESP research published in *English Teaching* by ESP types and discourse types, it was apparent that the bulk of the ESP research was dominated by EAP studies, while the number of EOP research papers was notably limited. When examining by discourse type, EAP research encompasses integrated studies that include both oral and written communication (e.g., Cho, 2012; Hafner, 2020; Shin, 2010, 2011), as well as research specifically related to written or oral communication (e.g., Choi & Ko, 2005; Chujo & Genung, 2003; Jin, 2015; Lee & Ro, 2020; Lee & Traynor, 2013; Odo & Yi, 2014), all of which occur at similar proportions. On the other hand, EOP research tends to focus slightly more on studies related to oral communication (Park, 2012; Shin & Kwon, 2005) than on integrated studies (Jeon & Choi, 2002) or those centered on written communication (Byun et al., 2006).

In the case of EAP research, when categorized by discourse type and specific genre, the results were as shown in Table 13.6. The primary

Table 13.4 Publication status of ESP Papers in *English Teaching* by Period

| Period | | ESP-related papers |
|---|---|---|
| 1965–1974 | | 0 |
| 1975–1984 | | 0 |
| 1985–1994 | | 0 |
| 1995–2004 | 1995–1999 | 3 |
| | 2000–2004 | 5 |
| 2005–2014 | 2005–2009 | 4 |
| | 2010–2014 | 9 |
| 2015–2023 | 2015–2019 | 3 |
| | 2020–2023 | 2 |

---

[10] The interpretation of ESP, whether broad or narrow, can influence the number of papers considered relevant. In this research endeavor, a narrow interpretation was adopted, focusing on English communication studies tailored for distinct objectives within specific sectors.

Table 13.5 Discourse types of ESP Research in *English Teaching*

| ESP Type | | EAP | EOP |
|---|---|---|---|
| Discourse Type | mixed | 7 | 1 |
| | oral | 6 | 2 |
| | written | 8 | 1 |
| | Total | 21 | 4 |

focus areas of EAP papers were science/engineering (e.g., Hafner, 2020; Hwang, 2013) and applied linguistics/TESOL (e.g., Choi & Ko, 2005; Jin, 2015). In terms of specific genres, oral communication research was predominantly on lectures and presentations (e.g., Kim, 2003; Lee & Traynor, 2013; Soh, 2005), while written communication research was mainly on research papers and theses (e.g., Choi & Ko, 2005; Jin, 2015). Notably, research on commonly studied fields abroad, such as law, medical science, economics, and business, was absent. Similarly, common EAP discourse forms abroad, like conversations or Q&A sessions in oral communication and letters, e-mails, and documents in written communication, were also missing. Upon categorizing EOP research by discourse type and distinct format, the outcomes are delineated in Table 13.7.

Table 13.6 Discourse areas and forms of EAP research in *English Teaching* (by discourse type)

| Discourse type | | Mixed | Oral | | Written |
|---|---|---|---|---|---|
| | | | Lectures | Presentations | |
| Discourse Area | One or more areas | 0 | 2 | 0 | 2 |
| | Law | 0 | 0 | 0 | 0 |
| | Medical science | 0 | 0 | 1 | 0 |
| | Medical science | 0 | 0 | 1 | 0 |
| | Science & engineering | 6 | 0 | 1 | 2 |
| | Applied linguistics/ TESOL | 0 | 2 | 0 | 4 |
| | Economics | 0 | 0 | 0 | 0 |
| | Business administration | 0 | 0 | 0 | 0 |
| | Others | 1 | 0 | 0 | 0 |
| | Total | 7 | 4 | 2 | 8 |

**Table 13.7** Discourse settings and specific discourse forms of EOP research in *English Teaching* (by discourse type)

| Discourse type | | Mixed | Oral | Written |
|---|---|---|---|---|
| Discourse Setting | Corporations | 1 | 0 | 0 |
| | Hospitals | 0 | 0 | 0 |
| | Aviation | 0 | 2 | 0 |
| | Nuclear power plants | 0 | 0 | 1 |
| Specific Discourse Form | Presentations | N/A | 0 | N/A |
| | Conversations/Q&A sessions | N/A | 0 | N/A |
| | negotiations | N/A | 0 | N/A |
| | Aviation communication | N/A | 2 | N/A |
| | textbooks/materials | N/A | N/A | N/A |
| | Business reports | N/A | N/A | N/A |
| | Letters | N/A | N/A | N/A |
| | E-mails | N/A | N/A | N/A |
| | Documents | N/A | N/A | N/A |
| | Computerized procedure system | N/A | N/A | N/A |
| | Total | 1 | 2 | 1 |

Within the realm of EOP research, certain studies have honed in on specialized discourse environments like aviation (Park, 2012; Shin & Kwon, 2005) and nuclear power facilities (Byun et al., 2006). Surprisingly, there was a noticeable dearth of research targeting corporate contexts. When examining specific discourse forms, a few studies emerged on aviation communication in the oral sector (Park, 2012; Shin & Kwon, 2005). However, there was an absence of research on prevalent workplace activities such as negotiations, presentations, or conversations/Q&A sessions. In the written sector, besides a distinct study analyzing computerized procedure system (see Byun et al., 2006), there was also a lack of research on routinely required written forms like letters, emails, and official documents.

When classifying ESP research in *English Teaching* by content and methodology, the outcomes can be observed in Table 13.8. In examining the content, both EAP and EOP research predominantly focused on understanding the characteristics of specific discourse communities or target discourses (e.g., Jin, 2015; Shin, 2010, 2011). In terms of instructional methods, research was consistently conducted in both EAP and

Table 13.8 ESP studies from *English Teaching*: research content and methodology

| ESP Type | | EAP | EOP |
|---|---|---|---|
| Research Content | Understanding the characteristics of the target discourse community | 7 | 4 |
| | course design/curriculum development | 3 | 0 |
| | Teaching methods | 4 | 1 |
| | Materials development | 2 | 0 |
| | Assessment | 1 | 3 |
| | Others | 1 | 0 |
| Research Method | Literature review/meta-analysis | 3 | 1 |
| | Genre analysis/corpus analysis | 3 | 0 |
| | Case reports/needs analysis | 5 | 2 |
| | Surveys/interviews/observations/experiments | 6 | 3 |
| | Mixed methods | 1 | 2 |
| Total | | 23 | 8 |

EOP domains (e.g., Chujo & Genung, 2003; Hafner, 2020; Lee & Ro, 2020). Within EAP research, there has been a focus on investigations related to course design/curriculum development (Kim et al., 1999), and material development (e.g., Noguchi, 1997). Conversely, in the EOP sector, there was a noticeable lack of studies covering these areas. Regarding research on assessment, the EOP domain presented three pertinent articles (e.g., Shin & Kwon, 2005), whereas the EAP domain yielded just one (Kim & Joo, 2018).

From a methodological standpoint, there is evident diversity in the research techniques utilized. While genre analysis and corpus-centric studies are present in EAP research (Choi & Ko, 2005; Chujo & Genung, 2003; Jin, 2015), such methods are conspicuously lacking in EOP studies.

## Conclusions and Recommendations

In this chapter, we embarked on an analytical journey, scrutinizing articles from the esteemed journal *English for Specific Purposes* from its inception until 2014. Leveraging corpus methodologies, we distilled high-frequency words and subsequently undertook content analysis, finding ESP types, Discourse types/genres, and central themes. Looking at the domestic journal, *English education,* in a retrospective analysis spanning six decades, a mere 26 ESP articles out of 1,767 research articles were found. A significant portion of these articles emerged post-2000, with a discernible uptick post-2010.

Evidently, when looking through one of the most esteemed and dedicated academic journal for English education in Korea, the state of ESP research in Korea is notably insufficient. There is an imperative need to expand research in the following ESP domains:

1. There is a pressing need for studies that discern the English communication requisites within specific discourse communities where learners are anticipated to engage. It is paramount to ascertain the nature of English communication students will employ post-graduation, the potential challenges they might confront, and the kind of pedagogical strategies universities should implement. Duff (2002) underscores that English communication, especially in a global milieu for educational or occupational purposes, should not merely be confined to linguistic facets but should also encompass the real-world contexts in which the language manifests. For individuals necessitating English communication for educational or professional endeavors, an exhaustive exploration of the specific contexts in which such communication transpires is indispensable.
2. One of the salient objectives for Korean learners studying English is to proficiently communicate within their professional domains in a global setting (Tarone, 2005). Consequently, research endeavors are required to foster a lucid comprehension of the discourse situations, structures, and intrinsic characteristics of discourse communities. Continuous research endeavors should encompass analyses of moves and steps across discourse genres (Flowerdew, 2005, Flowerdew & Wan, 2006), juxtapositions between domain experts and novices (Pecorari, 2006; Planken, 2005), and comprehensive needs assessments (Jackson, 2005). Through these analytical endeavors, one can delineate the requisite English communication proficiencies essential for learners to function efficaciously within their chosen discourse communities.

3. The realm of EAP research calls for a broader spectrum of exploration. Within EAP research, there are two primary pathways: the first, anchored in corpus-driven approaches, highlights the Academic Word List (AWL) and suggests a consistent foundational core spanning various academic fields (Coxhead, 2000; Paquot, 2010). Conversely, the second pathway, informed by corpus studies of distinct academic writing styles, underscores the intricate lexical clusters inherent to particular academic domains (Hyland & Tse, 2007), placing a premium on the specificity of each domain (Hyland, 2002). To equip students with the proficiency to effectively engage in English communication in their respective academic domains after their tertiary education, it is imperative for research to rigorously examine both the prevailing educational frameworks across academic settings and the bespoke English courses designed for distinct academic specializations.
4. In the current climate of interdisciplinary collaboration, there remains a discernible gap in genuine integration across academic fields and various societal domains. A salient challenge within the ESP sphere is the potential misalignment between having an in-depth understanding of English pedagogy and lacking proficiency in the specific content domain, or the inverse. This highlights the imperative for collaborative endeavors between experts in English pedagogy and specialists within specific domains.
5. EAP research should be inclusive of disciplines that are regularly examined in global academic contexts, including areas like law, medicine, economics, and business management. Beyond the realm of academic theses in EAP settings, it is imperative to explore written communication modalities pertinent to both research and pedagogical endeavors, encompassing formats such as letters and emails. Moreover, investigations into the students' comprehension of English lectures, feedback mechanisms in instructional settings, classroom conversations, Q&A sessions, and assessment methodologies within EAP contexts are of paramount necessity.
6. Within the scope of EOP, despite the inherent challenges associated with data collection compared to that of EAP, there is a

compelling need to bolster research efforts. It is imperative to undertake case studies that discern the specific English communication demands across diverse professional landscapes and comprehend the inherent challenges therein. Comprehensive investigations into routinely encountered discourse genres in these professional domains, such as negotiations, presentations, conversations, Q&A sessions, letters, e-mails, and official documents, are of significant importance.
7. EOP research in multifarious discourse communities is of the essence. Given that one of the cardinal objectives for Korean English learners is to communicate in English for professional purposes within a global framework, universities should not only proffer EGP courses, akin to foundational English, but also specialized EOP courses. When students exhibit ambivalence regarding their future professional trajectories, it becomes imperative to establish English for General Occupational Purposes (EGOP) courses. Once specific English communication requisites are discerned, the provision of English for Specific Occupational Purposes (ESOP) becomes crucial. The realization of such pedagogical offerings mandates extensive research.
8. In diverse discourse communities, there is a pressing need for EOP research. Given the trajectory of Korean English learners, who are likely to employ English for vocational objectives, higher education institutions should not only facilitate foundational English communication skills through courses like EGP but also curate EOP modules that align with their prospective professional domains. When students' future professional engagements within their chosen fields remain ambiguous, it becomes pertinent to introduce courses such as EGOP that address broad communicative requisites. As the precise communicative demands are discerned, specialized courses, namely ESOP, should be incorporated. The development and implementation of these curricular offerings necessitate rigorous academic inquiry.
9. Kim (2011) postulates that, from an individual's economic vantage point, while prodigious time and effort are invested in English pedagogy, there exists a discernible variance in English utilization across diverse professions. To efficaciously acquire the English competencies

requisite for professional endeavors, students harboring aspirations to engage in the corporate realm necessitate pedagogical interventions in business documents, emails, letters, reports, resumes, etc. (Boyd, 2002). Similarly, law students necessitate pedagogical strategies to comprehend legal documents in English and draft them (Feak & Reinhart, 2002), while nursing students require pedagogical paradigms to report patient conditions, conduct patient interviews, participate in team meetings, and scribe nursing logs in English (Hussin, 2002). The provision of these indispensable EOP programs mandates rigorous research. Research endeavors should not only encompass studies related to English as a lingua franca in business contexts (Chew, 2005), the development of contextually relevant instructional materials (Bosher, 2010), and assessment methodologies (Douglas, 2000) but also studies that explore the nexus between English communication in diverse professional terrains and EOP pedagogical paradigms (Bargiela-Chiappini et al., 2007).

An extensive examination of ESP literature in this study uncovers the numerous benefits of ESP education in Korea, such as its relevance, ability to motivate, efficiency, specificity, and capacity to enhance job prospects, which are instrumental in addressing ELT challenges (Hyland, 2002; Kim, 2011; Kwon, 2020). Specifically, ESP increases the learning's relevance for students, encouraging the application of their English knowledge in areas of personal interest. This engagement promotes interaction with both speakers and textual material. Utilizing learned vocabulary and grammatical structures in practical contexts not only solidifies the learning outcomes but also elevates motivation. Educators can harness the knowledge students have of their specific subjects to facilitate faster English language acquisition. Furthermore, ESP contributes to better job opportunities and academic achievements.

From these observations, several conclusions emerge: Firstly, effective strategies from ESP education should be integrated into EGP education. This entails performing needs assessments, establishing levels according to those needs, and providing learners with options. Despite the sporadic nature of ESP research and the evident divide between well-explored areas and those less attended to, suggesting potential for further ESP research, the foundational principle of needs analysis in ESP education is vital and should be adopted by EGP education. Contextual learning, aimed at making education more engaging and pertinent, along with emphasizing specific skills such as listening and speaking tailored to the learners' needs, exemplify how EGP could benefit from ESP methodologies.

Secondly, ESP differs from EGP in its division into specific fields like law, medicine, business, and the military, highlighting a pressing need for ESP to evolve further. Education within these fields lacks the depth provided by specialized modules, limiting personalized learning experiences. For example, the field of military English necessitates the development of specific genre analyses, vocabulary lists, teaching materials, activities, and curricula catering to areas like military training, security, and diplomacy. Segmenting modules in such a manner would create avenues for education more closely aligned with learners' needs.

Last but not least, a noteworthy pedagogical innovation for Korean EFL educators might well be a "back to basics" strategy, applicable across both ESP and EGP. In the modern educational landscape, 'personal choice' is paramount for both students and teachers, mirroring the evolving expectations and competencies. Shifting away from a hierarchical learning approach to a modular one that supports the integration of varied content can more effectively engage learners in areas they are passionate about. Educators are encouraged to adopt established ESP pedagogical frameworks, such as multimodal pedagogies, task-based learning, and CLIL, customized for diverse learner profiles based on a thorough needs analysis (Laadem & Mallahi, 2019; Rodríguez-Peñarroja, 2022; Shabani & Ghasemi, 2014; Vega & Moscoso, 2019; Yang, 2020). Offering educators the flexibility of hybrid teaching methods and reducing the limitations imposed by physical locations and schedules will promote a more adaptable curriculum, leading to a sustainable educational model. Ultimately, honoring the choices of students bolsters their willingness to learn, communicate, and continue studying.

Purpose-driven ESP education stands as a conduit for more effective and efficient English learning in Korea. With the broad aim of mastering English as a foreign language after mastering one's mother tongue, a focused, purpose-centered approach makes achieving specialized communication in English within specific discourse communities more attainable. Looking ahead to a globalized future, there is an aspiration for a landscape enriched with varied and comprehensive ESP research, geared towards nurturing Koreans adept in essential and professional English communication. To sum up, while ESP and EGP each have their distinct benefits, selecting between the two is primarily determined by the learners' particular needs and goals. ESP provides a more focused and efficient path to English proficiency for individuals with clear professional or academic goals. On the other hand, EGP is ideal for those aiming for a broad understanding of the language. Importantly, combining these two methods could lead to a well-rounded English learning approach, potentially addressing the challenges faced by Korean ELT effectively.

# References

Amano, T., Ramírez-Castañeda, V., Berdejo-Espinola, V., Borokini, I., Chowdhury, S., Golivets, M., ... & Veríssimo, D. (2023). The manifold costs of being a non-native English speaker in science. *PLoS Biology, 21*(7), e3002184.

American Psychological Association. (2001). *APA publication manual of the American Psychological Association* (5th ed.). American Psychological Association.

Bargiela-Chiappini, F., Nickerson, C., & Planken, B. (2007). *Business discourse.* Palgrave Macmillan.

Belcher, D. (2009). What ESP is and can be. In D. Belcher (Ed.), *English for specific purposes in theory and practice* (pp. 1–20). University of Michigan Press.

Bosher, S. (2010). English for nursing: Developing discipline-specific materials. In N. Harwood (Ed.), *Materials in ELT: Theory and practice* (pp. 346–372). Cambridge University Press.

Boyd, F. (2002). An ESP program for students of business. In T. Orr (Ed.) *English for specific purposes* (pp. 41–56). TESOL.

Byun, S., Jeon, J., & Kim, E. (2006). The interface of discourse analysis and ergonomic issues on computerized procedure system. *English Teaching, 61*(4), 247–275.

Chew, S. K. (2005). An investigation of the English language skills used by new entrants in banks in Hong Kong. *English for Specific Purposes, 24*(1), 423–435.

Cho, D. W. (2012). A level-and proficiency-based English language program of a science university in Korea. *English Teaching, 67*(4), 25–55.

Choi, Y. H., & Ko, M. S. (2005). Hedging in EFL academic writing of Korean postgraduates. *English Teaching, 60*(1), 3–27.

Chujo, K., & Genung, M. (2003). Vocabulary-level assessment for ESP texts used in the field of industrial technology. *English Teaching, 58*(3), 259–274.

Coxhead, A. (2000). A new academic wordlist. *TESOL Quarterly, 34*(2), 213–238.

Douglas, D. (2000). *Assessing languages for specific purposes*. Cambridge University Press.

Dudley-Evans, T., & St. John, M. J. (1998). *Developments in English for specific purposes*. Cambridge University Press.

Duff, P. A. (2002). Teaching and learning English for global intercultural communication: Challenges and opportunities. *English Teaching, 57*(2), 245–263.

Eggly, S. (2002). An ESP program for international medical graduates in residency. In T. Orr (Ed.), *English for specific purposes* (pp.105–115). TESOL.

Feak, C., & Reinhart, S. (2002). An ESP program for students of law. In T. Orr (Ed.), *English for specific purposes* (pp.7–23). TESOL.

Flowerdew, J., & Wan, A. (2006). Genre analysis of tax computation letters: How and why tax accountants write the way they do. *English for Specific Purposes, 25*(2), 133–153.

Flowerdew, L. (2005). An integration of corpus-based and genre-based approaches to text analysis in EAP/ESP: Countering criticisms against corpus-based methodologies. *English for Specific Purposes, 24*(3), 321–332.

Frank, R. A. (2000). Medical communication: Non-native English-speaking patients and native English-speaking professionals. *English for Specific Purposes, 19*(1), 31–62.

Gollin-Kies, S. (2014). Method reported in ESP research articles: A comparative survey of two leading journals. *English for Specific Purposes, 36*, 27–34.

Guo, P. J. (2018, April). Non-native English speakers learning computer programming: Barriers, desires, and design opportunities. In *Proceedings of the 2018 CHI conference on human factors in computing systems* (pp. 1–14).

Hafner, C. A. (2020). Digital multimodal composing: How to address multimodal communication Forms in ELT. *English Teaching, 75*(3), 133–146.

Howatt, A. P. R. (1984). *A history of English language teaching.* Oxford University Press.

Hwang, P. A. (2013). Target discourse in oral presentations by science and engineering graduates in the U.S. *English Teaching, 68*(1), 85–109.

Hussin, V. (2002). An ESP program for students of nursing. In T. Orr (Ed.) *English for specific purposes* (pp.25–39). TESOL.

Hutchinson, T., & Waters, A. (1987). *English for specific purposes.* Cambridge University Press.

Hyland, K. (2002). Specificity revisited: How far should we go? *English for Specific Purposes, 21*(4), 385–395.

Hyland, K., & Tse, P. (2007). Is there an "academic vocabulary"? *TESOL Quarterly, 41*(2), 235–253.

Jackson, J. (2005). An inter-university, cross-disciplinary analysis of business education: Perceptions of business faculty in Hong Kong. *English for Specific Purposes, 24*(3), 293–306.

Jeon, J. (2015). Studies on English for Specific Purposes: Current status and directions for the future. *English Teaching, 70*(3), 243–263.

Jeon, J., & Choi, Y. (2002). A three-round Delphi study on the contents of business English tests. *English Teaching, 57*(2), 451–479.

Jeon, J., Lee, W., & Kim, J. (2011). Investigating the English-speaking proficiency level Korean people want to achieve. *English Teaching, 66*(2), 273–305.

Jin, H. (2015). A corpus-based study on engagement in English academic writing. *English Teaching, 70*(2), 27–54.

Jung, Y. (2020). Perceptions of team-teaching between native and nonnative English teachers in Korean secondary schools. *Modern English Education, 21*(2), 49–61.

Kanoksilapatham, B. (2005). Rhetorical structure of biochemistry research articles. *English for Specific Purposes, 24*(3), 269–292.

Kim, E. J. (2003). A comparative study of academic oral interaction in English-medium lectures and Korean-medium lectures. *English Teaching, 58*(3), 3–20.

Kim, D., Jung, D., Chang, S., & Uhm, C. (1999). A desirable curriculum model for Korean open universities' freshmen English and English department programs. *English Teaching, 54*(1), 253–296.
Kim, H. (2011). *A study on equity and efficiency of investment in learning English.* KDI.
Kim, J. (2018). A case study of nonnative English-speaking international students' adjustment to a Korean university. *The Sociolinguistic Journal of Korea, 26*(1), 1–23.
Kim, K., & Joo, K.-J. (2018). Korean culinary college students' desired careers and English proficiency needs. *English Teaching, 73*(1), 161–181.
Kwon, E.-Y. (2020). A study of research trends in ESP using python and text mining. *Foreign Languages Education, 27*(2), 111–139.
Kwon, H. S. (2015, January). *ESP and corpus-based research methods.* Paper presented at the 2015 KATE SIG Conference. Seoul.
Laadem, M., & Mallahi, H. (2019). Multimodal pedagogies in teaching English for specific purposes in higher education: Perceptions, challenges and strategies. *International Journal on Studies in Education, 1*(1), 33–38.
Lee, G., & Traynor, K. M. (2013). Two Korean content professors' English-mediated instruction: Issues and use of feedback. *English Teaching, 68*(4), 165–191.
Lee, J., & Ro, E. (2020). "I actually picked up a physics textbook:" Complexities of the freedom principle in extensive reading. *English Teaching, 75*(1), 3–23.
Mackay, R., & Mountford, A. (1978). *English for specific purposes.* Longman.
Noguchi, J. (1997). Material development for English for specific purposes: Applying genre analysis to EFL pedagogy. *English Teaching, 52*(3), 303–318.
Odo, D. M., & Yi, Y. (2014). Engaging in computer-mediated online feedback in academic writing. *English Teaching, 69*(3), 129–150.
Orr, T. (2002). *English for specific purposes.* TESOL Inc.
Paquot, M. (2010). *Academic vocabulary in learner writing.* Continuum.
Park, P. (2012). An analysis of military ATCs' perceptions of English proficiency test for aviation. *English Teaching, 67*(4), 267–285.
Pecorari, D. (2006). Visible and occluded citation features in postgraduate second-language writing. *English for Specific Purposes, 25*(1), 4–29.
Planken, B. (2005). Managing rapport in lingua franca sales negotiations: A comparison of professional and aspiring negotiators. *English for Specific Purposes, 24*(4), 381–400.

Rodríguez-Peñarroja, M. (2022). Integrating project-based learning, task-based language teaching approach and YouTube in the ESP Class: A study on students' motivation. *Teaching English with Technology, 22*(1), 62–81.

Shabani, M. B., & Ghasemi, A. (2014). The effect of task-based language teaching (TBLT) and content-based language teaching (CBLT) on the Iranian intermediate ESP learners' reading comprehension. *Procedia-Social and Behavioral Sciences, 98*, 1713–1721.

Shin, D., & Kwon, O. (2005). Issues in the assessment of English oral proficiency for civil aviation personnel in Korea. *English Teaching, 6*(4), 261–275.

Shin, I. (2010). The importance of English for Korean postgraduate engineering students in the global age. *English Teaching, 65*(1), 221–240.

Shin, I. (2011). Necessary skills in English from Korean postgraduate engineering students in the academic community. *English Teaching, 66*(2), 233–252.

Soh, Y. (2005). Students' preparation, perception and attitudes toward an oral class presentation. *English Teaching, 58*(34), 69–94.

Swales, J. M. (1990). *Genre Analysis: English in academic and research settings.* Cambridge University Press.

Tajino, A., & Tajino, Y. (2000). Native and non-native: What can they offer? Lessons from team-teaching in Japan. *ELT Journal, 54*(1), 3–11.

Tarone, E. (2005). Schools of fish: English for access to international academic and professional communities. *The Journal of Asia TEFL, 2*(1), 1–20.

Vega, M., & Moscoso, M. D. L. (2019). Challenges in the implementation of CLIL in higher education: From ESP to CLIL in the tourism classroom. *Latin American Journal of Content and Language Integrated Learning, 12*(1), 144–176.

Yang, W. (2020). The development, adoption and evaluation of the integration of an ESP and CLIL textbook: Perspectives from the CLIL learners. *ESP Today, 8*(1), 68–89.

# 14

# Innovation in ELT in Korea: Looking to the Future

**Ju Seong Lee, Hayo Reinders, and Joo-Kyung Park**

## Government as the Main Driver of Korea's ELT

As highlighted in the introduction, the Korean government has been pivotal in spearheading innovation in English Language Teaching (ELT). To enhance English communication skills, the government has implemented several key initiatives. These include introducing English education in early elementary school, launching the Native English-Speaking Teachers (NESTs) Recruitment scheme, expanding 'English villages' and immersion facilities both inside and outside schools, promoting Teaching

---

J. S. Lee (✉)
Education University of Hong Kong, Hong Kong SAR, People's Republic of China
e-mail: jslee@eduhk.hk

H. Reinders
King Mongkut's University of Technology, Bangkok, Thailand

J.-K. Park
Honam University, Gwangju, South Korea

© The Author(s), under exclusive license to Springer Nature Switzerland AG 2025
H. Reinders et al. (eds.), *Innovation in Language Learning and Teaching*, New Language Learning and Teaching Environments, https://doi.org/10.1007/978-3-031-83561-2_14

English in English (TEE), developing the National English Ability Test (NEAT), and integrating Information and Communication Technology (ICT) into practice (Ahn, 2017; Lee & Lee, 2016).

However, such top-down, innovative policies and initiatives often change every few years due to new political motives and inadequate preparation by each new government administration (Ahn, 2017). This has led to unsustainable practices. For instance, despite significant investments, the NEAT program was short-lived, and many English Villages went bankrupt (Lee & Lee, 2016). Additionally, programs like the English Program in Korea (EPIK) and Teach and Learn in Korea (TaLK) primarily recruit teachers from 'inner circle' countries (e.g., USA or UK), limiting Korean EFL students' exposure to diverse varieties of English in today's multilingual and multicultural world (Jeon, 2009; Kiaer et al., 2021).

## Field-Driven ELT: Insights from Our 13 Chapters

Due to the limitations of government-led ELT initiatives in Korea, we have seen a surge in grassroots, bottom-up innovations in ELT. Our 13 chapters provide various examples of such field-driven approaches.

***Elementary English Literacy Education***: Hae-Ri Kim (Chapter 2) emphasizes that young EFL learners' English abilities, along with their creative and critical thinking skills, can be significantly enhanced through the effective integration of educational technology and collaboration between researchers and teachers.

***Artificial Intelligence Digital Textbook (AIDT)***: Starting in 2025, Korea is introducing AIDT for primary and secondary schools. Lee and Bang (Chapter 3) explore its grassroots effectiveness for students and teachers. AIDT offers AI-driven learning analytics, adaptive learning, and human-centered design. These features enable personalized learning, fostering student engagement and ownership. For teachers, AIDT enhances teaching by providing data-driven insights, optimizing curriculum design, and refining teaching strategies. Teachers remain crucial in curating content, facilitating personalized learning, interpreting data, and offering social and emotional support. However, potential challenges such as learning gaps, data management, AI divide, and inequity should be addressed.

*Willingness to Communicate (WTC)*: Korean EFL learners, particularly secondary students preparing for the Korean College Scholastic Aptitude Test (K-CSAT), often exhibit low WTC. Joohyun Bae (Chapter 4) addresses this by demonstrating how Informal Digital Learning of English (IDLE) can boost WTC through exposure to English as an international language (EIL). Bae found that middle school students who engaged more frequently in IDLE had a more positive perception of EIL, leading to higher WTC. This interdisciplinary research highlights the potential of utilizing out-of-class digital resources to enhance communication skills in secondary students with limited opportunities to speak English.

*AI-Driven Language Learning*: The pressure of K-CSAT is particularly intense for high school students. Rakhun Kim (Chapter 5) designed AI-driven language learning programs to improve reading comprehension for the K-CSAT. The study revealed that interactive engagement with generative AI significantly improved students' ability to identify main ideas through top-down processing. Additionally, human teachers' guidance further developed students' receptive skills, while AI-assisted corrective feedback enhanced their ability to produce complex sentence structures, thereby improving their productive skills. This interdisciplinary approach demonstrates that teachers who are well-versed in both classroom dynamics and new technologies can create effective, locally appropriate programs for EFL learners.

*Teacher-Driven Language Teacher Education (LTE)*: Traditional top-down LTE programs often fail to reflect the realities of the classroom and the true needs of teachers. Dissatisfied with these programs, master teacher Eun-kyoung Jang, along with Ahn Gyemyong and Mun Woo Lee (Chapter 6), developed the innovative "Snowball" LTE program. This teacher-driven, field-oriented program combines action research and learning communities, allowing teachers to research and address the most pressing issues in their local schools. The "Snowball" program grants teachers autonomy in identifying and solving real-life classroom problems, addressing students' genuine needs, and fostering authentic learning communities. Through customized special interest groups, teachers can reflect on and share their experiences, cultivating a culture of collaboration and leading to long-term action research.

***English for Peacebuilding Purposes (EPP)***: Peace is a critical global need, yet it is seldom addressed in ELT classrooms. Jocelyn Wright (Chapter 7) created and implemented innovative EPP courses for Korean EFL university students. Unlike traditional EFL writing courses, EPP courses involve a cyclical writing process, emphasizing both expressive and reflective writing (intrapersonal) and interactive and responsive writing (interpersonal). Students actively contributed content based on their personal stories or situations, such as voicing complaints, and shared their views on a virtual exhibit on Padlet. Although this EPP course is currently small-scale, Wright cites Galtung (2008), who noted that even small-scale innovations can have a broader impact. The 47 EPP students and this chapter could positively influence other students, researchers, policymakers, educators, and activists.

***Localized Critical Literacy***: Korean ELT scholars often adopt critical literacy models from Western scholars. However, Young-Mee Suh and Seonmin Huh (Chapter 8) argue for developing localized critical literacy practices tailored to the Korean EFL context. Based on their extensive research, they propose an innovative critical literacy model that combines conventional literacy instruction with a holistic approach, integrating personal engagement, critical thinking, empathy, social-political action, and language development. They emphasize that Korean ELT teachers play a crucial role in guiding students from challenging the status quo to taking action for social justice through activities like editing articles, emailing, small campaigns, surveys, game creation, and donations.

***Integrating Content and Language in Higher Education (ICLHE)***: While ICLHE is common in Europe, it is rarely adopted by Korean universities. Eun Gyong Kim (Chapter 9) has successfully developed and implemented ICLHE at the Korea Advanced Institute of Science and Technology (KAIST). She integrated content and language in undergraduate courses (biology, chemistry, math, physics, and programming) and graduate courses (discipline-specific scientific writing). Kim acknowledges that interdisciplinary collaboration is essential for the success of content-language integrated classes, but it is challenging due to the time constraints and responsibilities of content professors and the need for EFL professors to develop content knowledge. Therefore, support from departmental and central administration is crucial for the development of such courses. ICLHE offers valuable insights for teachers and EMI policy.

*Content and Language Integrated Learning (CLIL)*: Similar to Kim (Chapter 9), Eunjou Oh (Chapter 10) developed and implemented a CLIL model aimed at fostering global citizenship and competence in a Korean EFL tertiary setting. Oh's innovative approach included using machine translation as a pedagogical translanguaging tool. She provided a mini-lesson on machine translation, offered guidelines for machine translation-assisted writing for personal response essays, and evaluated the essays with feedback. Additionally, Oh facilitated out-of-class English learning activities with the help of a co-teacher, enriching the learning experience for Korean EFL students. For students with lower proficiency levels, Oh suggests using Generative AI tools, such as ChatGPT, to tailor the CLIL model to their needs.

*Critical-Project-Based Language Learning (Critical-PBLL)*: Unlike traditional English teaching that focuses on reading and listening, Mi Kyong Kim (Chapter 11) developed a Critical-PBLL framework for a general English course. PBLL is a student-centered inquiry activity where learners construct knowledge about the English language and the subject of inquiry through their own explorations. Kim integrated text-based generative AI tools (e.g., ChatGPT and Google Bard) into Critical-PBLL, allowing students to use automated translation systems, grammar checking tools, and text generation AIs. As a result, university students not only enhanced their language skills but also fostered reflective and critical thinking. Kim emphasizes the importance of collaboratively developing prompt literacy guidelines with learners to maximize educational value.

*Flipped Learning*: Flipped learning has been shown to boost Korean EFL students' motivation, engagement, and English skills, leading to its increased integration into Korea's ELT classrooms. As knowledge on flipped learning has grown, Hye-Kyung Kim and Sumi Han (Chapter 12) conducted an innovative bibliometric and keyword analysis of flipped learning trends from 2015–2022 using big data technology. They identified three areas for future research: (a) extending research beyond universities to include K-12 and vocational training centers, (b) balancing the focus on reading and writing with other skills like listening and speaking, which are crucial for real-life communication, and (c) exploring affective aspects of L2 English learning, such as self-efficacy, resilience, and emotional engagement.

*English for Specific Purposes (ESP)*: Similar to Kim and Han's work in Chapter 12, Jihyeon Jeon and Eun-young Kwon conducted a review analysis in Chapter 13, focusing on ESP in Korea. Both authors have extensive experience teaching ESP in classrooms. ESP involves learning a specialized form of English used within specific professional groups, such as doctors discussing medical procedures in a hospital. Jeon and Kwon utilized AntConc (version 3.4.3) to analyze trends in articles published in *English Teaching*, the oldest academic journal on English education in Korea, established in 1965. They compared their findings with data from *English for Specific Purposes*, a leading international journal in the ESP field. Their analysis revealed a need for more research on ESP in Korea. They also recommended that ESP research should include disciplines commonly studied in global academic contexts, such as law, medicine, economics, and business management.

Overall, these chapters highlight how Korean ELT teachers and educators have identified themes and objectives, addressing them through innovative approaches, methodologies, models, technologies, and activities.

## Looking to the Future

Drawing from the insights of our 13 chapters, this section offers concrete suggestions for future research and practice.

## Enhancing Researcher-Teacher Collaboration

We encourage Korean ELT educators to foster more researcher-teacher collaborations. Researchers often have deep knowledge of second language acquisition theory and research methodologies but may lack practical context knowledge, such as understanding specific school environments, student needs, and available ICT infrastructure. Conversely, teachers possess this crucial context knowledge but may lack theoretical and methodological expertise. By combining the strengths of both researchers and teachers, innovative ELT research can be effectively designed and implemented to address real-life classroom issues (Sato et al., 2022). For example, in Chapter 2, Professor Kim, a university professor and teacher educator, collaborated with teachers to understand local classroom dynamics and integrate suitable educational technologies to enhance elementary students' English literacy and critical thinking skills.

Another exemplary model is presented in Chapter 6 by Jang, Ahn, and Lee. Jang, a master teacher with extensive ELT experience, identified gaps in the existing English LTE program in Korea. In collaboration with university researchers Ahn and Lee, Jang developed and implemented the teacher-driven, field-oriented "Snowball" LTE program. This program successfully addressed real-life issues in local schools and inspired other educators to conduct action research and share their experiences. In Chapter 5, Kim, a secondary school teacher with over 15 years of experience and an adjunct professor, combined theoretical knowledge with practical experience. Kim designed and integrated AI-driven language learning programs to enhance high school students' K-CSAT performance. Based on these three models of researcher-teacher collaboration, we encourage Korean ELT educators to pursue similar partnerships to bring more innovative practices into Korean classrooms.

## Empowering Students to Become Autonomous English Learners

After completing their course, EFL students need to continue learning English independently, without teacher intervention (Lee, 2022). Given the limited opportunities for Korean EFL students to engage with English in real-life contexts, it is crucial to foster their ability to learn autonomously and use English in everyday situations (Lee et al., 2024).

Lee and Bang (Chapter 3) discuss how the Artificial Intelligence Digital Textbook (AIDT) enables personalized learning tailored to individual strengths and weaknesses. This fosters active student engagement and ownership. The authors emphasize the crucial role of teachers in curating and sequencing content for each student. Bae (Chapter 4) explored how students who engaged in IDLE outside the classroom developed their language skills independently. Bae discovered that Korean EFL students who frequently participated in IDLE activities had a more positive attitude towards English as an International Language (EIL), which increased their WTC. This study provides valuable insights for designing programs that help students become more autonomous and proficient English speakers.

Wright's (Chapter 7) English for Peacebuilding Purposes (EPP) courses aimed to enhance university students' writing skills by having them create and share personal stories in a virtual exhibit. This approach not only improved their writing but also raised awareness about peacebuilding, potentially motivating students to engage in peace-related activities independently. Similarly, Suh and Huh (Chapter 8) developed localized critical literacy practices tailored to the Korean EFL context. Their course encouraged students to take action for social justice through activities like editing articles, emailing, running small campaigns, conducting surveys, creating games, and making donations, preferably in English. Both EPP and critical literacy practices have the potential to expand the scope of ELT and inspire students to take small-scale actions for social justice. Based on these examples, we encourage Korean ELT educators to create learning environments that foster student autonomy and responsibility for their own English learning, both inside and outside the classroom (Reinders et al., 2022).

## Adopting Innovative Research Methods

Innovative research methods can provide fresh insights and drive advancements in ELT research and practice (Yi et al., 2022). For instance, Kim and Han (Chapter 12) used bibliometric and keyword analysis with big data technology to study trends in flipped learning. They recommend future research to explore other linguistic and affective aspects of L2 learning, such as listening, speaking, self-efficacy, and resilience, across different student groups and age levels. Jeon and Kwon (Chapter 13) utilized the software AntConc to analyze trends in English for Specific Purposes (ESP) in Korea. By comparing findings from Korea's English Teaching journal and international ESP journals, they offered new directions for future research. Bae (Chapter 4) investigated extramural digital settings using surveys. Future researchers could enhance this approach by collecting real-time data through the Experience Sampling Method (ESM), where participants report their IDLE experiences and related variables (e.g., emotions, self-efficacy, WTC) multiple times daily over one or two weeks (Lee & Chiu, 2024). ESM has proven effective in capturing phenomena in natural settings (Reinders & Lee, 2023). Additionally, descriptive ethnographic interviews could involve participants recording short videos of their IDLE activities and elaborating on them, providing rich, comprehensive data (Jensen, 2019). By adopting these innovative methods, researchers can gain deeper insights and contribute to the development of more effective ELT practices.

## Designing Optimal Learning Environments Using Innovative Technology

People often mistake the use of the latest technology for true innovation. However, innovation goes beyond merely adopting new tools (Reinders et al., 2023). In August 2024, the first author, Lee, conducted a workshop on AI for school teachers at a university in Hyderabad, India. He emphasized that AI is a tool that can enhance teaching in ELT classrooms. Later that day, Lee visited a nearby school and observed a classroom where the only teaching aid was a blackboard. The teacher used a government textbook and her first language to explain English words and sentences. Despite the lack of advanced technology, the teacher effectively managed a class of over 15 young EFL learners. She achieved this by actively listening to and empathizing with her students, understanding their unique needs, and designing engaging activities using the available resources—blackboard, translanguaging skills, and textbooks. This example illustrates that innovation can be as simple as introducing a blackboard in a resource-limited setting if it meets the students' needs (Mitra, 2020). A similar example can be found in Oh (Chapter 10), who designed and implemented the Content and Language Integrated Learning (CLIL) model to cultivate global citizenship and competence in a Korean EFL tertiary setting. Recognizing the needs of lower-proficiency students, Oh suggested integrating ChatGPT to create an engaging and optimal learning environment. Future ELT educators should first understand their students' true needs and then design optimal learning environments using available resources, whether a blackboard or AI tools (Reinders et al., 2023).

## Strengthening Concept Design Capability

Korean ELT educators often adopt theories or models suggested by Western scholars. While these mainstream SLA theories and models are useful, they may not always fit Korea's unique EFL context. Suh and Huh (Chapter 8) addressed this issue by developing localized critical literacy practices relevant to Korean EFL educational contexts. Similarly, Mi Kyong Kim (Chapter 11) created a Critical-Project-Based Language Learning (Critical-PBLL) framework tailored to Korean ELT classrooms.

While adopting Western models can be beneficial, future researchers should strive to develop original theories or models and share them with the global ELT community. For instance, the concept of Extramural English (Sundqvist, 2009) originated in Europe. Instead of merely adopting this concept, Lee (2022) developed the IDLE concept, which is more suitable for digitalized Korean EFL contexts. Initially focused on Korea, IDLE research has expanded globally, including Europe, the

Middle East, and Central/South Asia, and has been adapted for languages other than English, such as Korean (Lee et al., 2023; Taherian et al., 2023; Zadorozhnyy & Lee, 2023). It has also evolved into AI-mediated IDLE and teacher-supported IDLE intervention models (Liu et al., 2024a, 2024b). While designing new concepts or models is challenging, it is essential for future researchers to strengthen their concept design capabilities. Developing original ELT models and theories will foster innovation and progress in Korea's ELT field.

# References

Ahn, H. (2017). *Attitudes to World Englishes: Implications for teaching English in South Korea*. Routledge.

Jensen, S. H. (2019). Language learning in the wild: A young user perspective. *Language Learning & Technology, 23*(1), 72–86. 10125/44673

Jeon, M. (2009). Globalization and native English speakers in English Programme in Korea (EPIK). *Language, Culture and Curriculum, 22*(3), 231–243. https://doi.org/10.1080/07908310903388933

Kiaer, J., Morga-Brown, J. M., & Choi, N. (2021). *Young children's foreign language anxiety: The case of South Korea*. Multilingual Matters.

Lee, H., & Lee, K. (2016). An analysis of the failure(s) of South Korea's National English Ability Test. *The Asia-Pacific Education Researcher, 25*(5–6), 827–834. https://doi.org/10.1007/s40299-016-0301-6

Lee, J. S. (2022). *Informal digital learning of English: Research to practice*. Routledge.

Lee, J. S., & Chiu, M. M. (2024). Modelling trait and state willingness to communicate in a second language: An experience sampling approach. *Studies in Second Language Learning and Teaching, 14*(3), 483–514. https://doi.org/10.14746/ssllt.37541

Lee, J. S., Kiaer, J., & Jeong, S. (2023). The role of informal digital learning of Korean in KFL students' willingness to communicate. *Journal of Multilingual and Multicultural Development*, 1–17. https://doi.org/10.1080/01434632.2023.2216671

Lee, J. S., Xie, Q., & Lee, K. (2024). Informal digital learning of English and L2 willingness to communicate: Roles of emotions, gender, and educational stage. *Journal of Multilingual and Multicultural Development, 45*(2), 596–612. https://doi.org/10.1080/01434632.2021.1918699

Liu, G., Darvin, R., & Ma, C. (2024a). Exploring AI-mediated informal digital learning of English (AI-IDLE): A mixed-method investigation of Chinese EFL learners' AI adoption and experiences. *Computer Assisted Language Learning*, 1–29. https://doi.org/10.1080/09588221.2024.2310288

Liu, L., Guan, W. J., Qiu, Y., & Lee, J. S. (2024b). Effects of extramural English activities on willingness to communicate: The role of teacher support for Chinese EFL students. *System, 124*, 103319. https://doi.org/10.1016/j.system.2024.103319

Mitra, S. (2020). *The school in the cloud*. Corwin Press, Inc.

Reinders, H., Lai, C., & Sundqvist, P. (Eds.). (2022). *The Routledge handbook of language learning and teaching beyond the classroom*. Routledge.

Reinders, H., & Lee, B. J. (2023). Tracking learner engagement in the L2 classroom with experience sampling. *Research Methods in Applied Linguistics, 2*, 1–13. https://doi.org/10.1016/j.rmal.2023.100052

Reinders, H., Phung, L., Ryan, S., & Thomas, N. (2023). *The key to self-regulated learning: A systematic approach to maximising its potential*. Oxford University Press.

Sato, M., Loewen, S., & Pastushenkov, D. (2022). 'Who is my research for?': Researcher perceptions of the research-practice relationship. *Applied Linguistics, 43*, 625–652. https://doi.org/10.1093/applin/amab079

Sundqvist, P. (2009). *Extramural English matters: Out-of-school English and its impact on Swedish ninth graders' oral proficiency and vocabulary*. Karlstad University.

Taherian, T., Shirvan, M. E., Yazdanmehr, E., Kruk, M., & Pawlak, M. (2023). A longitudinal analysis of informal digital learning of English, willingness to communicate and foreign language boredom: A latent change score mediation model. *The Asia-Pacific Education Researcher*, 1–14. https://doi.org/10.1007/s40299-023-00751-z

Yi, Y., Cho, S., & Jang, J. (2022). Methodological innovations in examining digital literacies in applied linguistics research. *TESOL Quarterly*, 1–11. https://doi.org/10.1002/tesq.3140

Zadorozhnyy, A., & Lee, J. S. (2023). Informal digital learning of English and willingness to communicate in a second language: Self-efficacy beliefs as a mediator. *Computer Assisted Language Learning*, 1–21. https://doi.org/10.1080/09588221.2023.2215279

# Index

## A

action research 32, 137, 142, 144, 145, 149–151, 204, 333, 334, 337
AI Digital Textbook (AIDT) 10, 49–51, 53–55, 58–65, 67, 68, 98, 99, 332, 338
Artificial Intelligence (AI) 4, 10, 11, 14, 37, 50, 51, 54–65, 67, 68, 97–100, 102, 104, 106, 109, 111–114, 116–122, 186, 221, 234, 260, 262–271, 273–276, 332, 333, 335, 337, 339–341

## B

big data 14, 282, 288, 336, 339

## C

changes and developments 1, 38
chatbot 98, 100, 102, 111–114, 116–118, 120, 121, 260, 262
ChatGPT 10, 103–110, 114, 116, 119–121, 253, 254, 260, 262–270, 272, 273, 276, 335, 340
Communicative peace 160, 161, 164, 165, 181
Comprehensive peace 160, 164, 181
Concept design capability 341
Content and language integrated learning (CLIL) 10, 13, 226, 229, 231, 233, 234, 248, 325, 335, 340
Content-based instruction (CBI) 307
Content-based language teaching (CBLT) 263

creative thinking competencies 33
Critical affective pedagogy 198, 199, 201
Critical literacies 12, 185, 186, 189, 190, 196, 201–204, 207–209
Critical-PBLL 14, 260–264, 266–276, 335, 340
critical thinking skills 34, 35, 189, 260, 285, 332, 337
*culture of sharing* 12, 144, 154

D

data bias 65

E

educational equity 11, 50, 65, 67
EFL models of critical literacies 189, 190, 202, 206
elementary English 4, 10, 19–23, 25–27, 30, 31, 34, 36–38
English as an International Language (EIL) 2, 4, 7, 11, 75, 78, 80–82, 84–87, 89, 91, 92, 333, 338
English for Academic Purposes (EAP) 214, 216, 306, 309, 310, 312–315, 317–320, 322
English for Occupational Purposes (EOP) 306, 309, 310, 312, 313, 315–320, 322–324
English for Peacebuilding Purposes (EPP) 10, 12, 159, 160, 162–165, 168, 171, 172, 174, 176, 177, 179–181, 334, 338
English for Specific Purposes (ESP) 10, 14, 214, 215, 217, 219–225, 304–322, 324–326, 336, 339
English language skills development 78
English medium instruction (EMI) 5, 6, 213–216, 219, 226, 230, 231, 335
EPIK and TaLK 5, 7, 332
ESP and EFL education 14, 202, 284, 305, 309, 324, 325
ESP research trends 310

F

feedback 12, 27, 54, 57–59, 62, 63, 65, 67, 88, 89, 102, 104, 113, 116–121, 133, 135–138, 142, 144–147, 153, 165, 166, 172, 175, 178, 180, 181, 221, 222, 225, 236, 239, 249, 251, 265, 273, 288, 297, 322, 335
Field-driven ELT 332
Flipped learning 14, 139, 267, 282–286, 288, 290, 291, 293–299, 335, 336, 339

G

global citizenship 13, 36, 161, 229, 232, 234, 236, 237, 239, 240, 244, 245, 247, 249, 251, 335, 340
global competence 13, 229, 232, 234–237, 239–244, 248, 249, 251, 253
Google Bard 10, 260, 263–270, 272, 273, 276, 335

## H

Higher education 10, 12, 162, 213, 214, 229–232, 323

## I

IDLE approach 73, 75–80, 90
incorporating Edtech into literacy activities 36
Informal Digital Learning of English (IDLE) 11, 73–75, 77–82, 84–92, 333, 338–341
innovations 10, 12, 14, 20, 38, 65, 132, 136, 151–154, 159, 162, 181, 230, 281, 293, 297, 325, 331, 332, 334, 339–341
Innovative research methods 339
Integrating Content and Language in Higher Education (ICLHE) 10, 12, 214, 334, 335
integrating four language skills 26, 28
Intercultural citizenship 194, 195, 197, 203, 205, 207
issues and challenges 6

## K

Korean context 286, 296, 297
Korean high school EFL students 111, 117, 121
Korean university students 78, 205

## L

Language Teacher education (LTE) 12, 129–132, 135, 136, 140, 144, 146, 149–153, 333, 337
learning analytics 49, 51, 54, 57, 63, 65, 332

literacy education 10, 20, 21, 23, 28, 37, 38, 186–188, 190, 194, 198, 199, 202–205, 207

## M

Machine Translation (MT) 13, 79, 229, 230, 233, 234, 236, 237, 239–242, 244–246, 248–254, 335
master teacher system 134
middle school 20, 75, 76, 79–82, 84, 87, 90, 91, 292, 333
MOE and KICE 1, 7, 98, 100, 163, 293

## N

National Curriculum (NC) 1–4, 6, 8, 19–21, 36, 76, 98, 163
native-speakerism 7, 9
near peer role model 131, 144, 150, 151
NEAT and CSAT 6, 76, 77, 163, 332
NESTs and NNESTs 5, 7, 8, 331

## O

Optimal learning environments 340

## P

Peace 12, 159–162, 164, 167–177, 179–181, 203, 235, 334, 338
Peace language education (PLE) 160, 161, 181
Peace Linguistics (PL) 160–162, 181

personalized learning 10, 50, 51, 54–57, 59, 60, 67, 98, 100, 284, 325, 332, 333, 338
problem-solving abilities 270

R
reading to learn 29
Remotivating strategy 164
Researcher-teacher collaboration 337
research trends 287, 288

S
Science, Technology, Engineering, and Mathematics (STEM) 291
situatedness of teacher learning 132
Social action in critical literacy 204
Special Interest Group (SIG) 144, 145, 148, 149, 305, 334
student agency 50, 58, 59, 251

T
teacher cognition 130, 151
Teacher learning community (TLC) 142, 145, 146, 150, 152–154
translanguaging 229, 231, 234, 246, 248–252, 254, 262, 264, 335, 340

W
Willingness to Communicate (WTC) 11, 74, 75, 78, 79, 81, 84, 86, 87, 89, 91, 92, 333, 338, 339
Writing 6, 7, 10, 12, 13, 20, 22, 24–29, 32–34, 37, 74, 76–78, 80, 82–84, 133, 160, 164–174, 176–181, 198, 200, 202, 203, 208, 215, 216, 220–224, 232, 233, 236, 237, 239–241, 246–249, 253, 254, 262, 263, 266–268, 275, 294, 295, 297, 298, 308, 309, 314, 322, 334–336, 338

Printed in the United States
by Baker & Taylor Publisher Services